To KATHY

GREAT TO BE
ON THE SAME TEAM
WITH YOU. ENJOY IT (I HOPE)

CAPITALIZING ON THE GLOBAL WORKFORCE

CAPITALIZING ON THE GLOBAL WORKFORCE:

A Strategic Guide to Expatriate Management

MICHAEL S. SCHELL
CHARLENE MARMER SOLOMON

McGraw-Hill

New York San Francisco Washington, D.C. Auckland Bogotá
Caracas Lisbon London Madrid Mexico City Milan
Montreal New Delhi San Juan Singapore
Sydney Tokyo Toronto

McGraw-Hill

A Division of The **McGraw·Hill** Companies

Cover Photo: Schell Brothers

Library of Congress Cataloging-in-Publication Data

Schell, Michael S.
    Capitalizing on the global workforce: a strategic guide for expatriate management/by Michael S.
Schell and Charlene Marmer Solomon.
        p.   cm.
    Includes bibliographical references and index.
    ISBN 0–7863–0895–8
    1. International business enterprises—Personnel management.
2. Employees—Recruiting. 3. Employment in foreign countries.
I. Solomon, Charlene Marmer. II. Title.
HF5549.5.E45S34 1997
658.3—dc20   96–28992

Printed in the United States of America
 3 4 5 6 7 8 9 DOC/DOC 9 0 2 1 0 9

To Lynne for your confidence, encouragement, and love;
To Freida for the courage to pursue dreams, and to
Alexander for the strength and determination to make
them come true;
And a special dedication in memory of my friend and
business associate Susan Jacobson. You left the party too
early, Sigi.

Michael

To Alan for 30 years of love. Thank you for nurturing the
creative person within.
To Bobbie and Irv for teaching me that adventure begins
when you open doors.

Charlene

And to the next generation: Andrew, Elizabeth, Adam,
Jonathan, and Angela who own the future.

CONTENTS

FOREWORD

Michael S. Schell and Charlene Marmer Solomon have written a valuable addition to the literature on expatriate management. The explosion of global businesses in the 1990s has highlighted the need to manage expatriates from throughtout the world who are venturing abroad to meet the competitive needs of their enterprises. This book will be welcomed by those responsible for expatriate management as an excellent primer on the key issues in the selection, support, and development of the expatriate population who play such a valuable role in today's global business.

For many years, it has been clear that expatriate management should be conducted in a holistic manner that considers the *cultural* as well as the *administrative* aspects of relocation. Yet, the field has been traditionally divided between cross-cultural specialists who furnish cultural orientation and training for people moving abroad, and company human resource specialists who develop compensation plans, relocation policies, and career paths to meet individual and corporate needs. In *Capitalizing on the Global Workforce,* Schell and Solomon have done an admirable job of integrating these two areas, both of which are necessary for expatriates and their families to have a successful overseas experience.

For many years, the intricacies of cross-cultural adjustment and management have been neglected by the business community. It is estimated that less than 50 percent of expatriates today receive any cross-cultural preparation. Yet, over the last 40 years, the newly emerging field of intercultural relations has developed theories, researched experience, and tested methods of cross-cultural selection, training, and development. When used properly, this can save companies millions of dollars in relocation costs, and expatriate families years of heartache and trauma. The authors deal in a clear and useful way with the important and difficult issue of preparing employees and their families for expatriate assignments. They examine the responsibilities that companies have to expatriate families and partners, and the costs of not supporting families well. They recommend a series of practical steps to ensure effective family and partner support before, during, and after the expatriate assignment.

Schell and Solomon not only develop a case for the importance of understanding cross-cultural differences in expatriate living and adjustment, but make a major contribution to understanding the impact of culture on business relations and international management. The Windham International Cultural Model © provides a practical guide to understanding the impact of culture on colleague and customer relations. Building on studies by Edward Hall, Geert Hofstede, and Fons Trompenaars, the model provides practical, specific, and straightforward advice on how to behave in a wide range of cultures throughout the world. Using a generic approach to cross-cultural analysis that examines differences on a series of dimensions, the authors provide insightful guidance on how to communicate and manage relationships across cultures. Their perceptiveness makes significant interpretative additions to the general literature on cross-cultural relations.

But this is not just a book about cross-cultural adjustment, communications, and management. It is also a practical guide about the basic issues of expatriate selection, development, and administration. As expatriate assignments become a *sine qua non* of global career paths, an increasing number of companies are facing the difficult task of determining what criteria should be used in selecting people to go abroad. Expatriate selection requires finding the right person with the right technical and cross-cultural skills whose family situation allows him or her to take on an overseas assignment. For the first time, the work of Michael Tucker, one of the pioneers in expatriate selection through his development of Overseas Assessment Inventory, is documented and explained. The OAI has been used for many years by U.S. companies as a self-selection and coaching instrument designed to improve the effectiveness of expatriate selection and performance. This instrument probes expatriate expectations, open-mindedness, tolerance, flexibility, and a range of other characteristics that experience has proven are important in successful expatriate adjustment. Schell and Solomon use it as a practical example of instruments that are available to improve the expatriate selection process.

If companies are to compete successfully on a global basis, they must develop international service programs that are more thorough and sophisticated than those currently in place. International relocation will increasingly become a critical component of global competitiveness, ensuring that the right skills are in the right place for maximizing the timely delivery of corporate products and services to global customers. Developing an effective formula for expatriate management will therefore become a competitive weapon to provide a distinct advantage in a world of rapid change, requiring the ability to deliver all corporate resources—techinal, financial, *and* human—to the appropriate place anywhere around the globe on short notice.

Schell and Solomon have made a significant contribution to two of the most complex areas of expatriate management—compensation and program administration. They provide excellent frameworks for understanding the basic components of these issues. One particularly worthwhile area of advice is the road map they constructed for paying and rewarding expatriates and locals, one of the thorniest areas of international human resource management.

The authors end with an intriguing look at human resource management in the 21st century and its impact on the way that global business is conducted. Drawing a scenario for the year 2001, they highlight the potential impact of developing trends in international human resource management, including the new role of human resource development (HRD) as a strategic business partner and the impact of technology on the HR function. This is done in a way that provides guidance for professionals interested in developing their own skills and talents for expatriate management in the 21st century.

Schell and Solomon have given all of us the gift of a practical and informative guide to the selection, support, and management of the world's new global citizens. This is a contribution not only to the families who will benefit from better preparation and assistance, but to the companies who have sent them, the customers who will benefit from their services, and all human resource professionals concerned with improving the quality of life and effectiveness of people working and living internationally.

Stephen H. Rhinesmith

PREFACE

The inspiration for this book came to us just after we met in the spring of 1994. We had both attended a conference that brought together human resource practitioners from all over the world. Charlene, a contributing editor for *Workforce* magazine, (formerly *Personnel Journal*) had just begun writing a Global Human Resource series. Michael, who had recently launched Windham International, was one of the professionals being interviewed for the series. In short order we realized that the field—and all the literature we knew about—was segmented into two distinct groups, one dealing with the cultural impact of global business, and the other addressing the weightier descriptions of compensation and tax on expatriate administration.

As we completed our interview for the *Personnel Journal* article, we began to discuss the works in the field and the need for an authoritative book that viewed the international business opportunity as a melding of intercultural understanding and practical/tactical business functions. We found several excellent companies and literary works that maintained a focus on either the cultural or administrative side of the international human resources. It was as though a wall stood between those who administered international HR deployment and those who felt a need to prepare people to succeed in the global business arena.

While there was a general consensus that cultural training was important, it was not seen as the "gotta have" in order to send people into unfamiliar countries and cultures. Although no expatriate would leave on assignment without a session on the tax implications of foreign compensation, people thought nothing of sending an unprepared middle-level engineer who had never been out of Texas to manage a facility in Jakarta—an environment with a completely different way of doing everything. Even when a cross-cultural program was arranged, it was a struggle for assignees to find time to attend it.

We also found practitioners paying lip service to the importance of spouse and family issues. There was almost no field of study—and certainly only few remedies offered—for the trauma that awaits an expatriate family when they arrive in a strange location. Spouses, in particular, known for being fundamental to the success or failure of the assignment, were virtually ignored in terms of policy provisions, preparation, and ongoing support. Why? This important activity, which has tremendous influence on the success of an expatriate assignment, was an area in which managers felt they had no responsibility or control.

How could smart businesspeople not see that a holistic view was required? Our experience in the field and all the research we had done, convinced us that there was a need for this book. A book that integrates these ideas into a single work and through it, to influence the field itself. That was particularly important to us because we observed that as companies globalize, their human resource leadership function seems to go to the tactical practitioners—those with the fundamental skill to manage all the necessary tasks that must take place before an employee can go on an international assignment. These practitioners, caught in the inevitable crush of administrative requirements, were not particularly concerned about integrating cultural training and family support into the many pre-departure tasks.

We hope that by providing equal weight to all the expatriation activities, this work will alert practitioners to find equal-time to take care of the "gotta have's" without forgetting or downplaying the cross-cultural experience that limits the potential success of an assignment for the organization as well as for the expatriate family.

So we set about to write a book that bridged these two bodies of knowledge into a single work that mirrored the myriad activities of the global manager with responsibility for international deployment. We also believed it was important to write a book that would be accessible and understandable for any company officer looking at new opportunities in the global arena.

During the writing of this book, we have each experienced—and heard—some terrific, interesting, real-life cultural challenges encountered by business people and global travelers. These experiences bring home the complexities and richness of culture more than the written word can. We wish to thank all the people along our travels who so generously added to the depth of our understanding, and the fun and fascination of writing this work.

ⓑ ⓑ ⓑ

- After getting off the subway in Tokyo during a recent business trip, I asked a street laborer for directions to the Tokyo Tower. He didn't understand English but got the gist of the request and, with pointing fingers and other forms of sign language, told me where to go. After about two blocks, I noticed a small shop with a telephone and went inside to use the phone to call the hotel and pick up phone messages. When I emerged from the phone booth, my "guide" was panting, dreadfully concerned that I had misunderstood the directions and was turning in the wrong direction.

- Culture can be seen in a microcosm in the Four Seasons Hotel in Bali, Indonesia. When I checked in to the hotel, I was escorted to my room by a Balinesian young man who took great lengths to explain that the satisfaction of my entire stay was his responsibility. He told me that everyone serving me—from the housekeepers to the bell men—reported to him. With graciousness and warmth, he stated again and again that my satisfaction was his most important job. He was committed to my enjoying the stay. And, indeed, he did his utmost.

  I later learned that the entire staff had chosen to share the automatic 10 percent gratuities that were added to every bill—equally—no matter what their position, rather than divide it proportionally based on a graduated, hierarchical basis, as the rest of the hotel group does around the world. While hierarchy was very clear, the staff believed that the well-being of a guest was a group effort and should be acknowledged as such. Apparently, hierarchy and status had come to a face-off in a group-oriented culture, and the group affiliation was strongest.

- When I visited with Mary Beth, an expatriate wife, she told this story: When she first arrived in Den Haag, The Netherlands, she was summarily instructed that she'd better not act in the same way as one of her compatriates. One of her neighbors refused to sit down and have tea with the workmen whenever she needed the plumbing fixed or the house painted. And, no matter what the work, the laborer would not start until tea—and conversation—had been served. Mary Beth realized it was a cultural situation, indicating that jobs don't define status in relation to one another. And, if you don't treat everyone with great respect, nothing will get done.

- In a conversation with an oil company executive who was doing business in a traditional Moslem country we learned that the company had prepared a guidebook for expatriates. In it, one of the illustrations was a cartoon of a woman in shorts and halter top. There was an X through the picture. Obviously, the company considered this universal symbol (**X**) to signify that this is inappropriate dress. When the employee guidebook was shipped into the country, it was seized by local customs as being pornographic.

- On a trip through Asia, a female colleague was constantly referencing the subtle sexism she experienced. It culminated when the flight attendant asked me if I wanted a newspaper. I declined. She then went on to the next male passenger. My colleague said, "Wait. What about me? I can read." "Certainly, sir," said the flight attendant, "which one would you like?"

- For two years, Bill (an American senior manager) would order pizza from a local pizzeria in Tokyo—once or twice a week. When the entire management staff came to work on a Saturday, he asked the Japanese secretary to call in the pizza order. She tactfully returned to him and suggested that he should be calling a different phone number next time. It turned out that for the last two years he had actually been phoning his Japanese neighbor who would take his order and then, in turn, call the pizzeria.

And there are also countless business anecdotes. The secretary in Taiwan who felt that her boss lacked confidence in her because he didn't ask her to take care of his personal errands; the Australian managing director who arrived in Germany slapping people on the back and telling them they should use his first name; and the American engineer who asked to be repatriated early from Israel because he couldn't stand the constant "bickering" and challenge to his authority. People who never thought about doing business outside of their countries now think of little else.

We wrote *Capitalizing on the Global Workforce: A Strategic Guide to Expatriate Management* with those people in mind. It is designed to be a primer for those entering the field, a refresher for those who have been in global HR for a long time, a quick reference for human resource professionals whose responsibilities are expanding in the rapidly changing environment, and a guide for businesses first capitalizing on international opportunities. With these objectives, we structured the book to recognize that intercultural understanding is the foundation for global business, and based on that we develop the various business applications necessary to function in the international arena.

Along the way, our mission was reinforced by the numerous professionals we met who reconfirmed the need for such a book. We conducted strategic roundtable discussions around the world with experts in the field, and built a knowledge base to complement our experience and background that we brought to this endeavor.

It is a book we both wished we'd had at our disposal to gain knowledge as we ventured into this new area. We decided to build the book around the concept of global cultures because we believe it is the essential cornerstone of success in a global marketplace. Indeed, one of the surprises we encountered was that even though culture is fundamental, there are virtually no books that weave together the technical aspects of compensation and expatriate administration with culture while taking into account the pivotal role of personal and family dynamics in protecting the international business investment.

Although we chose the title, *Capitalizing on the Global Workforce,* we are well aware that we would have to write several more volumes to adequately fulfill the scope of the title. So, while we may not cover the entire subject, the book does take a reasonable first slice of this evolving business reality. In addition, the book initially focuses on our *Weltanschauung*— our world view—which is, admittedly, the expatriate experience from the United States–British perspective. We believe that this is appropriate because global cultural understanding can only come after we each appreciate the impact that culture has on us individually and the role it plays in coloring our own perceptions. So what more appropriate point of departure is there for the exploration of cultures' influences than our admittedly geocentric perspective? You, as the reader can use that perspective to enhance and differentiate your own perceptions of culture's impact. We selected the title, *Capitalizing on the Global Workforce* because we envision the present and the future as being a melding of global talent. Indeed, the Information Age dictates the need for a level of technical competence that is available only through a well-educated workforce. And since that talent will be recruited from a worldwide talent pool, the global workforce will quickly become a reality. We remain firmly convinced that intercultural competence is now, and will become the ever-more important underpinning of a successful global business enterprise.

Many individuals helped in conceptualizing and writing this work. A few were exceptional in their time, support, and effort.

Both of us thank Marian Stoltz-Loike, Ph.D., contributing author and co-creator of the Windham International Cultural Model. For the

past four years, intellectual dialog with Marian has honed our appreciation for national and corporate culture as well as human interaction,
which are not only a part of this book, but also a core to the concept of
Windham International. Marian's discussions with both of us have
covered a wide breadth, and been enlightening not only in the areas of
culture, but also in the arena of women's work, dual-career, and family
concerns.

We also want to thank Alan Chesters, contributing author, as well
as operations director of London-based ECA International and managing
director of ECA Windham. Alan is another individual who has been actively involved in this work since its inception. His wisdom on global
compensation is already widely acknowledged by his colleagues and
peers in the field. Alan's knowledge, however, is even surpassed by his
patience and wit, both a tremendous source of support and encouragement. Working with him is a pleasure.

We'd also like to thank Ilene Dolins, senior vice president of Windham International, who actually first suggested that we write this book
and the entire staff of Windham International and ECA Windham, whose
research and hard work added enormously to the book's depth and insight. In addition, we want to thank the staff of the Windham Companies
who held down the fort while Mike worked on "the book": Susan
McDonald and Lee Ann Southorn for the contribution of case studies in
the culture chapters; Gary Parker, Valerie Greenly, Claudia Quinones,
Claudia Feehan, Samantha Gold, Shurlan Tran and Stephanie Rappoport
for their support.

There are other individuals who have added to this book in significant ways. We would like to thank them. Michael Tucker, Ph.D. who
provided wisdom and information on expatriate selection. Rick Swaak,
who so generously shares wisdom, insight, and his years of experience.
Eric Stern, whose sense of humor and understanding of the field of relocation, along with MaryLou Belmont, helped us with the chapter on expatriate policy.

We want to extend special thanks to Stephen H. Rhinesmith, Ph.D.,
who shared not only his experience as a noted international business
consultant, but also his wisdom as a writer of some noted works in the
field. His book, *A Manager's Guide to Globalization: Six Keys to Success in a
Changing World,* is, itself, a milestone work in the field of international
business. Steve, who preceded Michael as president of Moran, Stahl &
Boyer, again generously shared his wisdom and experience.

We each have individual acknowledgments as well.

Michael would like to thank his clients, for their confidence and the opportunity they have provided, and his partners in the Global Relocation Partnership (GRP) for making the vision of Windham International a reality.

Charlene would like to add a special thank you to Allan Halcrow, publisher and editor in chief and Margaret Magnus, CEO of *Workforce* magazine (formerly *Personnel Journal*) and ACC Communications, for providing the opportunity to write dozens of stories about—and research—this ever-changing field of global human resources. As important as affording the opportunity to develop expertise about this topic, Allan has always been a thoughtful advocate and good friend, who has supported and encouraged the vision and intuition about what makes a good story—even when it was trendsetting and going out on a limb. In addition, many people, both in major corporations and in consultant firms, were generous with their time, their knowledge, and, in effect, served as teachers for the last five years. In editorial endeavors, Charlene also thanks Samuel Greengard, Lynn Newman, Michelle Cutrow, and Jody Welborn.

We'd like to thank the following companies who participated in our global Strategic Issues Roundtables: ABB Vetco Gray, Allied Signal, Alltel Information Services, ANZ Bank, Aramco, Arco, AT&T, Avon, Barclay's Bank, Bates Worldwide, Brown & Root, Inc., CAMCO International, Caltex, Chase Bank, Citibank, Colgate-Palmolive, Continental Grain Company, EDS, Employment Conditions Abroad (ECA), General Electric (GE), GTE Directories Service Corporation, International Flavors and Fragrances, Marathon Oil, Marks & Spencer, Merrill Lynch, JP Morgan, Reed Tool Co., Shell International, Shell Oil Company, Smith International, RTZ, Tenneco, Inc., and Warner Lambert.

Michael S. Schell
Charlene Marmer Solomon

I

CROSS-CULTURAL CHALLENGES OF THE GLOBAL WORKFORCE

CHAPTER

1

⑥ **CAPITALIZING ON GLOBAL BUSINESS OPPORTUNITIES: THE CRITICAL ROLE PEOPLE PLAY**

This chapter will cover
- An historical overview of the impact of globalization on business.
- What is expected of a globally astute manager.
- The business and personal challenges of operating in the international arena.
- The hard realities about the "soft subject" of culture.

While much of the world has been involved in the global marketplace for some time, the United States is a relative newcomer. For most of our history, we've been a completely self-sufficient economic entity with vast natural and human resources. Other nations less well endowed needed to engage in international trade for their very survival.

World history bears witness to the fact that the pursuit of international trade has inspired mankind's greatest adventures. It has been the precursor to the very best and the very worst chapters of history. The quest for international trade has started wars and made peace, encouraged scientific innovation, and advanced civilization. Today, the pursuit of global trade is accelerating at an ever faster pace. International trade has long been a magnet for adventurers, entrepreneurs, monarchs, and nations. From Marco Polo and Columbus to today's international teams of astronauts, international trade has served as an impetus for adventure, discovery, and the generation of wealth.

Such opportunities are still out there. Monarchs and nations have been replaced by CEOs and corporations; new adventurers are entering uncharted territory in search of greater wealth and power. Called corporate expatriates, they are still in search of wealth and many are still armed with advanced technology. Now, however, these voyagers are coming to partner, not to conquer. Whatever their motivation, they know that to win in today's game of global trade, they must create opportunities for mutual gain and work together with the local nationals. These adventurers need an entirely different set of tools and skills to succeed. That is what this book is all about.

BECOMING GLOBALLY ASTUTE

Becoming *globally astute* is something we all must do. Most of us think that our culture and frame of reference is universal, but once we venture outside our national boundaries, we realize that this simply isn't the case. Becoming globally astute means being able to understand behaviors and to translate that knowledge in a variety of cultures into appropriate responses and winning tactics.

Because of its great resources and powerful economy, the United States has been able to avoid many of the issues that Europeans and Asians have long been concerned with. In the past, our enormous power and open markets have caused *others* to adapt to the American way of doing things: English became the language of business and U.S. business schools set the norms. Others had to learn our language, our customs, and our business practices because their markets were in the United States.

What has happened to change all that? The answer is threefold: First, the United States has become a fertile marketplace for foreign products, resulting in a weakened balance of trade and balance of payments. To equalize that imbalance, and fend off the competition, we must not only sell more in the world marketplace, but produce better and more inexpensive products within the United States. That requires global materials and labor sourcing. Second, the middle class throughout the world is growing at an extraordinary rate. It has a thirst for products and services that will soon eclipse that of the United States and Europe. Third, with the advent of technology—capital and education are almost equally accessible worldwide—competition in every aspect of business is intensi-fied. No one organization or country can maintain an undisputed domi-nance or can support a business of global stature. The traditional advan-tages that the United States had—access to capital, a technological lead, and a highly educated workforce—are being neutralized. The Microsofts and Merrill Lynches of the world have made the flow of capital and tech-nology equally accessible in Kansas City or Kuala Lumpur.

U.S. EXPANSION IN THE GLOBAL MARKET

As a result, we now find ourselves rushing with great speed into global competition—as much to protect our domestic markets as to conquer new ones. Our historic commercial dominance is no longer impenetra-ble. As we look around, we see emerging countries and economies that represent opportunities far greater than many of the traditional markets we're familiar with. We, too, are striking out beyond our shores.

But, are we prepared for this contest?

In the short span of 10 years, many U.S. companies have discov-ered that more of their revenues are coming from international markets and alliances than from traditional domestic activities. Motorola, for ex-ample, estimates that at least 60 percent of its revenues will come from foreign investment by the year 2000. The $5 billion McDonald's gener-ated from its 7,000 restaurants outside the United States attests to its spectacular success abroad,[1] and 56 percent of Citicorp's employees re-side outside the United States.[2]

Indeed, American corporations are expanding into the global arena at a staggering pace. They already employ 5.5 million people abroad, among whom are at least 350,000 expatriates, and they sent 30 percent more American expatriates overseas in 1994 than the previous year.[3] In 1970, only 7,000 corporations were listed as multinationals (half of them were United States and British); in 1993 that number grew to 35,000.[4]

No question, the stakes are enormous. In 1993, $4 trillion dollars in goods and services were traded across national boundaries, with inter-national trade growing one and one-half times the rate of production.[5] Overseas investment by American companies surged to more than $716 billion in 1993.[6]

The result? A global business village that is redefining behavior and action. Yet, experts say that U.S. business is often held back *not* by lack of technical know-how or financial capital, but by human capital.

Businesses often have trouble finding talented individuals who are willing and able to relocate and conduct business abroad. Many managers and human resource professionals shudder at the thought of staffing these global operations with the required number of expatriates. Furthermore, managers have to learn an entirely new set of rules about employment and new management practices in every country where they employ locals.

THE CHALLENGES OF OPERATING IN THE INTERNATIONAL MARKETPLACE

How does a company operate in this complex international arena? How does it select, prepare, and manage people who will run these businesses? How does it adjust domestically to capitalize and absorb the profound lessons it learns in the global village?

This is the new challenge for business and for traditional human resource practices. HR managers will need to take a leading role in solving these complex business issues, which heralds a profound change from their historically service-focused role. Helping companies succeed in this life-and-death struggle for economic survival is a new breed of manager—a globally astute executive—an individual whose elaborate duties encompass responsibilities as complex as the global business environment itself.

The ramifications are many. Whether the industry is soap, automobiles, pharmaceuticals, or petroleum, the scenario is much the same. For a business to succeed, it needs to effectively staff the worldwide marketplace with people who have savvy and ingenuity. As the world's workforce becomes increasingly mobile and skill based, it is clear that organizations will recruit with far less regard for national boundaries and country of origin. This has already taken place in many of the world's leading organizations. Likewise, multinational organizations will move employees from one location to another in response to business needs, with little concern for the national boundaries they are crossing. Eventually, people will need to be able to cross national borders as easily as computer data and automobiles.

However, unlike computers and cars, which need only minimal reengineering to succeed in a foreign environment, people require great care, and reengineering people skills demands careful consideration. As the global marketplace expands and the need for qualified people grows, senior managers and human resources professionals increasingly face an array of new and complex issues. At the core is the need for cultural awareness and an understanding of the effects of culture on day-to-day business operations.

Unfortunately, cultural horror stories abound, showing that people need a great deal of training to reach the skill levels to function effectively in the global village. Simple things such as finger pointing, laughing at the wrong time, raising one's voice, or touching someone can create problems.

Although cultural blunders are almost always avoidable, so is walking through a minefield if you know where all the explosives are located. In other words, it isn't easy and you have to know the path. It takes a great deal of effort to be sure we know enough about each other to conduct business. The real challenges lie more deeply in intercultural transactions. They are found in the different way people react to leadership styles, management behaviors, and the importance they ascribe to building trust and long-term relationships. In other words, we may all speak English, but that doesn't mean we understand one another.

These *faux pas* occur all the time overseas. Witness the American manager in Beijing who tried to critique his Chinese colleague's idea. Knowing how respectful the Chinese people are with each other, he said very respectfully, "That's a very good point, but I don't agree with you." The American never realized that he caused his Chinese colleague a major loss of face and was baffled that the deal was never consummated.

There are countless examples: in Mexico, asking opinions of junior people when their superiors are present; in Venezuela, inviting people to a party that runs from 8:00 to 11:00 P.M.; in France, dressing casually when invited to someone's house for dinner; in Japan, declining to accept a gift or giving one in return that is of far less value.

These gaffes don't apply only to people's behavior. They happen even when we introduce new products to market. There's the ofttold tale about Procter & Gamble trying to sell Pampers in Japan. The only problem was that the Japanese have little space in their small dwellings to store full-size disposable diapers! And they change their children's diapers far more frequently than Americans, which means they need more of them. Then, there's the well-known case of Kentucky Fried Chicken translating its "Finger Lickin Good" slogan into Chinese: It became, "Eat Your Fingers Off." And everyone's heard of the fiasco when General

Motors introduced its Nova model into the Latin American auto market. The word "Nova" in Spanish means "No go."[7]

These cultural mistakes could be avoided with a little knowledge, a good bit of research, and a recognition of the importance of culture. However, the cultural traps that stall intercultural team functions and business negotiations, and stymie international business leaders, are far more subtle and omnipresent. Interactions involving interpersonal relationships need a depth of understanding, so that people can internalize this wisdom until it becomes second nature. Indeed, just as quickly and effectively as McDonald's has created McSpaghetti for the Philippines and McMutton pot pies in Australia, intelligent businesspeople realize that culture is bottom line.

This book probes the world of staffing an international organization: selection, compensation, benefits, understanding the impact of culture on international business, preparing people to function in a multicultural environment, providing cross-cultural preparation for those embarking on an expatriate assignment, and offering support to families on assignment so they can succeed. It is all borne out of effectively developing individuals who are comfortable in different cultures and skilled at dealing with the variety of people around the world. It affects all aspects of business, from dealing with customers and colleagues to creating products and marketing campaigns.

CULTURE: THE HARD REALITIES ABOUT THIS "SOFT SUBJECT"

Learned and absorbed during the earliest stages of childhood, reinforced by literature, history, and religion, embodied by our heroes, and expressed in our instinctive values and views, culture is a powerful force that shapes our thoughts and perceptions. It affects the way we perceive and judge events, how we respond and interpret them, and how we communicate to one another in both spoken and unspoken language. Culture, with all of its implications, differs in every society. These differences might be profound or subtle; they might be obvious or invisible. Ever present yet constantly changing, culture permeates the world we know and molds the way we construct or define reality.

Businesses can't be separated from people and their cultural milieu. Understanding culture—being sensitive to nuances and differences in people from country to country—is fundamental for success in the international marketplace. The corporate cultures of many global organizations are often so strong that they may appear to override local national cultures, misleading the international traveler into believing that the cultural similarity is more than skin deep. For example, the financial services industry has been able to introduce competitive pay-for-performance schemes in Japan. However, that individual competitiveness in no way abridges the Japanese reverence for team effort and hierarchy.

Although companies often refer to understanding culture as part of the "soft side," there is nothing soft or easy about learning culture, and it will profoundly influence the hard numbers on the bottom line. More than any other aspect of the business experience, our knowledge and understanding of culture affects the outcome of business ventures. Without insight into the ways of others, we can't expect to develop credibility, nurture goodwill, inspire a workforce, or develop marketable products. And that directly translates to bottom-line results. Culture affects the way we develop and maintain relationships. It plays a significant role in determining success with colleagues and partners, and helps us grasp how to evolve into respected leaders around the world. Understanding culture fundamentally affects how we run our business, what characteristics to look for in selecting people, how to develop global talent, how to conduct meetings, and how to manage employees and work with teams. In spite of its importance and growing acceptance by major corporations, culture may be the component most overlooked by expatriates preparing for work in the international business arena.

⑥ ⑥ ⑥

WHAT IS CULTURE?

Culture is multilayered. Created by myriad factors, including the history, religion, mythology, climate, and geography of a country, culture is defined by shared values and beliefs, and it forms the fundamental assumptions on which the whole society is built. Because no two countries share exactly the same influences, national cultures always vary. We can see what happens when countries artificially merge cultures based on political or economic motivations. When they try to create alliances between ethnic or religious groups without understanding and integrating cultures, the situation inevitably unravels. We need to look no further than the former Yugoslavia or the Soviet Union to see how cultural incompatibility can cause alliances to disintegrate. Even though several generations were raised in this artificial "nationality," the populations maintained their separate cultures and eventually sought autonomy.

To be sure, culture is a powerful force. We talk about it like the layers of an onion—the outer visible layer—to the less visible middle layer that carries a society's unspoken, intuitive value system, down to the core of the culture that embodies the values that are assumed because they're intrinsic. Cultural anthropologists have described culture as a shared way of solving dilemmas or processing ideas. A prerequisite for this is the existence of mutual expectations.[8]

Culture has three layers. (See Figure 1–1.) The outer layer or the

FIGURE   1–1

The Three Layers of Culture

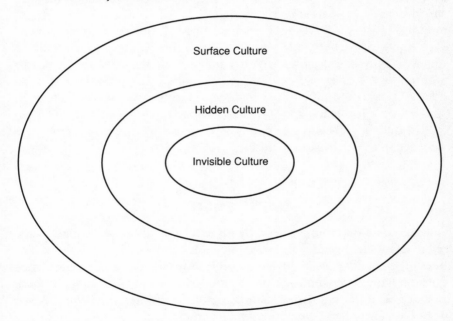

Surface Culture

Hidden Culture

Invisible Culture

Figure 1–1 shows the following:
Outer layer or surface culture—dress, food, architecture, customs.
Middle layer or hidden culture—values, religions, and philosophies about childrearing, views of right and wrong.
Core or invisible culture—the culture's universal truths.

surface culture is the obvious, observable behavior—food, language, dress, infrastructure of cities, structure of office space. The middle layer or the *hidden culture* is the values, beliefs, and philosophy that define the culture: attitudes toward time, communication, religion, and notions about good and bad. The inner core, the *invisible culture*, hearkens back to the essence of our innermost beliefs about universal, nonnegotiable truths. The invisible culture is so deeply embedded that it is difficult to recognize, but it is critical to forming our social fabric. The visible layers might change, but these changes are superficial and shouldn't delude observers to think that deep alterations in culture have been made.

Culture can be defined as the way a society has evolved to incorporate the fundamental realities dictated by its physical environment into its value system. These realities change as culture evolves and changes, but slowly, building on existing values and norms to incorporate changes that it must make.

For example, the dramatic evolution that took place in the American culture that went from a society that owned slaves to one that values diversity. Much of that change is still taking place. Since it was legislated and enforced by the state, the culture had no choice but to integrate it. And, it did so, but slowly. Now, with the population shifting and new entrants into the workforce expected to be comprised of two-thirds women and people of color, the United States is converting itself from a "melting pot" which was supposed to help everyone become the same, to a society that wants to capitalize on the differences in people and the unique, individual contributions each one makes.

To prepare global managers, expatriates, and others to interact effectively across cultures, we could theoretically provide them with a cultural briefing for every destination so they could learn how to live with their new neighbors and conduct business in that environment. That's obviously inefficient and not always possible, so we have developed a cultural training process that builds a foundation for both understanding new cultures and recognizing cultural behaviors. This preparation develops managers who are multiculturally fluent and capable of functioning in a global environment.

J. Stewart Black, Hal B. Gregersen, and Mark E. Mendenhall explain that just as the special international "driver" needs to understand that motoring behavior and expectations are different around the world, the globally astute individual desperately needs a cultural atlas.[9] We've developed the Windham International Cultural Model© to provide people entering the global arena with a multicultural road map.

Before we explore the Windham Cultural Model with its nine dimensions, let's look at culture as it affects everyday transactions.

NOTES

1. McDonald's Annual Report, 1995.
2. Citicorp Annual Report, 1995.
3. Figures based on estimates by Reyer A. Swaak of the National Foreign Trade Council.
4. Figures based on conversations with J. Stewart Black, associate professor of International Management, Thunderbird, The American Graduate School of International Management, Glendale, Arizona.
5. Anant Sundaram and J. Stewart Black, *International Business Environment,* (New York, NY: Prentice Hall, 1995).
6. *New York Times,* July 25, 1994.
7. David A. Ricks, *Blunders in International Business,* (Cambridge, MA: Blackwell Business Publishers, 1993).
8. Fons Trompenaars, *Riding the Waves of Culture: Understanding Diversity in Global Business,* Burr Ridge, IL: Irwin Professional Publishing, 1994).
9. J. Stewart Black, Hal B. Gregersen, and Mark E. Mendenhall, *Global Assignments: Successfully Expatriating and Repatriating International Managers,* (San Francisco: Jossey-Bass, 1992).

2

⑥ THE INFLUENCE OF CULTURE ON GLOBAL BUSINESS

This chapter will cover

- The role of culture in business.
- The layers of culture.
- How culture affects business operations.
- A fictional global case study.

SCENARIO: ORBOX TELECOMMUNICATIONS

The year: 1996

The place: Somewhere in central California.

The company: Orbox Telecommunications, a U.S. firm created in 1986 by Jonathan Orbox, now chief executive officer. The firm is a leading manufacturer of cellular phones and paging devices.

The sprawling campus of Orbox Telecommunications typifies the company's philosophy and approach. Perched on a bluff above the Pacific Ocean in central California are six ranch-style buildings—each two stories high—scattered amid a wooded courtyard that offers benches, picnic tables, a stream, and an outdoor running track. The informal atmosphere and people reflect the American version of a modern, individualistic, hard-driving, and entrepreneurial culture. It serves as a subtle metaphor for the company's attitude and spirit.

Created only a decade ago, Orbox, like many of its high-tech neighbors, has enjoyed phenomenal success. It began with only a handful of employees and now has more than 1,000 workers worldwide. Its annual revenues exceed $500 million. Such success is clearly a reflection of Jonathan Orbox's personality. Starting with a $5,000 loan from his grandmother, the brash, hard-driving 42-year-old built this empire which is the envy of the industry. That same "can do" spirit now permeates the company and its employees.

In 1994, Orbox began to expand its global reach into Asia and Latin America. Its foray into Asia involved a merger with a Taiwanese computer chip manufacturer, Jin Dian Nau. The expansion into Latin America began with the purchase of a Mexico City distribution facility named Grupo Communicación. The management team insensitively refers to that division as "Mañana Enterprises," a reflection not only of the current pace of the operation but also of the acquisition's future importance to Orbox.

Jonathan believes that with enough ingenuity, vision, and effort, Orbox Telecommunications can succeed anywhere in the world. He is ready for the contest. He is a strong leader who prides himself on developing and empowering key senior managers and then relying on their energy and creativity to rapidly build up the business.

In a recent speech to employees, Jonathan emphasized the most important points of Orbox's push towards the future:

These investments into new markets reflect the current nature of our business and the competitive environment we find ourselves in. The Asians are coming into our markets and competing for our customers. Despite the fact that we have outstanding products, they are winning away some customers, based on price and quality, and the open nature of our marketplace. They are expanding into other international markets faster than we are, and we can't let them gain any market share over us.

They are establishing strategically located manufacturing and distribution centers and as a result will be able to get their products to market more cheaply. Our advantage as innovators and creators is short-lived for each product since the competition is able to copy them at an ever-faster rate.

Asia and Latin America are the fastest growing markets in the world and they are price sensitive. We have to take advantage of our leading position and bring products and innovation to those areas. I firmly believe that the energy, creativity, and vitality that has made us the market leader in the United States can be replicated in these markets.

We have to be aggressive, bold, and undaunted by the challenge. If we can introduce our winning culture, and introduce the changes necessary in those new markets, we will continue to accelerate our growth with this international endeavor. We will continue to keep our vendors competitive, to source and buy from a variety of suppliers, to shop for best prices and highest quality, and to have zero tolerance for error and lack of quality in ourselves and our suppliers.

Toward that end, we need to continue our focus on cutting costs and always seeking new ways to reduce development time. The way we will stay on the cutting edge is to fill our company with innovators.

Orbox's entry into Asia presented dazzling opportunities to beat the competition and grab major market share, and Jonathan practically salivated with eagerness. At any time, he was ready to don gloves and step into the ring. If he didn't already have the responsibility of running the company, Jonathan would have planted himself in Taiwan so he could run the operation himself. Instead, he handpicked James Simon, senior vice president of production and a proven star who had played an integral role at Orbox Telecommunications since the beginning. He had gained tremendous respect from Jonathan for his ability to motivate the workforce, introduce new processes, and increase profit margins and revenues in a highly competitive market. Best of all was his ability to effect rapid change in a fast-moving, high-tech industry. James was also a long-time buddy of Jonathan's. He was 36, married for six years with two children, and a classic car collector.

James never professed much interest in living in Asia—or anywhere outside the United States for that matter. While he confessed an almost complete ignorance about what was involved with an overseas assignment, he was pleased to have landed such a plum opportunity. So, he casually waved off his wife's protests about leaving friends and giving up her role as president of the kids' school coordinating council and director of a local charity. He shrugged off his own concerns by focusing on the $50,000 relocation bonus atop his $250,000 annual salary and a chance to increase the value of his company stock by millions of dollars. In addition, and to allay his own fears, he told himself that his expatriate allowances would provide an excellent lifestyle for his family and, because they were outgoing and amiable, they would make friends and have a great time.

CENTRAL CALIFORNIA

Friday, March 10, 1995

The family swiftly packed its bags, enrolled the children in the American school, and jetted to Taiwan with an optimistic, fearless attitude. They were about to embark on a great adventure and reap many rewards.

TAIPEI, TAIWAN

Jin Dian Nau (JDN) had begun as a family-run operation 35 years ago and had slowly grown over the years. The company had always prided itself on manufacturing only the highest-quality products. It cherished its roots and paternalistic structure. Company picnics and group vacations weren't an obligation; managers and employees thoroughly enjoyed them. It was a chance to socialize and pay respect to one another.

Unlike Orbox, a company that had opted to go public and sell stock as quickly as possible, JDN had remained a family-run enterprise. Under the stewardship of company president Cheng Yi-Hwa, JDN had grown from a manufacturer of small handheld calculators to a major producer of personal computers and semiconductors for the cellular industry. Cheng Yi-Hwa, who had led the organization and its employees through a series of transitions, always invested significantly in the growth of the business. The goal was simple: ensure the firm's success during his lifetime and that of his children and grandchildren. Unlike Jonathan, Cheng believed in slow growth built upon consensus and mutual understanding.

A recent article in the *Taiwan Times* highlighted JDN, focusing on its ability to provide secure employment opportunities and the strong ties and devotion that existed between employees and management. The article also highlighted the company's special relationship with suppliers and customers. In addition to the local custom of gift giving at the New Year, the firm paid special attention to birthdays, the births of children, weddings, anniversaries, and other significant events. Moreover, Cheng Yi-Hwa would give gifts to his many friends around the world as a way of acknowledging their contributions. Executives often took clients and suppliers to dinner, and once a year gave a banquet in their honor at one of Taipei's finest restaurants.

Monday, March 13, 1995

During the negotiations that preceded the acquisition of JDN, James played a behind-the-scenes role and never actually visited Taiwan. But with the new responsibility of managing the integration of the two companies, James intended to "hit the ground running." He could hardly wait to get into his new job. "If I can drive this thing fast enough," he told his wife, "we can be back in California in a year, I'll have a real feather in my cap, and I'll be rewarded with additional company stock." Already, James's American perspective of time had become apparent. His bias toward short-term gains failed to take into account the time and energy it would take to establish relationships and trust with the Taiwanese. Although he knew that the cultures were different and that things would need to be moved along at a gentler pace, he was convinced he could win over the Taiwanese once they saw the near-term cash benefits of his rapid integration plan. He assumed that while it would take a little longer, the process would unfold as it always had during similar U.S. acquisitions.

Even before his family found a home, James arranged for the executives from JDN and Orbox to meet. They would discuss the vision of the company and some of the details related to the integration of the two firms. With most of his clothes still packed away in storage crates and his official start date for the project a week away, James headed off to meet his Taiwanese colleagues.

Tuesday, March 14, 1995

At their first meeting, Cheng Yi-Hwa gently shook James's hand with a serious expression on his face. He did not make immediate eye contact and James thought he sensed tension in his body—though it was really nothing more than Cheng Yi-Hwa's formality. James forged ahead with the meeting, figuring that the tension would evaporate after a few minutes of discussion or a joke or two.

"Yi-Hwa," James said, "I am so pleased to meet you. I am really looking forward to working together with you to develop this company into a truly great corporation." The two exchanged small talk for awhile, and then James suggested that they go to lunch to get to know each other. At lunch, Cheng Yi-Hwa and the other Taiwanese managers showed a pronounced interest in James's family, his educational background, and his hometown. They didn't seem to be as interested in discussing the business as they were in finding out about him. James asked a similar perfunctory question or two—just to be polite—but he was rather uncomfortable prying into nonbusiness activities.

After a half hour or so, James decided to move the conversation to business issues, "So, what do you think about the merger of our two companies?" He was greeted with a gallery of smiles and took this to mean that there was general satisfaction with the agreement. Yet, no one answered his question and nobody seemed inclined to discuss the issue.

Behind Cheng Yi-Hwa's smile was a deep feeling of discomfort. He wasn't intimidated by the foreign company coming to Taipei; from only a few minutes of conversation, James seemed like a nice enough fellow. But he wondered how could someone so young, so informal, and so direct could be given such an important responsibility? Why was he in such a hurry? Why wasn't he giving them ample time to become acquainted and develop a sense of trust?

James went on, "I have received a briefing, but I can't wait to see what is really going on here. Once we reduce your man-hours per unit to the same levels as we have at home, margins will be staggering." He smiled and took a deep breath: "What do you think about a general meeting on Monday of senior managers, including the other Americans?" His Taiwanese colleagues nodded, which he took to be a go-ahead. "Good, I'll have a memo sent out," James concluded.

Monday, March 20, 1995

Cheng Yi-Hwa began the meeting with a flowery introduction of James, referring to him as "Mr. Simon." James thanked Cheng Yi-Hwa for his introduction but continued by discussing his own career achievements within the company, saying nothing complimentary in return about Cheng. He also displayed his excitement at having the opportunity to lead the company to a higher level of success. "By combining our state-of-the-arts methods with the success you have been able to achieve here in Taiwan, I feel confident we will be able to raise Jin Dian Nau to world-class standards by the end of the year. And the bottom line is that this will translate into more money and success for each of us."

James continued with the meeting, discussing specific goals he had developed for the overall program. The key points of his vision: Increasing productivity, improving quality control, empowering employees, and slashing costs. As he scribbled each of these goals on a chalkboard, he called on the key managers of marketing, sales, finance, and production to suggest ways to reach each of these goals. To his surprise, the senior managers remained silent.

He looked over at Cheng Yi-Hwa. If James could have read Cheng's mind behind the stoic expression, he would have read, "What are you doing? Why are you asking questions of these people? How can they possibly make suggestions that will offend their colleagues who developed the systems? Don't you know they would never speak about such things without conferring with each other first?"

Finally, after a great deal of cajoling, Mr. Wu, manager of sales, commented, "This is a new way to look at operations. I need some time to think before being able to comment." Most of the other managers echoed his sentiments. Although he couldn't put his finger on the problem, James knew that his message wasn't getting through the way it did back home in the United States. He had always prided himself on being a great motivator and creating an environment that encouraged an outpouring of ideas.

Turning to his American colleagues—partly as a way to break the tension—James asked them for their thoughts. A former vice president of finance at Orbox, Michelle Arman,[1] chimed in, "First, I think we need to reduce the tremendous year-end bonuses that these people hand out." The Taiwanese executives glanced at the outspoken woman curiously thinking, *This American woman is interesting, but doesn't she know that everyone's salary is calculated over a 13-month period?*

CENTRAL CALIFORNIA

April 20, 1995

As the Asian fiasco was unfolding, Orbox's distribution plant in Mexico City was just beginning to ramp-up production. Thirty-year-old Reuben Jones was selected to manage the facility. He had been with the company for only three years and was considered one of the new breed of Orbox managers who had been recruited from the Kellogg School of Business. Most recently, he had served as the company's vice president of operations. Having heard about the company's move into Latin America, Reuben approached his boss and asked if he could be considered for the position.

While in high school, Reuben had been an exchange student in Italy. Fascinated by cultural differences and international business, he decided from the start to pursue a career that allowed him to conduct his work in the global arena. He had studied Spanish and had taken several college courses in international affairs and political science. On his way to getting an MBA, he continued to study languages and traveled extensively to Latin America and Europe.

Reuben's wife, Lilliana, whom he met at the International School in Rome, was an illustrator of children's books. Their only son was seven, heavily into soccer and an average student. While Reuben was eager to move to Mexico, he took great care to think about his family's needs as expatriates. Having already lived abroad once, he knew that they had to maintain a certain living standard while balancing the need to integrate into the local community. He and Lilliana discussed their concerns and weighed all the issues for several weeks before making a decision. One factor that played a major role in the final decision to accept the position, was Lilliana's ability to continue to work for her current publisher while living abroad.

With Reuben, as with James, the human resources department at Orbox had suggested that he and his family participate in an intercultural counseling program. While James considered himself too busy with work and family details to attend, Reuben jumped at the opportunity. He hoped the two-day program would provide him and his family with additional understanding. The Jones's also spent four days in Mexico City looking at available accommodations, checking out the international school, and meeting other expatriates in the community.

Despite all the preparations, Reuben approached the Mexico assignment with trepidation. Not only was he worried that Orbox's corporate culture and the values of the Mexican company might clash, but he was concerned about the company's rigid adherence to timeline commitments and the need to boost the financial performance in only two quarters. He knew that Latin culture viewed time in a very different way.

Because of these and other cultural concerns, as well as an understanding of the importance of relationships in the Latin environment, Reuben invited Señor Jiménez, the senior manager of his Mexico City team to California to spend several days touring Orbox headquarters. Not only would this help Reuben develop a bond with the highly respected executive, but also it would provide an opportunity for Jiménez to become acquainted with his U.S. colleagues.

CENTRAL CALIFORNIA

May 5, 1995

During the week, Señor Jiménez helped Reuben understand a great deal about how Latin managers ask and respond to questions. He also helped Reuben gain insight into how they function in a hierarchical environment, including how they conduct meetings and other interactions with peers, superiors, and subordinates. Reuben also learned about the operation in Mexico City. Seeing the environment at Orbox—with its wide open spaces and casual appearance—Jiménez was struck by the differences in the two workforces and knew that it was important to alert Reuben to this fact. In carefully crafted words, he suggested to Reuben that the Mexican workforce would have different expectations and needs. Mexicans would not respond well to the American style of empowerment, Jiménez said, because they expect their leaders to be formal and authoritative. Reuben was fascinated by the Mexican gentleman's appearance in relation to his colleagues in California. Although Reuben mentioned that he should dress as casually as Orbox employees, Señor Jiménez, a quietly assertive man in his late 40s, arrived at the office wearing a dark suit and tie. But Reuben noticed that he fell into step calling his U.S. cohorts by their first names.

MEXICO CITY, MEXICO

June 5, 1995

When Reuben arrived at his office in Mexico City dressed in the appropriate conservative, formal attire—company officials gave him a tour and introduced him to the key managers he would be working with in the months ahead. At a special luncheon in his honor given by Jiménez, they discussed their jobs, families, and backgrounds. They also engaged in small talk about a recent soccer match between Grupo Communicación and a competitor. They shared the highlights of the match they had won, and Reuben could see how much they valued teamwork and group spirit. Reuben walked away from that day's luncheon feeling he had begun to establish a relationship with his colleagues.

June 9, 1995

During the first few days, Reuben eased himself into the new environment, paying special attention to names and the nature of relationships. He requested a meeting of the people who reported directly to him. At that meeting, Reuben presented Orbox's overall global agenda along with the specific contribution expected of the Mexican business unit. He began by demonstrating his grasp of the current business situation in Mexico based on a detailed reading of company data while making a painstaking effort to show respect for the performance of the Mexican company and its current management.

At the meeting, he allowed plenty of time for everyone to speak. Then, over another leisurely lunch, Reuben talked about Orbox's corporate values: speed, change, integrity, equality, work dedication, and continuous improvement. He understood that these were essentially American values, so he expressed a desire to find ways they could define those Orbox corporate values at Grupo Communicación.

At the afternoon meeting, Reuben once again advanced the uncompromising commitment to achieving the goal Jonathan had set: to triple production of high-quality cellular telephones in the next two years. The discussion meandered, but Reuben surmised that his colleagues had gotten the message. He committed to deliver specific plans and to outline tactics that would make the achievement of these goals possible. What he needed from the Mexican staff was a commitment to those tactics. He communicated his confidence that the managers and employees would be able to accomplish this enormous mission.

TAIPEI, TAIWAN

November 17, 1995

After six months of working at JDN, James was confused and feeling overwhelmed by a growing sense of futility. Despite cuts in overhead spending for entertainment, gifts, and other expenses, the faster drop in worldwide sales was causing both gross and net revenues to plummet. Moreover, the new vendors brought in because they offered lower prices were missing delivery commitments, and quality was suffering across the board. As if that weren't enough to fill his head with grave doubts about his abilities, James was further surprised that some of JDN's most talented employees had resigned. The remaining members of the Taiwanese management team appeared to him to be useless in coming up with any recommendations. Invariably, the implementation of the suggestions of his California team seemed only to make things worse. He felt absolutely helpless.

January 8, 1996

James was not surprised when he received a phone call from Jonathan. Jonathan's attitude was different than it had been in the past, and his voice was very tense. "James, we cannot afford to let this situation go on much longer. If things don't turn around soon, I'm going to have to slot someone else into the top position and bring you back to the United States. You've cut overhead and expenses, but your revenue and market share are dropping and there's no sign of a turnaround. We have real problems."

James sat down and pondered the conversation for a long while. He decided that it would be best to cut his losses and return to the United States while Jonathan still considered him an asset to the company. When he notified Jonathan of his decision, the CEO accepted it and told him that he would have a replacement in Asia by the end of the month. James breathed a giant sigh of relief. He suddenly realized how unprepared he had been for the assignment.

CENTRAL CALIFORNIA

February 16, 1996

Jonathan had always prided himself on learning from his mistakes. But this situation had him perplexed. Not only had one of his most knowledgeable executives created a disaster in one location, but a less experienced executive was succeeding in a locale about which he had initially had doubts. While James's operation was suffering, Reuben's Mexico City division was growing steadily. Reuben didn't have the same kind of labor problems. In fact, when Jonathan paid a visit to Grupo Communicación several weeks earlier, he wondered whether Reuben hadn't underestimated production capability in his initial projections. He was impressed that while Grupo had retained its Mexican personality, Orbox's values were beginning to be visible.

After considering where things had gone wrong, Jonathan realized a fundamental lesson: Just because a manager succeeds in the United States doesn't mean he or she will succeed anywhere in the world. Technical competence may not have cultural boundaries, but managerial skills certainly do. He realized that in the future he would have to look for other skills in selecting his international managers. Cultural literacy is not necessarily an innate skill. Like learning a new language, it's something that often doesn't come naturally.

THE WINDHAM INTERNATIONAL CULTURAL MODEL©*: NINE CULTURAL DIMENSIONS

The Windham International Cultural Model was designed to provide a behavioral definition of culture, a way for people working in the global business arena to understand different cultural morés and behaviors. Because individuals make so many assumptions about the way people should act and think based on their own culture, it is important to see how assumptions differ from those of people around the world.

The Windham International Cultural Model (WICM) is an easy-to-understand cultural template which takes an amorphous subject and concretizes it, giving it distinct definitions called *cultural dimensions*. WICM is intended as a tool for businesspeople who find themselves in other cultures and who need to understand their own behaviors and those of the people they're working and living with. The model defines nine specific cultural dimensions: relationships, time, communication, hierarchy, status attainment, space, group dependence, diversity receptivity, and change tolerance.

The model was developed by Michael S. Schell, Marian Stoltz-Loike, and other members of the Windham International organization. It is grounded in the work of respected sociologists and anthropologists, including Fons Trompenaars, Geert Hofstede, and Edward T. Hall,[2] but it takes a different approach. Tailored to be easy to learn, WICM builds on familiar terms and experiences, and is intended as a business tool to use in this mobile, ever-changing expatriate world where international business people travel from culture to culture. The model has been used as a core component in cross-cultural training and counseling programs to

*Contributing author to the chapters on culture, Marian Stoltz-Loike, Ph.D., is vice president of Windham International.

FIGURE   2–1

Windham International Cultural Prism

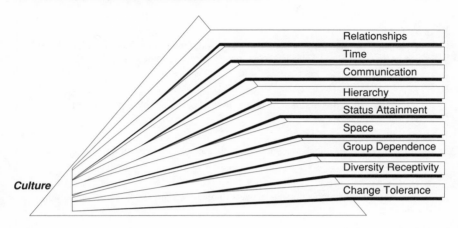

provide hundreds of expatriates with a blueprint for understanding culture and adjusting to behavioral differences in people.

By understanding the model, expatriates have a context into which they can place the cultures they know and the new ones they might encounter. The result is that they can modify their own behavior to be effective in both business and social situations.

Once you understand culture and its manifestations, you can adapt your behavior as you recognize cultural differences. When you visit another culture, you will be aware of differences in language and the way people dress, but many cultural ingredients aren't visible. To explain how these factors come together, the Windham International Cultural Model contains a cultural prism (Figure 2–1). Just as a prism separates light into its component parts, the cultural prism can be used to examine the nine cultural dimensions which are never independent of one another, but are components of a total culture. The nine cultural dimensions are shown in Figure 2–2.

Although we have broken down cultural definitions into nine dimensions, there is obviously a great deal of overlap between these dimensions. Clearly, human behavior doesn't easily separate into clean slices (or dimensions), and there can be a great deal of debate where those slices are made or whether there should be 8, 9, or 10 of them. For example, Hall has three fundamental dimensions; Hofstede has four, and

FIGURE   2–2

The Nine Cultural Dimensions

- **Relationships**
  Focuses on whether an organization places primary importance on completing a job or devoting time to building relationships among business associates.

- **Time**
  Measures the degree to which a society believes an individual can focus on one or more tasks and evaluates the importance of personal relationships verses adherence to schedules.

- **Communication**
  Addresses the way societies communicate, including the use of nonverbal gestures.

- **Hierarchy**
  Measures the way individuals interact with one another within an organizational hierarchy.

- **Status Attainment**
  Measures the importance of personal achievement and accomplishment to an overall sense of well-being.

- **Space**
  Views how individuals in societies use space to define themselves, including spatial distances used when speaking, and the amount of space needed for comfort in business and living environments.

- **Group Dependence**
  Measures the importance of the individual vis-à-vis the group in diverse social and business situations.

- **Diversity Receptivity**
  Defines how roles, power, and authority are associated with each gender. Also measures the attitude towards people of different race, religion, national orgin, and so forth.

- **Change Tolerance**
  Identifies group responses to change, the need for rules, and the ability to take risks. Also measures the perception of how much control we have over our destiny.

Danielle Walker in her Training Management Corporation (TMC) model has 10.[3] The Windham International Cultural Model, has a specific breakdown that relates more to experiences of business people and expatriates than to anthropologists. Although individual differences account for variety in the way everyone expresses these dimensions, there is no fundamental disagreement on the cultural manifestations. Furthermore, individual differences between people will prevent the possibility of unanimous agreement on specific cultural behavior within a society.

An Important Note

In the following three chapters, we will discuss the nine cultural dimensions and their ramifications for business and personal interactions. As you read these chapters, you will see how pervasive culture is, and you will gain a greater appreciation of how the culture in which you were raised has affected your beliefs, biases, and attitudes. As international business people, the more you know about the cultural background of the people you work with and the culture in which they are operating, the more effective you can be.

Keep in mind as you read these chapters that in order to define cultural differences, it has been necessary to make generalizations. Such generalities often are inadequate to address the span of individual differences within a culture. For example, there are people who are never prompt in a culture that puts high emphasis on time, and there are others who are concerned about nurturing and maintaining relationships in very transactional cultural environments.

Furthermore, cultural behaviors are being modified all the time. This is a result of accelerated intercultural contact and the increasing multinational ownership of major corporations and the corporate cultures that their employees adhere to. Traditional cultural behavior is also being modified by the influence of worldwide media and the increasing access to technology.

As you read, it will be helpful for you to focus on the culture in which you live and compare it to those that we're examining.

We have clustered the nine dimensions into three groupings (see Figure 2–3.) in order to enhance conceptualization and facilitate understanding. Clearly, all the dimensions overlap and there are interrelationships between the dimensions within and between clusters.

FIGURE   2-3

The Cultural Dimensions

Time/Relationship Cluster
- **Relationships**
  Focuses on whether an organization places primary importance on completing a job or devoting time to building relationships among business associates.

- **Time**
  Measures the degree to which a society believes an individual can focus on one or more tasks and evaluates the importance of personal relationships compared with adherence to schedules.

- **Communication**
  Addresses the way societies communicate, including the use of nonverbal gestures.

Power Cluster
- **Hierarchy**
  Measures the way individuals interact with one another within an organizational hierarchy.

- **Status Attainment**
  Measures the importance of personal achievement and accomplishment to an overall sense of well-being.

- **Space**
  Views how individuals in societies use space to define themselves, including spatial distances used when speaking, and the amount of space needed for comfort in business and living environments.

Societal Interdependence Cluster
- **Group Dependence**
  Measures the importance of the individual versus the group in diverse social and business situations.

- **Diversity Receptivity**
  Defines how roles, power, and authority are associated with each gender. Also measures the attitude toward people of different race, religion, national origin, and so forth.

- **Change Tolerance**
  Identifies group responses to change, the need for rules, and the ability to take risks. Also measures the perception of how much control we have over our destiny.

NOTES

1. Not her real name.

2. Edward T. Hall, *Anthropology of Everyday Life,* Doubleday, 1993; Edward T. Hall, *Dance of Life,* Doubleday, 1984; Edward T. Hall, *The Hidden Dimension,* Doubleday, 1966; Edward T. Hall, *The Silent Language,* Doubleday, 1959; E.H. and Mildred Reed Hall, *Understanding Cultural Differences,* Intercultural Press, 1990; Geert Hofstede, *Cultures and Organizations,* McGraw-Hill, 1992; and Fons Trompenaars, *Riding the Waves of Culture: Understanding Diversity in Global Business,* (Burr Ridge, IL: Irwin Professional Publishing, 1993 and 1994).

3. Terence Brake, Danielle Medina Walker and Thomas Walker *Doing Business Internationally: A Guide to Cross-Cultural Success,* (Burr Ridge, IL: Irwin Professional Publishing, 1995).

3

⑥ THE TIME/RELATIONSHIP CLUSTER*

Time, Relationships, and Communication

This chapter will cover

- The impact time has on social and business interactions.
- The importance of relationships in working and living in another culture.
- How different cultures convey information to each other in their verbal and nonverbal communication.

This group of cultural dimensions has a dramatic impact on intercultural success across the spectrum of business and social interactions. These attributes fundamentally define people's ideas about human interaction. They are so all-encompassing that they are the pivotal factors influencing negotiations, sales and marketing, product positioning, and social and business dealings. Anyone functioning in the international arena, whether in business or social situations, will immediately recognize the emphasis that each culture places on time and relationships and the way they communicate with each other.

---

*Contributing author to the chapters on culture, Marian Stoltz-Loike, Ph.D., is vice president of Windham International.

DIMENSION: TIME

Time is such a complex dimension that we divide it into three subsections.

Time refers to:

1. The idea of time as a controllable commodity.
- Do we control time or does time control us?
- Is the management of time possible, and is the ability to manage it a positive attribute?

2. Where do societies see themselves on the time spectrum— present, future, or past?
- Are today's behaviors influenced more by past, present, or future events?

3. Is a society monochronic or polychronic?
- How does the society believe an individual can or should focus on tasks? Are people expected to be able to perform only one function at a time (monochronic) or several functions at once (polychronic)?
- The importance of involvement with people versus adherence to schedules.

As the definitions indicate, cultural perception of time is both complex and multifaceted. Because it is also a readily recognizable behavior, it provides early clues for understanding and adjusting to other societies. As everyone can attest, the use of *time* may be one of the most misunderstood—and therefore most important—dimensions for the international business person to understand and adjust to. The fundamental questions are (1) whether time is seen as a controllable commodity that can be saved and spent much like money; (2) whether behaviors in relationship to time are dictated by focus on the present, future, or past; (3) whether people tend to accomplish one activity at a time or perform several activities simultaneously; and (4) whether adherence to schedule and tasks takes priority over concern for people.

Not surprisingly, the concept of time ranges from having almost no material value (low time) to being the most important commodity you own (high time). High-time cultures, such as those of northern Europe and North America, view time as something that is finite—an entity that can—and must be—controlled or it will be wasted and used up. Activities must be carefully scheduled to fit within a limited number of hours, and individuals must continually select and prioritize those activities. These cultures so value time that they are often encouraged to take courses on time management.

In contrast, people in the world's many low-time cultures, including southern Europe, Latin America, and the Middle East, believe that time is uncontrollable. Time is not their taskmaster. Many things can be done simultaneously, and greater attention is afforded to relationships rather than to deadlines and schedules. Moreover, time—and scheduling it—is viewed as a very limiting activity. In action, this means that plans change frequently and unexpectedly. Consequently, when someone is late, it doesn't reflect negatively on the person's character or ability to be organized. Since plans are expected to change; everything must be kept fluid. After all, how could you offend a friend by not stopping to talk just because you might be late for work?

In low-time cultures, people are convinced that careful scheduling is futile because so many chance circumstances can legitimately interfere with deadlines. Traffic jams, car breakdowns, meetings that take longer than anticipated, problems at home, are only a few of the everyday elements of life that interfere with routine. In some instances, people think it's absurd to try to schedule appointments precisely. They believe that time should not be sliced into units of seconds, hours, or days that can be managed and planned. Instead, the fluid, changing character of time should be respected and serve only as the framework for one's life. Thus, anyone wandering into work late one day probably wouldn't feel the need to stay late. Being tardy was simply beyond their control.

Those living in high-time cultures approach life from a completely opposite point of view. Being late to work or to meetings is not only stressful, but implies that the time will need to be made up. Just as one might delve into a bank account to repay a "loan," the employee who is late to work must "repay" time owed. Deadlines and commitments are taken very seriously, and those who are unable to adhere to those schedules are considered irresponsible and unreliable.

The potential conflict between people operating in high-time and low-time societies is obvious. Imagine how difficult it is for this Latin American executive. He traveled to a New York conference to make a presentation. To his bewilderment and shock, people got up and left his talk after he exceeded the 25-minute time slot for his presentation. He perceived them as rude; they perceived him as insensitive to their schedules. Neither was wrong, but all were offended.

In high-time cultures, making oneself available, or "giving up time," is considered a great compliment to a friend or colleague. "Time is money" and free time is "discretionary funds"—which carries an additional premium—so time is the most valuable gift one high-time individual can give to another. When this gift isn't appreciated by a low-time recipient, everyone feels dissatisfied.

Schedules are adhered to rigidly; people who are "considerate" and "responsible" usually confirm plans far in advance of a proposed meeting date in high-time cultures. Low-time recipients of such a phone call view this as strange behavior indeed. Consequently, interpreting behavior becomes a challenge. Think of the phone call confirming a business appointment. To someone in a high-time culture, this simply assures an efficient use of time. No one is confused about the beginning of a meeting, which prevents one individual from waiting for another (and thereby wasting time); in a low-time culture this confirmation phone call would simply be a courtesy because no one would be concerned with the time.

In low-time cultures, a concern for the needs of others dictates that a person spends time to help solve the problem. In fact, spending time with others is considered quite normal and expected. It doesn't reflect a unique concern or interest in the other person. As a result, a manager in a low-time culture might routinely have several people in his or her office simultaneously, and each might have different problems or concerns. Interruptions are commonplace and expected.

The ways in which societies utilize strategic or tactical planning to achieve business solutions is another enormous difference between low- and high-time cultures. While both may agree on a long-term strategic objective, extremely time-sensitive cultures will immediately set forth an elaborate, comprehensive tactical timeline and adhere to it. Low-time cultures will take a more fluid approach, always focusing on the strategic end, but feeling no compunction about modifying it as it progresses.

You can see how stressful this would be for an intercultural team working together on a single strategic mission. The German members of the team, for instance, would be frustrated by the constant schedule and tactical adjustments made by the Italians. In essence, their differences come down to what governs the process. Does the timeline govern? Do the tactical steps govern? Or does the most comfortable way to achieve the result govern?

Another example: High-time cultures schedule a beginning and ending time for meetings and social gatherings. In contrast, planning the length of a meeting or party in a low-time culture is considered impossible or rude. How can people plan the amount of time necessary to discuss specific topics or when the "good time" at a party will be over and people should leave.

Another important differentiation is whether people are focused on the past, present or future. Does the society look at past victories? Does it focus on present, immediate rewards? Or, does it concentrate on long-term, future-oriented strategic objectives? This is another area in which people of different cultures can learn a lot from one another.

Kluckohn and Strodtbeck describe three different types of societies:

1. *Present-oriented,* which is timeless and traditionless, and ignores the future.

2. *Past-oriented,* which is concerned about maintaining traditions from the past into the present.

3. *Future-oriented,* which sets out to design and implement an improved future.[1]

Distinctions in the perception of time become evident in business discussions to establish schedules and timetables. Even though most business development takes place in a future-oriented environment, the cultural influence of past or present values and thinking influences the long-term strategic plans and immediate tactical objectives.

Finally, Hall's definitions of time should also be taken into account.[2] He identifies cultures as being *monochronic* and *polychronic.* Monochronic cultures fall into our definition of high-time societies. Hall says these groups focus on doing one thing at a time, while polychronic cultures do several things at the same time. He also notes the correlation between polychronic cultures and high-relationship cultures, and observes that monochronic cultures tend to place more importance on accomplishing activities than on people. Imagine the distraction of a high-time "monochronic" manager dealing with a polychronic joint-venture partner who kept him waiting for an appointment. Once the meeting started, the partner took phone calls and spoke with several people throughout the time instead of focusing on the single agenda item the monochronic executive had set forth.

Time: Beliefs and Behaviors

Low	High
■ Time is uncontrollable. If you are late, it cannot be helped.	■ Time can be measured, saved, and controlled. Therefore, if you're late, you're being disrespectful or disorganized, and wasting a tangible commodity.
■ People who place less emphasis on the absolute dictates of time will focus on numerous things at the same time and be more concerned about people's feelings than adhering to a schedule (polychronic).	■ People who ascribe a great deal of importance to controlling time also generally prefer to do one thing at a time (monochronic).
■ Maintaining a harmonious working environment is more important than adhering to arbitrary schedules.	■ If you help people to accomplish time-driven deadlines, you are considered a good manager and admired even if you make everyone work late and surrender their personal time. If you do not know how to use time effectively, especially in business, you're viewed in a negative way as not very serious. One of the highest compliments people pay each other in business is to say that someone is extremely efficient with time.
■ People change plans often and easily.	■ People tend to schedule events and plans as if they are fixed. Schedules are sacrosanct.
■ Individuals don't expect to allot a certain length of time to business meetings because they consider it impossible to plan *a priori* how long it would take to discuss relevant business concerns.	■ People set times for the beginning and end of social and business engagements, viewing time as precious and not easily compromised.
■ Scheduling business meetings ahead of time isn't expected, especially because people often will not arrange their schedules until the last minute.	■ Providing significant lead time before an event or meeting is a sign of respect, reflecting the individual's status as well as the significance of the business goals. Short lead time shows that business is not very important or an unexpected situation has come up.

TIME IN BUSINESS

In low-time cultures, meetings rarely begin on time and persistent tardiness isn't viewed as a problem. It simply provides those waiting with an opportunity to strengthen relationships and build networks. This approach is quite different from high-time cultures, where schedules are detailed down to the last minute and agendas are followed with meticulous precision.

It's important to note that subsidiaries of American companies in low-time cultures—and companies that are experienced in dealing with high-time cultures—demonstrate their cross-cultural understanding by adhering to schedules and structuring agendas. It shows their respect for high-time cultures. This is, of course, a learned behavior on their part and demonstrates an accommodation to a dominant business/corporate culture.

In the low-time cultures of Latin America or the Middle East, for instance, government bureaucracies operate in a fashion similar to those in the markets and souks (Middle Eastern open markets). Offices of important officials often include a large reception area in addition to the private office space. In that large space, small groups of people wait to be visited by the minister or an aide who comfortably moves from group to group. Not only does this make things easier for the minister, it provides an opportunity for the groups to interact among themselves and conduct other forms of business. Again, during the waiting period, people develop their networks and engage in relationship building.

For northern Europeans or Americans who live by the clock, this way of conducting business can be stressful and projects an appearance of disorganization. Therefore, instead of meeting in the public space, a visitor might request a private meeting in the inner offices, thus missing the opportunity to network with other business people in the outer, more public, spaces.

In low-time cultures, where adherence to timelines is difficult and viewed as somewhat illogical, the decision-making process can be lengthier. However, by the time the decision is made, more people are familiar with the information and action might be taken more quickly. Had James Simon's team spent more time discussing Orbox's business strategies with the Taiwanese managers and given them time to look over the evidence, the implementation plan might have had a chance of success. The Western business world nevertheless finds it difficult to respect the process and frequently imposes its time values on cultures not prepared to accept its logic.

DIMENSION: RELATIONSHIPS

Relationships refers to:

- The importance of developing a personal relationship before conducting business.
- The value of knowing the "right people" to get things accomplished.
- Whether trust is assumed and protected by legal contract or established prior to the commencement of a business relationship.
- The merit of relationships over other credentials when choosing associates and setting goals.
- The implied obligations associated with friendship.

This dimension describes the importance individuals place on people—people versus products, people versus schedules, and people versus price. It focuses on the importance of knowing one another before significant interactions can occur. Does the culture encourage rapidly developing transactional interactions or does it require a fuller relationship in order to work together? Are superficial social friendships made quickly or are relationships slower in developing but also more enduring?

Trust is a major component of the relationships dimension. In low-relationship cultures such as Sweden and the United States, associations develop quickly, but they also may last for only a short period of time. Neighbors who see each other socially every day might not stay in touch at all if one of them moves to another city. Social relationships may be superficial, with people sharing few of their private feelings. In high-relationship cultures people develop friendships slowly, but they're built atop a framework that transcends time and place. These relationships tend to endure even if one friend moves to another city or country. Likewise, friendships are likely to be multidimensional. For example, in the United States we're discouraged from doing business with friends and family, whereas in high-relationship cultures, such as Italy, friendship is the best criterion for a business relationship.

These ideas about the importance of relationships fundamentally affect the way individuals approach business. In low-relationship cultures people expect to engage in business immediately, whereas in high-relationship cultures, people spend a lot of time in activities such as playing golf and sharing meals as a way of getting to know each other first. Low-relationship cultures move directly into business dealings without first forming a personal bond based on trust. They tend to rely heavily on legal systems and penalties to protect the rights of business and individuals. Those in high-relationship societies believe that trust compels people to act honestly and fairly with each other and use that framework for constructing deals and handling problems.

Think about Orbox Telecommunications. When Americans such as James Simon or Reuben Jones interact with people who place a high value on relationships, they simply cannot plow into business dealings as though they were in the United States. They are expected to take time to get to know their peers and the people they are working with. James Simon was met with confusion when he neglected to build a foundation of trust with the Taiwanese business people. He was confronted by silence when he callously skipped the relationship building and abruptly told his colleagues that he was eager to look at the firm's finances so he could find ways to generate greater production. Their wordlessness masked surprise and annoyance at the disrespect shown. It is little wonder they could not comply. Nor is it any wonder that revenue and productivity declined when relationship-building activities, such as gift giving and entertainment, were eliminated. The low-relationships mind-set that James displayed was a direct contradiction to the values of the Taiwanese to whom loyalty, commitment, and family ties were far more important than profit levels. Both groups suffered.

RELATIONSHIPS IN BUSINESS

In relationship-focused societies like France, Italy, Mexico, and Japan, human interactions are resilient, develop slowly over time, and are viewed as long term. The way these individuals approach personal relationships parallels their approach to business planning. For example, in Japan and other Asian countries, such planning is rarely done on a quarterly-to-annual basis. Plans of 5, 10, and even 50 years are common. Of course, the definition of "long range" varies from culture to culture, but it is almost always associated with the expectation that business success builds upon and honors prior business arrangements. When new business plans are created, they might address business concerns for three months, three years, or three decades, depending upon the culture's view toward time horizons.

Relationships: Beliefs and Behaviors

Low	High
■ Relationships and business agreements may continue only for a short period of time.	■ Relationships and friendships are extremely stable over long periods of time.
■ Individuals are willing to engage in many activities immediately on the assumption that if it doesn't work out, they can always end it. Personal trust isn't a prerequisite to business dealings.	■ Trust is a prerequisite to business dealings and must be established and nurtured over a period of time. It is essential for initial and further business dealings.
■ Business agreements must be protected by contracts and lawyers.	■ People won't do business with someone until they've built a relationship and know they can trust the person. Recourse to the law is secondary to honoring a commitment to a "partner."
■ Fax and phone suffice for most business interactions. Only high-level decisions and information exchange are necessary in person.	■ Face-to-face meetings are always preferred.
■ Conversations in both business or social occasions tend to focus on business issues. Getting to know the other individual is considered irrelevant to business.	■ It's important to show an interest in the individual as well as in the business issues. It is helpful to gather information about the individual and the business before meetings, so that it is apparent that you care about the person, not just the success of the joint business endeavors.
■ People begin relationships easily. There is more transience in friendships.	■ It takes time to build relationships, but they are impermeable to distance and the passing of time.
■ Relationships are seen as transactional and a necessity of working together. Even on a social level, neighbors who consider themselves fairly close may have little to do with one another if one moves to a new location.	■ Relationships tend to remain stable even if great distances separate the people.

For example, the United States is a transactional society. Americans willingly do business with people they hardly know. They make sales and establish partnerships and alliances based on opportunity and circumstance, not on long-standing relationships. They enter these transactions with the assumption that if things don't work out, they can use legal means for breaking them. Trust is of negligible importance before beginning negotiations because legal contracts are all-encompassing and binding. Americans expect to take individuals at their word, and if things don't work out, they simply walk away from the deal. Few subtleties are implied. In other words, if it is not spelled out as part of the deal, it is not expected in the transaction. American contracts often have a clause spelling out that what is on paper is the entire deal and that nothing else exists.

In transactional cultures, people generally frown upon the idea of doing business with friends, and they hesitate to "impose" on friends for special consideration or favors, particularly in the business arena. This is exactly the opposite of the way those in high-relationship cultures act, where people expect others to favor their friends and family and to do special things for them. When choosing suppliers and service organizations, relationships and trust are at least as important as price and product.

In high-relationship cultures, face-to-face business dealings become extremely important, whereas in low-relationship cultures, only business dealings at the highest level are considered important enough to be conducted in person. This is illustrated in the different ways the two cultural perspectives approach contemporary communication. Busy executives in low-relationship cultures may choose to not follow through on the details of a telephone discussion, but they will rarely ignore the printed word on a fax or e-mail. The exact opposite is true in high-relationship environments where more personal commitment is implied by the closeness of the voice communication.

What's more, in low-relationship cultures, managers are expected to be task oriented, rather than people oriented. This means that getting the job done is more important than the personal toll it might extact. Building bonds with subordinates or supervisors can even interfere with achieving stated business goals. Similarly, creating connections with peers is simply an outgrowth of working together well and recognizing the other's business abilities. It doesn't necessarily extend into friendship.

With this in mind, we can see why James's initial directives to the Taiwanese to curtail entertainment expenses and consider staff reductions in order to meet near-term objectives resulted in failure. The Taiwanese cultural filter saw these as poor decisions that would sever relationships built up over 50 years and would require another 50 years to reestablish.

DIMENSION: COMMUNICATION

Communication refers to:

- How societies use language, both verbal and nonverbal.
- How much specific data is needed to convey understanding.
- The amount of information considered appropriate in communications. Is it only task relevant or is it background information as well?
- The way people use words or gestures to express feelings and display mood.

The way a society communicates provides remarkable insights into the way it thinks . . . and conducts business. Indeed, communication transcends the actual words. It encompasses the way people transfer verbal and nonverbal messages through voice, body language, and actions. Of course, much of this behavior becomes unconsciously embedded into the collective psyche and isn't even acknowledged. However, the differences become glaringly apparent when cultures try to speak. Suddenly, a question that's phrased in an inappropriate manner or a gesture that's not expected can send the wrong message. If too much information is provided, the recipient might not be able to distinguish what is important, whereas too little information could leave the reader unable to complete the task.

Hall refers to cultures as being either high or low context in conveying information.[3] In low-context cultures, individuals expect only as much information as they need to accomplish the specific task. When provided with more data, they end up confused and annoyed at the wasted time. By contrast, people in high-context cultures are paralyzed without a comprehensive picture of the entire project, their role in it, and the role everyone else is playing. In other words, they need to know the context of the communication.

Imagine the frustration of a pressured American executive trying to convey succinctly a straightforward task to a Spanish colleague. Kept on the phone for an hour being asked questions that appear to the American to be irrelevant to the task, the executive can inadvertently appear to be rude because of a lack of understanding of the Spanish colleague's need for context. Imagine then, the American's total astonishment when, at the end of the conversation, the Spaniard asks when he's going to get a briefing on the project. The Spaniard, on the other hand, turns to his colleagues at the conclusion of the phone call and complains that it's so difficult to understand Americans who call requesting help without describing the project.

Even low-context cultures have high-context individuals, the people who share stories at the water cooler and over two-hour lunches as people might in high-context cultures. While others consider this a waste of time and rarely give more than two-syllable answers, high-context individuals know more about the entire process of a project as it is progressing. Not surprisingly, low-context cultures need frequent meetings to review progress on projects during which participants share new information while high-context cultures will have fewer meetings with relatively little new information being shared.

Nonverbal communication is no less important. It is conveyed through body language, eye contact, hand and body gestures, seating positions at business meetings, and even how much time one spends with others. Regardless of the culture, nonverbal communication either enhances or detracts from the verbal message. In many societies, how people look when they're saying something—as well as how they look *at* another person—is as important as the words they use.

A repatriated American related his experiences about the importance of nonverbal communication. A group of Korean employees came to him, apologizing profusely for their inadequacy on the job. He was stunned and expressed his surprise, immediately telling them they were excellent performers. When he asked them what he had done to give them the wrong impression, they replied that his serious demeanor, absence of smiles, and distracted answers left his Korean staff feeling they were the cause of his unhappiness.

An individual's eloquence and how elaborate he or she is at communicating details also can be significant. Colleagues, subordinates, friends, and the world at large all judge a person based somewhat on their image.

Another cultural communication characteristic that can lead to confusion and frustration is the directness or indirectness of speech, which varies tremendously across cultures. Some cultures pride themselves on direct, open communication and ask to be taken at their word. Individuals in these cultures are blunt and specific, and assume that the recipient doesn't take it personally (i.e. he or she is able to separate professional critique from personal validation). Imagine a manager from a culture that believes in direct communication doing a performance evaluation with an employee from Asia, who is sensitive to the subtlety of speech and innuendo of word choice. The Asian experiences a blunt evaluation as a sledgehammer that undermines his sense of well-being and leaves him virtually incapable of continuing in the business relationship. Many cultures use an indirect style of communication and place great value on the context of the talk and eloquence of the speaker. Recipients use this context and nonverbal cues as important elements of the communication.

In contrast, Americans, who tend toward a low-communi-cation approach, value "logic" and linear thinking. It's expected that ideas will be presented directly and clearly. While this approach works fine for Americans, it can easily insult those who come from a high-communication culture where deductive reasoning is far less important.

COMMUNICATION IN BUSINESS

The key business issues related to communication are:

- Understanding and comprehending what the other person is saying.
- The nonverbal behaviors that convey and reinforce the message.
- Varying the degree of detail that's necessary or expected.
- The directness and subtlety of the language used.
- The location of the conversation.

George Bernard Shaw said that the British and Americans are di-vided by a common language. Shaw's quip cuts to the core: Just because we use the same words doesn't mean we use the same language. This has never been more true than in global business where the international lan-guage might be English, but that doesn't mean it's understood universally. People who make that assumption do so at considerable peril. If com-mon expressions differ in the United States and the United Kingdom, and proper ways to ask questions also differ, how difficult must it be for individuals who are not native speakers of English?

Furthermore, it's important to recognize that even though people might speak well, their comprehension of English may lag far behind. It is more difficult to understand native speakers of a language than to con-struct and speak that language yourself. No matter what language is

Communication: Beliefs and Behaviors

Low	High
■ People look for content, not what surrounds the content. They expect that all the information they need to communicate is contained within the words they use. What is spoken matters, not *how* or *where* it is spoken. Even the expressions used are not that important.	■ The context of the communication is very important. It isn't only *what* people talk about that is important, it's the tone of voice and *where* the conversation takes place. What is being said might not be as important as how it is said.
■ Information is held very closely and shared on a need-to-know basis. People in positions of power have more information.	■ People share more information and expect to have a constant flow of input. Even mundane bits of information are valued.
■ People are direct and expect to be taken at their word.	■ People tend to be indirect. Listeners are expected to interpret statements and questions to infer what the speaker is saying.
■ Body language usually won't be acknowledged as having a major impact on the content of the message. Verbalized information is key.	■ Nonverbal nuances, including gestures and voice quality, are important. The same verbal message may mean something totally different to three people because of the nonverbals that accompany the words at the time they are stated.
■ Clarity of communication in words is paramount and open dialogue with probing/challenging questions is acceptable. Simplicity is admired and language may be punctuated with vulgarity for effect.	■ Speaking eloquently but indirectly is a prized art.
■ Saving face is not important. As a matter of fact, openly challenging someone you disagree with is often admired.	■ In some high communication cultures, the idea of saving face is an essential part of information exchange.

used, in international business we often deal with people whose native language is not the one being spoken. The result? At least one party to the communication is having to struggle with both comprehension and word selection.

At the same time, this individual is having to work harder to understand the communication. Then there's the added challenge of trying to decipher an accent and idiosyncratic word usage. What must a non-American think when we talk about *a boot-strap operation, grassroots support,* or *movers and shakers*? What does an American think when a British person uses the word *puncture* or *flat*? Add to all this the nonverbal communication that's taking place, and the potential for problems begins to expand exponentially.

Of course, communication patterns and styles vary greatly. Members of a low-communication culture tend to be direct. Managers provide direct feedback on issues of performance. Employees are expected to accept this feedback—no matter how painful—as "constructive." They are not supposed to take any comments personally. In high-communication cultures, a manager would never offer direct feedback publicly, although he or she might criticize an employee behind closed doors. More likely, criticism would be couched in indirect words and stated more softly than in a low-communication culture. The environment in which the interchange takes place is at least as important as the verbal message.

High-communication cultures use business meetings for discussion and eloquent demonstrations of understanding. Imparting new information is a secondary and much less important purpose. Discussion of the topic and the agenda almost always occurs prior to the meeting. Subtleties in speech and language are extremely important. People react to everything around the conversation as more than mere words. Indirect language and nonverbal messages impart important information. Cultures that place a premium on communication reward eloquent speeches, which become the cornerstone of a successful meeting. Likewise, important meetings must be held in a place that allows participants to recognize its significance.

Within low-communication cultures, meetings are called to deliver information. Discussions are limited to general information and to understanding what is needed to get the job done. It's expected that one asks questions if he or she needs additional information. Everyone expects decisions to be reached at the conclusion of a meeting, and there is impatience if a second meeting must be held to continue the discussion.

In low-communication societies, presenting an agenda—and adhering to that agenda—is essential because the agenda is what moves the meeting along and assures that all the information is covered. Low-communication cultures also rank high on time. The societies are blunt and to the point with language, even if it involves criticism. Body language, while observable, is not confused with the real message, which is contained in the words.

Executives in low-communication cultures are typically insulated from the people around them by closed doors, secretaries, and the placement of their offices away from the center of activities. Information is compartmentalized and the executive only receives information from the few people he or she sees on a daily basis. Needless to say, having a good support staff is essential, because they are the gatekeepers of the information flow and control what the executive knows and who the executive sees. Furthermore, having information is viewed as having power, and many people guard it with intense fervor.

However, this is exactly the opposite in high-communication cultures, where a constant flow of information takes place. Business leaders value having their fingers on the pulse of the organization, so that information flows effectively and rapidly. Secretaries don't act as gatekeepers to insulate the boss from information. Individuals know a lot about one another and typically have excellent information networks among friends, family, and colleagues, from whom they constantly receive new information. Consequently, when they communicate with one another, they need little background information because they keep themselves well informed about everyone important in their lives. Since nothing is compartmentalized, all information flows to all relevant individuals and the organization is able to gather, process, and distribute information.

Not surprisingly, the issue of *face* is of great concern in high-communication cultures. This concept refers to the honor and respect afforded to another person by treating him appropriately. In Asian cultures, where the concept of *face* has been raised to a fine art, it is possible to act in a way that *gives one face* or helps one *save face*—or to act in a way that causes someone to *lose face*. A public reprimand directed at a subordinate or the singling out of one person from a group is a reason for that person to lose face.

It can be far more subtle than that, though. Think of the first meeting James Simon had with the employees at Jin Dian Nau. Cheng Yi-Hwa introduced him with a lengthy, complimentary prologue as a way of framing the speech to come and offering vital information about the speaker—and of course giving him great face with the Taiwanese employees. When James made no attempt at a similar, complimentary repartee because he assumed the audience would understand his low-context speech, he not only revealed his ignorance of communication in the culture, but also insulted Cheng Yi-Hwa, creating a loss of face for the revered gentleman.

TIME/RELATIONSHIP GROUP BUSINESS APPLICATIONS

Throughout the rest of the book, we will explore how these specific cultural dimensions express themselves in the business environment.

In Chapter 8, we discuss the process of selecting expatriate families and predicting their success in the international arena. People who place high value on relationships, are flexible in their use of time, and are adaptive in their communication styles will obviously be better candidates for international assignments.

Furthermore, understanding time/relationships/communication is also extremely useful when settling a family into a new environment where they will immediately encounter these different styles when dealing with neighbors, tradespeople, teachers, and so on. We talk about these issues in Chapters 9 and 10.

NOTES

1. From Fons Trompenaars, *Riding the Waves of Culture: Understanding Diversity in Global Business* (Burr Ridge, IL: Irwin Professional Publishing, 1994).
2. Edward T. Hall, *Anthropology of Everyday Life,* Doubleday, 1993; Edward T. Hall, *Dance of Life,* Doubleday, 1984; Edward T. Hall, *The Hidden Dimension,* Doubleday, 1966; Edward T. Hall, *The Silent Language,* Doubleday, 1959; E.H. and Mildred Reed Hall, *Understanding Cultural Differences,* Intercultural Press, 1990.
3. Ibid.

4

⑥ THE POWER CLUSTER

Hierarchy, Status Attainment, and Space

This chapter will cover
- The way in which cultures recognize and manifest society's expectations of power and hierarchy.
- What constitutes status and recognition.
- The physical configuration of cultural values in interior and exterior usage of space.

Three dimensions—hierarchy, status attainment, and space—are called the power group because they define how authority and position are demonstrated in different societies. These important aspects of gaining and showing respect are critical in business and social interactions. As you read this chapter, you will also see the dramatic influences of these attitudes in interacting with and managing local nationals. You will see that fundamental beliefs of good management practices in one culture can be devastating in another.

DIMENSION: HIERARCHY

Hierarchy refers to:

- How people view their status in relation to others.
- Whether a culture believes that all people are created equal—or not.
- How individuals define their innate belief in social mobility. Is social ranking flexible or is it fixed by birth?
- Who in the society is responsibility for decision making?

One of the most important cultural definers is how a society perceives power and authority: how you get it, how you act when you have it, and whether anyone is entitled to it. How does a culture react to individuals with power? What is its belief about social mobility and equality? In some societies, there is a precise order that carries with it specific rules about behavior, dress, and language. In others, social interaction is fluid and unrestrained by rigid rules and protocol.

In societies where hierarchy doesn't play an important role, such as Canada or Australia, anyone can grow up to be the president of a multi-million dollar business. It's not just a fairy tale told by mothers to their children or a fantasy people read in books. Indeed, American culture is full of rags-to-riches success stories, and a favorite American pastime is to recount tales about individuals such as Abraham Lincoln, Henry Ford, Bill Clinton who overcame meager beginnings to attain great power or wealth.

However, in high-hierarchical cultures such as India and China, individuals believe a person's social rank is fixed at birth and is unlikely to change. These societies have a different set of heroes and stories that become embedded in their folklore and psyche. They believe that people should know their place and not only make the best of it, but dignify their position by accepting their rank.

In emerging economics, education is highly valued and becoming more accessible to all social levels. As a result, the hierarchical rankings become less fixed and these societies begin to experience more social mobility. Nevertheless, cultural mores and values run very deep, and while visible culture is changing, the underlying values are far less fluid.

High-hierarchical societies show great deference and respect to power and authority. They believe in overt manifestations of wealth and power, whereas low-hierarchical societies will often intentionally try to blur the power distinction. For example, a plumber coming to repair a faucet in a Dutch household can expect to be invited to sit with the owner of the house and have a cup of tea before he embarks on any work. Individuals are viewed as equals regardless of the work they do. Contrast that to Indonesian household help, who are confined to the "wet kitchen" and would never dream of entering the home itself.

In high-hierarchical societies, individuals are expected to demonstrate their position by the way they dress and by the accoutrements and trappings that surround them. They limit social interaction to people of similar status.

HIERARCHY IN BUSINESS

Hierarchy—and people's perceptions of their rightful place in society and expectations of their leaders—has an immediate impact on how people react to empowerment as opposed to authoritative management practices. What is good management in one society won't work in another.

What happens when these two cultural ideas collide? Orbox Telecommunications is a good example. Jonathan Orbox is the epitome of the self-made man who believes that everyone can rise to the heights they desire. Social ranking, class distinctions, and fixed hierarchical structures mean nothing to him. Consequently, when his company began its global expansion, he believed completely in empowering the people who surrounded him, knowing that they too believed they can achieve anything. Such a philosophy works well as long as it is applied in a culture where people respond positively to such empowerment. But it causes confusion in cultures where people expect to be told what to do.

From the beginning, Jonathan's ideas, as translated and delivered by James Simon to his Taiwanese cohorts, were doomed to failure. In a culture that reveres hierarchy and structure, a casual egalitarian approach was completely foreign and unnerving. Although the Taiwanese owners and senior managers might understand theoretically that Americans do things differently, they would be completely confused when action was taken without preparation or sensitivity. Simon hadn't taken the necessary time to learn about the importance of hierarchy in Taiwan's culture and, therefore, he had no way of understanding how much formality and structure were revered.

The hierarchical thinking of a society is woven throughout its busi-

Hierarchy: Beliefs and Behaviors

Low	High
■ People believe in egalitarian principles.	■ People assume that social levels truly exist.
■ People are mobile. They are able to change their rank.	■ Individuals believe that one's position cannot easily change.
■ Individuals at different levels are quite similar and should be treated with the same rights, privileges, and entitlements.	■ People at different levels of the hierarchy have—and should have— different rights.
■ People believe in empowerment. Everyone has a right to be heard.	■ People observe class distinctions and believe that behavior, dress. and speech reflect hierarchical differences. They dress expensively and should be addressed only with honorifics.
■ Obvious symbols such as a fancy car, a big office, and elegant clothes are optional and sometimes even viewed as pretentious and an insensitive flaunting of power and wealth.	■ Status symbols such as cars, fancy clothes, and jewelry are important cues to a person's rank in society.
■ People typically call one another by their first names.	■ Everyone is addressed according to their status by a series of titles and honorifics. Even neighbors refer to each other with a title and never assume that they may call someone by a first name no matter how long they know their acquaintance.
■ People dress for comfort, not to demonstrate their position or status. Dress may be informal both in the office and at home. Organizations may have "dress down days" for the comfort of employees.	■ Dress is typically more formal. People also dress to show respect for others.
■ Language is typically direct and informal.	■ Languages have several words for "you," indicating different levels of familiarity.

ness environment. Hierarchical cultures reflect that status in office design and configuration, in closed versus open doors, and in titles and in dress. High-hierarchical organizations have distinct layers and everyone expects to see visible trappings of power and authority. Written and verbal communications are formal. For example, managers are referred to by surname with honorifics and titles, such as Herr Doktor or Herr Direktor, which are not considered superficial niceties. These honorifics are a reflection of good manners and respect. They are cues that express organizational responsibilities and authority, and provide information to others about how they should behave. Because organizations have distinct lines of command, it is not only poor manners to go outside the lines of authority but also disrespectful and undermining.

Reuben Jones recognized this fact when he addressed Señor Jiménez formally and paid him great deference during his visit to California. On the other hand, James Simon's informal behavior completely baffled his Taiwanese managers because they had no point of reference. How could a person in a position of authority dress and speak so casually?

In cultures with a complex set of hierarchical rules, managers are expected to be decision makers who tell employees what they should be doing, and they often are paternalistic, watching over all aspects of their subordinates' lives. In such cultures, decision making and delegating authority follow rigid hierarchical structures. Subordinates don't expect to participate in the decision-making process, but they also bear no responsibility for management's decisions. The person at the top is ultimately responsible. Employees at all levels adhere to strict organizational lines and report to their superiors and subordinates as rank dictates. These hierarchical culture structures present problems to low-hierarchical organizations in the United States which scoff at traditional chains of command, considering them bureaucratic and dysfunctional.

Participation in meetings also follows these distinct hierarchical levels. Consequently, it is considered embarrassing and inappropriate to ask subordinates for their opinion in the presence of senior managers. Another blunder by James Simon when he asked and expected everyone to participate in the meeting.

In some high hierarchical cultures, all the trappings of power become extraordinarily important. As such, they must be accorded great respect. For example, business cards take on immense significance because they indicate a person's status and communicate that status to others who don't know the individual personally. Thus, the way people exchange cards is meaningful because the business card itself is viewed as an extension of that person. People handle cards with great care and take pride when they exchange them. Just as you would not mistreat a favorite possession or someone's photograph, you handle business cards respectfully. Even individuals who are not employed outside the home carry and exchange personal cards.

Offices also often reflect an individual's status. The greater the status, the larger the office, the more windows, the better the location. The role of the secretary can be important because it symbolizes individual status through the actual tasks and responsibilities the secretary fulfills. This person not only handles correspondence, but runs errands, makes travel arrangements, and generally takes care of the boss. He or she is expected to perform a wide variety of activities that secretaries in low-hierarchy cultures would not. Even in the United States, which is a medium-hierarchical society, managers don't dare ask a secretary to pick up the laundry because this is deemed entirely unacceptable. However, transfer that same individual to a hierarchical country such as Japan or Chile, and that request would be entirely appropriate. Indeed, if the boss doesn't request certain tasks, subordinates might wonder what they've done wrong.

In contrast, low-hierarchical cultures approve of anyone making a decision, and with decision making comes responsibility. Employees expect to move up the organizational ranks based on exemplary performance and good decisions. Because managers are viewed as facilitators— people who help employees do their best work—and not simply as decision makers, they empower employees and expect them to take responsibility. Furthermore, it's entirely acceptable for employees to freely cross management levels and speak directly to senior managers. This freedom is particularly apparent at meetings where participation is open and encouraged of everyone in attendance.

Outside the business setting, hierarchies also play an important role. It's rare that individuals in high-hierarchical societies mingle across social strata, and you'll find those at the top consider drivers and domestic help essential. The boss's spouse is routinely accorded the same respect as the boss. Indeed, after visiting California, Señor Jiménez couldn't envision his wife living in the United States. His wife had always had domestic help to cook and clean and a chauffeur to drive her from place to place. He was surprised at the amount of work expected by Mrs. Jones.

In low-hierarchy environments, on the other hand, informality is the way at the office and at home. People who have just met address each other by their first names and comfortably socialize across levels. Language is freer and more casual, as is dress.

DIMENSION: STATUS ATTAINMENT

Status attainment refers to:
- How people define their status in society. Is it inherited or personally achieved?
- The need for personal accomplishments versus connections.
- Whether status in the society comes to individuals because of what they know or who they are.
- How one's work influences self-image and self-perception.
- Motivation for success: why people work and what it means.

Status attainment is the cultural dimension that relates to how people in a society connect what they do to how they feel about themselves. It refers to the importance of personal achievement compared to family position or connections. It relates what they do for a living to whom they think they are as members of their community. It is either a motivator for achievement or a precursor for the inevitable. For example, do you speak about someone in terms of what he or she does or who their family is and how important that family is in the society? Is it more important to know *what* you've studied in school or *where* you went to school? Do you work to live or live to work? How important is your work and what you achieve to your self-image? Those are the questions that distinguish cultures in the status attainment dimension.

Attitudes toward status attainment impact the hours individuals work, the willingness to let organizations interfere in their personal lives, and the relationship between how you think about yourself and what you do for a living.

You can think about this dimension historically. Possibly the most revealing example of the Status Attainment dimension is seen by looking at British society. From its earliest beginnings, status at birth has been an accepted part of British culture: You were born to landowners or nobility or peasantry, and there you remained. But over the years, entitlement by birthright was superseded by status based on achievement. No longer are wealthy but unproductive gentry admired unequivocally; they may be re-spected because of family lineage, but individuals must and now can achieve and alter their status. However, even today clear signs remain of the two notions of status attainment operating simultaneously—in the House of Commons and the House of Lords, for example. As a backlash to the British hierarchical structure, Americans developed a culture in di-rect contrast with that of their British ancestors. Americans sought to de-fine status strictly by personal achievement. Titles were illegal in the United States and the culture reveres individuals who strive to achieve and succeed.

In countries of high-status attainment, people feel that one can ac-complish many things and what one does achieve is determined by hard work. These accomplishments should be rewarded and recognized. In countries of low-status attainment, personal achievement is ascribed far less value. Success in the business place is determined more by proper connections than hard work, and recognition and promotions are awarded accordingly. Indeed, without proper connections, it is unlikely that a person would aspire to reach the top or ever get there. For exam-ple, people in high-status attainment cultures will readily talk about their own achievements—what they do for a living, and even how much money they make and how much they paid for their home. This would seem strange—and even bad manners—to people from low-status attain-ment societies, because these cultures assume that personal worth is be-stowed by birth and social position.

In high-status attainment environments, what one achieves defines his or her importance and status in the world. Hard work and personal achievement leads to a sense of well-being. Status and recognition is ob-tained by personal accomplishment and a job well done. People are val-ued for their measurable contributions. High-status achievement cultures are goal oriented, measuring people's values against their abilities to achieve those goals. Performance objectives are clearly defined and on-the-job performance is measured against these objectives for bonuses, promotions, retention, or recruitment for special projects.

In low-status attainment cultures, great value is placed on connec-tions and personal characteristics. In addition, job satisfaction and posi-tion or title are often more important than setting and reaching some-what arbitrary career goals. Social status isn't controlled by individual accomplishments alone, and great importance is placed on family con-nections and inherited position. Since attaining wealth doesn't, in-and-of-itself, confer status or provide the sense of well-being and satisfaction, people are not motivated by money as much as they are in high-status attainment societies.

Americans who have status talk about their job responsibilities and titles first and then move on to family or personal issues. In contrast, people from Latin America, Africa, and the Middle East—low-status attainment societies—talk first about their family or clan name. Europeans will often provide a short description of their humanistic or philosophical outlook early in an interaction.

Status Attainment: Beliefs and Behaviors

Low	High
■ Connections and who you know are more important than anything else. Nothing can be achieved without connections to key people.	■ Hard work, intelligence, and the ability to be a useful employee lead to success.
■ Status is related to whom you know and your status at birth. People can hardly be blamed for not being born into the best family or having the best connections.	■ Since achievement is the responsibility of individuals, those who don't make it are often looked down upon.
■ Business is typically based less on individual initiative. Hierarchies are more clearly defined and structures are more rigid.	■ Business encourages individual creativity and rewards hard work.

STATUS IN BUSINESS

In low-status attainment cultures, people work to live rather than live to work. The organization cannot easily interfere in the private lives of individuals. Since expectations directly affect motivation, status is closely tied to reward structures. People aren't as likely to be motivated strictly by compensation (money isn't a source of status). As a result, finding common ground for rewarding and motivating workers is a significant challenge when dealing with people from opposite ends of this cultural dimension.

Going back to the Orbox example, James thought that replacing the 13-month pay schedule with a performance bonus package would encourage people to work longer hours and bring unit productivity up to

U.S. standards. He was wrong on both counts. The role of compensation as a motivator was based on erroneous cultural assumptions. And James underestimated the importance of the relationships he severed with people of high status who endorsed the company's product and expected recognition in return.

Furthermore, simply because people in these societies are reluctant to talk about their personal accomplishments doesn't mean they don't have them. This is a grave error high-status attainment individuals make when interviewing potential job candidates from low-status attainment societies. In high-status attainment cultures, people are more comfortable talking about what they've accomplished. When going on job interviews, they'll be coached to emphasize the amount of money they've earned for the company and the number of people they've managed. The objective is to show that they were an integral component in their company's success. In low-status attainment cultures, individuals might consider it highly inappropriate to flaunt personal achievement. Instead, résumés are expected to be more comprehensive and to outline the jobs and skills individuals have mastered. Recommendations from prominent individuals are considered of great value. In addition, information related to age, schools attended, and other affiliations may be more significant to an interviewer in a low status attainment culture.

In high-status attainment cultures where achievement is coveted, people are willing to work on weekends when necessary to get the job done. For example, in some of the low-status attainment countries of Europe, people would be loathe to surrender their six-week vacations and are unlikely to work on weekends just to earn more money. Contrast that with the United States where executives often do not take their allotted vacations and regularly take work home on weekends after putting in 60-hour weeks.

The status-attainment dimension is very subtle and sometimes difficult to recognize. Just because an Englishperson might find it intrusive to work on a holiday doesn't mean he or she is unmotivated. It means that a sense of well being and self-satisfaction is not attained by the long hours and Herculean efforts that rewards such behavior in the United States. Living to work is not part of the culture and long hours at the office do not constitute status attainment to an Englishman. Contrast the English afternoon high tea break with an American coffee break where people stand and gulp coffee from a Styrofoam cup. English society makes sure that it allocates time to pursue other interests on Saturday and Sunday.

But nothing in culture is absolute, and these generalities are often contradicted by individual behavior. Global competion will also bring about behavioral changes. For example, as worker productivity increases in Asian countries, it will put pressure on the custom of six-week vacations enjoyed by many Europeans.

In high-status attainment cultures, families readily tolerate work demands that interfere with a person's private life because working hard and showing the trappings of being very busy is a way of attaining status. It might mean carrying a pager or a cellular phone, so that you can always be reached by your clients, or simply handing out one's home phone number to important customers. If a crisis occurs over the weekend, it means dropping everything to head to the office. In low-status attainment cultures, your status depends on who you are. Moreover, work hours are shorter and weekends are spent relaxing with friends and family. A call from a manager would evoke feelings of anger and transgression because leisure time is considered sacred.

The concept of status attainment may best be described as what makes people feel good about themselves. Is it what they have done or who they are? Can individual accomplishments markedly change your social positioning or is social position conferred as a birthright and reinforced by where you went to school and the people you know as a result?

DIMENSION: SPACE

Space refers to:

- How individuals and societies use space.
- The amount of physical space needed for comfort in daily business and living environment.
- The amount of spatial distances people need when they speak and when interacting with others.
- Need for and definition of privacy.

How people use space and define it, says a lot about the culture and the way it thinks. Imagine two men in an Arab souk standing virtually nose to nose in conversation, holding hands. Contrast that to a similar conversation taking place in Munich where two men are standing three feet apart in an equally intense dialogue. Obviously, the comfort of personal space between them is enormously different. It would be comical if one of the Arabs were to speak to one of the Germans; you might see a dance in which the German constantly backs away to maintain a comfortable distance while the Arab moves forward to achieve the same objective.

The amount of physical space that different cultures need manifests itself in more than just interpersonal dialogue. It is visible in the size of offices, homes, and cars and it is underscored in the need for and expression of privacy and personal space. Then there's the issue of body space. People from low-space cultures are likely to stand quite close when they speak to another person. In high-space cultures, people might stand at least four or five feet apart during conversations. These individuals will feel uncomfortable if their "space bubble" is invaded. They are unlikely to touch people during conversations and feel uncomfortable when they interact with someone who constantly touches them to emphasize a point.

This further manifests itself in the way homes are designed, communities and cities developed, and offices arranged. You can see this in the thickness of walls or doors. In some societies, individuals experience a sense of privacy with a mere screen, whereas others need a thick concrete wall so they can't be seen or heard. If you find yourself in a culture that requires a good deal of space, you need to take care not to invade someone's privacy. Conversely, if you notice a culture that looks for closeness, don't become offended when people get really close to you or touch you as they speak.

This is not a frivolous matter. Individuals from certain societies need people in close proximity to be productive and comfortable. In other societies, the opposite is true; people need complete privacy and quiet to get their work done. Knowing a society's space requirement is particularly important when it comes to office design. The British, who like and can function well with limited space as long as it provides privacy, designed offices in Malaysia that left Malaysians terribly uncomfortable. The British separated the Malaysians from their peers and, by limiting close personal contact, inadvertently interfered with the Malaysian need to have people around and, consequently, their comfort level and productivity.

Hall closely examined the issue of space and made a connection between space and privacy, focusing on the German need for space with thick, closed doors, blinds, and screens for interior space and fences and hedges defining exterior space. He observed that standing in a German executive's open doorway would be deemed an invasion of his or her private space and be very bad manners. Additionally, many high-space cultures feel land and space are sacred, something that's reflected in the German love of hiking. Rarely will a stranger be invited into a German home; if they are, it's considered a singular honor. This sense of privacy is maintained in casual relationships; seldom do Germans chat casually with neighbors.

Hall points out that in high-space societies, the CEO or president of the company has an office close to the employees rather than being sequestered on a high floor away from "the troops." A society's use of space is reflected in its people, its organizations, and its cities.

A look at an American city and U.S. corporations can provide a dynamic model. The United States is a large country and Americans are used to wide open spaces. They prefer large homes with private rooms for their children and large yards. Through their language and hand gestures, Americans also command space when they speak. A city's downtown is surrounded by a seemingly endless array of suburbs, some of which house the rich and powerful and others that house the poor and downtrodden. Mobility is prized, so it's acceptable to live anywhere, provided that it's a "good" community. The corporate model reflects this thinking. Inside a building, departments usually aren't organized according to importance or status. They are laid out so that the entire company can interact efficiently. This might appear haphazard to an Argentine businessman who depends on structure and status to make decisions in his own country, but it is logical to the American way of thinking.

Our need for privacy is fulfilled with big open space, a German's need for privacy is satisfied by thick walls and other barriers, while the Arab need for close companionship with very little privacy is accommodated through overall closeness and slight partitions.

SPACE IN BUSINESS

In low-space cultures, people have little difficulty working in close proximity with each other. Psychological space and physical space can be cramped with no decrease in productivity. Noisy offices with a constant shuffle of bodies moving through will not interfere with performance. In fact, it might be expected and even preferred. Office doors remain open and large communal work rooms are acceptable.

In high-space cultures, where people need physical and psychologi-

Space: Beliefs and Behaviors

Low	High
■ People don't need a lot of space to feel comfortable. They can create it psychologically. In crowded countries such as Japan, people create their own sense of privacy.	■ People place a premium on space.
■ People use virtually no hand gestures as part of their conversational styles.	■ People often use large, sweeping hand motions.
■ Language is contained and vocabulary is not prone toward exaggeration.	■ Language may tend toward exaggeration and grandiosity.
■ Individual offices are unnecessary.	■ People prefer large offices with carefully selected pictures of their family or other personal items placed on their desks or hung on walls.
■ People do not need much body space during conversation.	■ People may want to stand four or five feet from the person they're speaking with.

cal space to function optimally, business environments are relatively quiet. Separate offices—or at the very least dividers—are required for employees to maintain their space. Consequently, workers in high-space cultures tend to be territorial. They assert their ownership of their offices by placing pictures and other personal objects inside. They often consider it rude if someone else touches the objects on their desks without asking permission.

Indeed, space is also used as a mark of recognition in high-hierarchical cultures. In Japan, for instance, employees feel uncomfortable taking an elevator with their superiors. Whenever possible they also show respect by standing at a greater distance.

POWER CLUSTER BUSINESS APPLICATIONS

In Chapter 7, which covers global compensation, you will see alternatives for compensating, recognizing, and rewarding local nationals and expatriates in a manner consistent with their interpretation of the Power

Cluster of cultural dimensions. You will see that while some cultures are motivated by money, others value different rewards for performance.

These cultural dimensions also comprise a significant portion of any expatriate preparation program as discussed in Chapter 9, "Preparing Employees and Families for Expatriate Assignments." They can be taught, understood, and integrated by expatriates to make them effective in a new culture.

5

THE SOCIETAL INTERDEPENDENCE CLUSTER

Group Dependence, Diversity Receptivity, and Change Tolerance

This chapter will cover

- Differences between societies that are individually versus collectively focused.
- How a society's attitudes toward diversity affect its business and daily life.
- The ways in which attitudes toward change impact how activities are accomplished.

This group of cultural dimensions explores a society's attitudes about individual versus group behavior, appreciation of strangers, and adaptability to new situations. This cluster is perhaps the most subtle of the three groups and, as a result, is not readily recognizable in different societies. However, it is often the cause of the unexpected resistance and defensiveness that people encounter, and serves as a reminder of the strength and pervasiveness of cultural behaviors and predelictions.

DIMENSION: GROUP DEPENDENCE

Group dependence refers to:

- How important the individual is in relation to the group.
- Whether people want to be distinguished from the group—seen as individuals—or be considered part of a particular group.
- The idea that group harmony is necessary to achieve business goals.
- How harmony with others and the environment is related to being able to successfully live and work together.

In social and business situations, a culture's attitudes toward this dimension say a great deal about their social, political, and economic system. We can readily distinguish cultures that are high and low on group dependence. Cultures low on the group dependence scale focus on individuality and individual achievement, have laws protecting the rights of the individual, and encourage individuals to distinguish themselves from the masses. Cultures high in the group dependence scale focus on group achievement, emphasize conformity with the group for the "good of the group," and discourage calling attention to oneself.

If you really want to see how cultures think, examine their heroes and their stories. The archetypical American superhero is Superman. He acts independently, disregards the accepted way of doing things, and saves people with his superhuman strength. And what does he do when he's low on energy or overly stressed? He goes off to his icy retreat where he's totally isolated. He derives strength by sequestering himself. The Lone Ranger, the one good guy who defeats all the bad guys in American Westerns, also reinforces the culture's attitudes toward the importance of the individual.

These ideas are also found in children's stories. Look at *The Little Engine That Could,* a popular children's tale in America. It is about a small train engine that dreams of pulling a big train and knows that if it tries hard enough—regardless of insurmountable odds—it can achieve its dreams. The story illustrates the American conviction that if you believe enough in yourself and work exceptionally hard, you can succeed single-handedly. French children's stories featuring the little girl Madeleine show that her independence can sometimes get her into trouble, but her cleverness always saves her and her friends.

In individualistic Western countries like the United States, people learn the lessons of the individual from the earliest moments of life.

Sleeping Beauty is rescued by the prince. Jack climbs the beanstalk, takes the treasure, and cuts off any means of escape for the ogre—all by himself. People are encouraged to display their individuality in the way they dress and the things they do. They are encouraged to "make it on their own."

By way of contrast, consider collectivist cultures like Japan where the same overriding lessons teach the value of being part of the group. Only through communal efforts can success be achieved. These values are reinforced in Japanese children's stories. One of the stories is the *Peach Boy,* a Japanese tale of a boy who goes off to fight the ogres on Ogre Island. In order to be able to do so, he collects a group of compatriots on the way, all of whom played a vital role in subduing the ogres. Think of how different that is from the Western story of Jack and the Beanstalk where Jack climbs through the clouds alone to slay the giant.

Look at the difference in proverbs from one culture to another. In the West people say, "The squeaky wheel gets the grease." This means that if you stand out in the crowd, your needs are more likely to be met. In Asia the saying is, "The nail that stands out gets pounded down" or "the pig that squeals goes to slaughter." This is an obvious reference to the dangers of being different. It carries a strong admonition to remain part of the group.

A Copeland-Griggs video illustrates just how these values take root in early childhood.[1] In the video, a teacher asks a group of American children to draw their families. Each child promptly picks up a pencil and sketches the family. However, when the same question is put to kindergartners in Asia, the children first consult with each other and then begin to draw. When children seemed confused over how to draw family members, American children were told to figure it out for themselves. Japanese children, in contrast, were offered specific suggestions about how family members should appear.

The concern for individual rights in cultures that rank low in group dependence, such as the United States, is pervasive. The societies tend to construct elaborate safeguards for the rights of people who are suspected of committing crimes. In some cases, the individual is more fully protected than the society that has been injured. Group-dependent societies, have little trouble imposing harsh punishments on people accused of committing crimes. Loyalty to the larger group is paramount for the individual in a high-group dependent society and is considered appropriate because the individual is cared for and protected by the family and group. Quite simply, people believe that the group is always greater than the sum of the individuals who comprise the group.

In high-group dependent societies, individuals find security in being part of a group. It isn't uncommon in high-group dependent cultures like Hong Kong for people to walk on the crowded side of a street just so they can feel part of the group.

Group Dependence: Beliefs and Behaviors

Low	High
■ Individualism reigns supreme. People are encouraged to be self sufficient, to "make it" on their own, to "think for themselves."	■ Values the team and the community. The individual's identity is important as he or she relates to the whole group.
■ Individual accomplishment is recognized and rewarded.	■ Harmony is important. Every person in a group must be comfortable for that group to work together.
■ Individual freedom is very important. There is an "I" consciousness and an orientation to one's self.	■ Taking into consideration how the group "feels" about an issue is more important than how an individual reacts.
■ Decision making is often done by majority decision. People are encouraged to speak up, but if they don't take responsibility for their own actions, no one in the group feels it is necessary to make their wishes known.	■ In group activities, everyone must be heard; consequently, decision making takes much longer.
■ Meetings are scheduled to maximize time. Decisions are expected.	■ Meetings may also take a considerably greater amount of time and people resent being forced to adhere to a schedule rather than be allowed to voice their concerns or perspectives.
■ Meetings are devoted to collaboration and the exchange of information.	■ The point of many meetings is simply to gather the group so everyone can voice his or her opinion. Meetings aren't simply for feedback and approval of ideas.
■ Individual taste and style is reflected in home decoration, offices, dress, and even choice of cars.	■ People don't value the need to "express themselves."
■ Focus is on nuclear family with fewer children.	■ Emphasis is on extended family and community.

GROUP DEPENDENCE IN BUSINESS

The significant issues related to group dependence have to do with the way people work together and how they can be motivated and rewarded. This impacts how managers make assignments and how people solve problems. Group dependence determines whether teams or individuals are given assignments and whether problems are solved individually or as a group process. Is decision making and production a group process? Do people like to work in close proximity to each other and share developments as the process continues, or do they prefer to work alone?

In low-group dependence countries, employees are singled out for praise and recognition. Incentive compensation and promotions for performance work well as a motivation. The opposite holds true for cultures with high-group dependence. They represent a culture with a "we" consciousness; one in which the individual is closely tied to the collective body. Success depends on a cooperative effort, so it seems absurd and inappropriate to single out one individual for praise or recognition.

In low-group dependent cultures, organizations often single out people with such things as employee-of-the-month awards to underscore the valuable addition made by individual contributors. Individuals are proud to be singled out for acknowledgment. Individuals like to work on their own and work out problems by themselves in low-group dependent cultures. An individual may be singled out for praise and criticism. The shared belief is that individuals are responsible for their actions.

Motivation in low-group dependent cultures is related to power and achievement. People are hired, fired, or promoted because of their skills, past achievement, and technical know-how. They are selected for international assignments because they are viewed as individuals who can get the job done. In high-group dependent cultures, people are motivated by the assurance of greater security and the opportunity for affiliation, which means that they expect their organizations to take care of them, develop their talents, and compensate them fairly. High-group dependent cultures are not meritocracies; instead, group membership and loyalty are the key in hiring, promoting, or firing decisions. People are selected for international assignment because of their loyalty to the company and their ability to fit into the group and get tasks accomplished by building consensus and working toward organizational goals. They focus on organizational policies, harmony, and the needs of the group. Promotions are based on seniority and are generated from within the organization.

Achievement originates from the creative talents of the group, not the capabilities of one outstanding individual.

People are often eager to hold meetings because of their affinity for working together. A common concern among Western business leaders when dealing with some Asian counterparts is the ongoing need for meetings in order to reach a decision. Part of the reason is that high-group dependent cultures never allow a single person to make decisions. Rather, a delegation is brought to business meetings. They confer before they make a decision and also need to discuss certain business issues with the home office. Anyone affected by a business decision is expected to be consulted, and decisions are made only after consensus has been reached.

When people in cultures that value collectivism work together with people from cultures that value individualism, challenges abound. Working in teams is a good example. Most Americans will tell you that teamwork is a noble endeavor—that team players are the best. Obviously, in business, work groups have become the accepted way to perform many tasks. However the American concept of teamwork is entirely different from the Japanese perspective.

Simply compare. When Americans are part of a team, they want to do their individual best to help the team succeed. When given a task, the individual works on it until satisfied that it's complete, whether or not a team member is struggling. Often, the best performer is acknowledged as the leader. Everyone acknowledges the status of that position. Individual contribution to the team is what's important, what's going to propel the team forward. In many parts of Asia, however, a good team player is aware of all his or her team members and is always available to help out if a colleague stumbles. The group moves ahead as *a group*. The group moves ahead as *a group*, and doesn't move forward leaving stragglers behind. Imagine how difficult it is for the American buyer to understand why the rep of the Japanese vendor company was reluctant to take a sales order until after all his team members in Tokyo could agree with the delivery schedules stated.

DIMENSION: DIVERSITY RECEPTIVITY

Diversity receptivity refers to:
- Gender's relationship to power, authority and societal roles.
- Gender based terminology in language.

- The position of women and their access to opportunity. (Men's roles are relatively static in every society.)
- Whether or not careers and jobs have gender-specific expectations.
- Perceptions and stereotypes of individuals who differ from the majority—in race, religion, or national origin.

The attitude a society has about gender role expectation is probably one of its most subtle defining cultural characteristics. This dimension breaks fundamentally into four areas: (1) Is the society masculine or feminine (using Hofstede's model)? (2) What are the behavioral expectations of each gender? In other words, what are the assumed gender-linked characteristics? (3) What access do women have to power, authority, and traditionally nonfemale roles? (4) What is society's attitude toward diversity and does it value differences among people?[2]

Hofstede defined *masculinity and femininity* as a cultural dimension and demonstrated how different societies identified behaviors, values, and roles as being either masculine or feminine. Masculine cultures encourage people to be assertive and aggressive while feminine cultures are nurturing and more collaborative. Does the society, for example, expect women to fulfill specific roles such as mother, caretaker, and housewife or is it equally acceptable for a woman's role to be more broadly defined to include provider and decision maker? Are men expected to be assertive, be primary wage earners, and take a dominant role in society or is it equally acceptable for them to fulfill nurturing, cooperative roles. Are little girls discouraged from being aggressive and forward?

The fundamental question: Is behavior defined in feminine and masculine terms? Hofstede observed that different societies identified certain professions and behaviors as traditionally masculine or feminine, and that those interpretations and expectations differed between national cultures. For example, are doctors and lawyers expected to be men because the society perceives doctors as making life-and-death decisions and lawyers as aggressive? Are nurses and teachers expected to be women because they are caretaking and nurturing?[3]

The United States and other Western countries are in the midst of redefining traditional masculine and feminine roles. These societies are reluctant to tolerate linking certain behaviors with gender. Unfortunately, these sociologically valid definitions and observations are broadly misinterpreted in today's climate of politically correct language and thinking. Some of the objections cultures now grapple with include the question of established barriers to people acting outside these behavioral norms. For example, are there glass ceilings limiting women's access to power?

Beyond the idea of masculine and feminine behaviors, diversity reflects the organization's willingness to incorporate different styles of learning and performance. Not surprisingly, tendencies toward linear or holistic thinking, or deductive or inductive reasoning, can lead to vastly different behaviors and learning styles. Similarly, attitudes about competition or cooperation can affect performance styles.

High-diversity cultures believe that the ability to succeed in business is not dependent on a person's gender, race, or cultural background. Indeed, these cultures believe that a diversity of backgrounds and perspectives enhance the business culture and create a breadth of performance styles that can make business function more effectively. James Simon is an excellent example of an individual from a high-diversity culture who believes that people's differences will enhance their ability to work together as a group. He brought together his American team, including a woman, with the Taiwanese because he believed that their variety of perspectives would bring about the best solutions and approaches to the situation. While applaudable in the United States and other high-diversity countries, this naive notion presupposes that all cultures share an appreciation for diversity.

The diversity dimension also reflects the culture's attitudes toward individual members of different genders, ethnicities, religions, and countries of origin. Does the society value differences or does it encourage a uniform national way? Americans, for example, speak of a tapestry that incorporates many cultures and heritages. Business cultures that value diversity are more likely to develop short mission and values statements and to encourage the formation of a "hybrid" office culture that borrows from and includes the business-related best that each culture has to offer.

In high-diversity cultures, jokes with negative overtones about gender, race, or background are not tolerated. This isn't the case in low-diversity cultures.

Customer relations, product development, and decisions about who should handle public relations are all based on diversity attitudes as well. In low-diversity cultures, individuals from the dominant culture will be chosen to focus on customer relations. In high-diversity cultures, however, the person with the best listening skills who can respond most effectively to customer concerns, is the likely candidate for the job regardless of his or her background.

Diversity Attitude: Beliefs and Behaviors

Low	High
■ Personal differences are seen as enhancing the business and social environment.	■ Differences are seen as part of the natural order of things. They are not necessarily an asset.
■ The roles of men and women are not clearly delineated and are viewed as fluid. Their abilities are more important than their gender.	■ Men and women do not have equal opportunity in all arenas. The roles and expectations of men and women are clear and rigid. It will be expected that women and men are ideally suited to different jobs, and that women will be nurturant, whereas men will be assertive.
■ While women may still be seen as the primary nurturers, women have equal access to the full range of professions and activities.	■ Women's roles will be typically confined to raising children, maintaining households and helping professions. People will be very surprised to find a woman in a "man's" job.
■ Jobs and roles do not have a gender definition or expectation.	■ Jobs have gender-linked definitions.
■ Differences in work style, performance style, and outlook characterize individuals who move ahead.	■ Governmental actions may be necessary to provide equal access to all society members.
■ People see diversity as an asset. The society sees it as enriching people's ability to perform rather than having just one right way to do things.	■ Uniformity and homogeneity are glorified.
■ Greater receptivity to foreigners. Differences may make them attractive. These cultures pride themselves on integrating people of many different backgrounds.	■ Less acceptance of foreigners. Even foreigners who have lived in the country for many years may not be fully accepted.
■ Universalistic—focuses on generalizations and consistency of rules	■ Particularistic—focuses on differences, uniqueness, and exceptions

Another interesting clue to diversity is the way women dress for business. Around the world, men wear business suits or shirts and ties, but women's fashion varies greatly. In the United States, successful business women are careful not to dress seductively. In South America or Europe, women who hold a position of authority dress in a far more feminine and—at least from the American perspective—more provocative manner. A somewhat open blouse or short skirt wouldn't raise eyebrows as it might in America.

Finally, in cultures such as Japan, which ranks low in diversity attitudes, women who excel in school are more likely to find their way into American businesses where they're promoted according to abilities and achievements. If they remain in their native country and play by the rules of their culture, they're unlikely to realize the same kind of upward mobility they would in high-diversity societies. They will hit the glass ceiling at a level that would shock members of a high-diversity culture.

In low-diversity cultures, people believe that sharing the same or similar perspectives makes you more effective in business. These cultures feel that business functions most effectively when everyone thinks in the same way. Conversely, in high-diversity cultures, individuals believe that different perspectives enhance creativity and the business outcome.

DIMENSION: CHANGE TOLERANCE

Change tolerance refers to:
- How people respond to change.
- Whether or not individuals view change as bringing opportunities.
- How the society views the environment. Does the individual control the environment or does the environment control the individual?
- Is change seen as part of the natural phenomenon or something to avoid?

As the name implies, change tolerance refers to attitudes toward change, newness, and doing things differently. This dimension is extremely important in today's change-driven world where technology is propelling social change at an ever-increasing pace. Contemporary organizations around the world have embraced the notion that change is good and vital for their success while they struggle internally to believe it. However, all cultures do not view change as a positive force. As a result, they create an important distinction for organizations to reckon with.

Cultures that are low in this dimension strive to maintain the status quo and look at new opportunities as creating problems. Leaders are expected to be champions of tradition. On the other hand, societies that are high in change tolerance expect transitions to take place constantly. They view change as part of the natural order; it is necessary and they accept it as such—like evolution. Leaders are expected to be change agents; they're looked to as the visionaries of change and the helpers who will direct its course. Think about the American political environment where even conservatives running for public office talk about the need for change.

Societies that tolerate change are interested in using their creativity and ingenuity to address the inevitable evolving challenges. For example, as American society moved from a manufacturing to an information-based structure—and computerization was introduced as a method for accelerating the process—Americans individually may have been intimidated by the rapid pace of technological advancement, yet the society as a whole embraced it and eagerly awaited the benefits that each new advancement would bring. Now, even individual Americans expect technological change to be positive and embrace it. They have rapidly adjusted to the idea of a computer on every desk.

In contrast, societies that have a low threshold for change cling to the status quo, even if adhering to the status quo comes at the expense of progress or profits. This is because they are rooted in history and traditions from which they draw rewards, satisfaction, and pleasure. We are all aware of how proud the French are of their language and contributions to the arts and philosophical concepts of freedom. It's not surprising, therefore, that they frown on words which they believe debase their language. Contrast that with the Americans, who periodically update their dictionaries to include new slang.

Think of the 1996 French labor strikes, for instance. In spite of clear evidence that a downsized public labor sector was critical for the economic well-being of France and, in turn, the European Union, the threat of change that accompanied that downsizing, paralyzed the country and halted the economic streamlining. Some cultures are so threatened by change that it's difficult for them to see any value in it. They take strong preventive steps to avoid the introduction of new and different thinking. Consider the Saudi need to keep U.S. troops segregated from its citizens during the Gulf War.

Of course, change tolerance, like the other cultural dimensions, is complex. While France may protect its language and historical institutions, its society is on the forefront of innovation in other aspects of culture. The world looks to Paris for changing fashion design and trends in art. Similarly, while Middle America may be at the forefront of technological discoveries, it is slower and more reluctant to modify fashion than the French. It's not a simple equation. So, if you're an American going to France or Japan, learn their values and find out what they will change and won't change, so that you can better accomplish your mission. Thus the danger of oversimplifying and stereotyping cultures.

This dimension defines the need for rules, the ability to take risks, and the ideas we all hold about how much control we have over our destiny. At the most fundamental levels of society, it affects the freedom we allow our children for self-expression, with low change tolerance cultures being quite restrictive while high change tolerance cultures encourage children's freedom to explore. Are children encouraged to express themselves freely or are they encouraged to be more reserved? Do changes take place in quantum leaps, such as in the United States or in incremental steps such as in Germany? Think of the changes in BMWs and Mercedes Benz as opposed to the changes in cars from General Motors and Chrysler.

CHANGE TOLERANCE IN BUSINESS

Examine organizations in high-change cultures, it is obvious that one of the mostimportant aspects of a corporate culture is rapid change. Such cultures view something new as synonymous with something good. They value individuals whose creative genius leads to fresh organizational plans and strategies.

Compare countries that have high-change tolerance with those that have low tolerance, and it's obvious that each has profoundly different ideas about lifetime employment, receptivity to new ideas,and attitudes toward moving or beginning new ventures. Today, few Americans would consider holding the same job for life; changing jobs is generally viewed as highly desirable because it can broaden one's knowledge and skills. Japan, in contrast, has a low tolerance for change as witnessed by the lifetime employment assumption (which is slowly being eroded by eco-

Change Tolerance: Beliefs and Behaviors

Low	High
■ Cultures with low-change tolerance are risk averse. They describe their ideals: "We have always done it this way, why change now?"	■ People tend to be receptive to new ideas. They like innovation and tend to accept alternative ways of doing things.
■ Change represents a threat to traditional ways. It must be controlled and limited.	■ Societal changes are more frequent. Creativity and experimentation is highly valued.
■ Low worker turnover; greater company loyalty.	■ High worker turnover and less loyalty to the company.
■ Child rearing tends to be strict. Children are given fewer freedoms.	■ Child rearing may be more permissive. Children are encouraged to be innovative and creative.
■ People believe that nature cannot be easily controlled. Instead, people must learn how to respond to the fluid, ever-changing character of nature.	■ People believe in their abilities to control the environment and harness the forces of nature.
■ Employees like clear outlines of requirement, rules, and instructions and believe that rules cannot be easily broken.	■ Employees prefer broad plans and guidelines and feel that rules can be changed for pragmatic concerns.
■ Employees are less willingness to compromise and view competition as inappropriate.	■ Greater readiness to compromise with opponents and perceive competition as acceptable.

nomic realities) and ancient traditions, dress, art, and music. Interestingly, while the Japanese have embraced change in technology and business, they continue to cherish and retain tradition and the status quo in social structure and personal life.

In cultures averse to change, companies demonstrate their aversion to risk by building structured organizations with clearly defined approval systems. Young employees do not present bold, new concepts. They leave the decision making to older and more senior managers. Organizations from cultures that embrace change view it as a means of self-improvement for both the business and the individual. Organizations tend to have far greater fluidity and flexibility in their organizational structure. Employees are often comfortable expressing their feelings about company policy to colleagues and supervisors.

Organizations in countries that view change favorably have higher employee turnover because employees see change as a positive step in their own careers. Industries tend to be more innovative and creative. These societies are usually the ones that develop new products, register a disproportionate number of new patents, and promote technological advances.

Whereas risk taking is rewarded in these cultures—even if it doesn't always lead to a breakthrough or bottom-line success—that isn't the case in more risk-averse societies. Furthermore, low-change tolerance societies are more comfortable with change in incremental steps, whereas high-change tolerance cultures expect innovation in quantum leaps. Therefore, turnover is very low. Job security is very important and, consequently, employees rarely disagree with corporate policy. Obviously, cultures with low-change tolerance can and do introduce innovations. One need look no further than Japan to see that the security created by this work environment can lead to innovation and consistent progress. For example, people in Japan are very receptive to introducing robots to do manual work because they don't feel that people will be put out of work as a result. Rather, they assume that people are necessary and will be used by their companies to perform more creative, challenging tasks. In addition, this conformity and lifelong loyalty approach allows the Japanese to succeed at manufacturing high-quality manufactured items such as TVs, VCRs, cars, and so forth at price points others can't match.

Predictably, companies in low-change tolerance cultures experience stress when organizational issues are not clear. As a result, they will detail job and task responsibilities at a level that might seem excessive to others. What's more, managers ensure that subordinates clearly understand all aspects of a project before a company sinks money into research and development (R&D) or manufacturing. Finally, loyalty is a legitimate basis for promotions. Structure is perceived as empowering employees. In contrast, high-change tolerance cultures develop broad project guidelines that focus on achieving the goal, but they don't define how to get there. Individual innovation and creativity will supply the fuel, and it's believed that multiple paths are possible. Loyalty to the organization is not highly valued, which translates into short-term planning.

SOCIETAL INTERDEPENDENCE GROUP BUSINESS APPLICATIONS

In Chapter 8, we discuss the selection of expatriate families. Obviously, personal predispositions toward such issues as group dependence, diversity and change tolerance are important factors when considering who to send on international assignments. Furthermore, preparing expatriates and international business people to function effectively in an intercultural environment means teaching them to recognize the subtle, and not-so-subtle, cultural behaviors described in this chapter. We discuss that in Chapters 9 and 10.

The following chapters in the book will assume a fundamental understanding of the cultural dimensions we have discussed in the first part of the book. This knowledge will facilitate the ease with which managers can tackle many of the business challenges they will encounter as they send individuals on assignment.

NOTES

1. Going International. 1983. Produced and directed by Lennie Copeland and Lewis Griggs. Seven-part series. Griggs Production, San Francisco. Videocassette.
2. Geert H. Hofstede, *Cultures and Organizations,* (New York; NY: McGraw-Hill, 1992).
3. Ibid.

II

⊚ # KEYS TO EXPATRIATE MANAGEMENT

6

⑥ DEVELOPING
RESPONSIVE POLICIES
AND EFFECTIVE
PROGRAM
ADMINISTRATION

This chapter will cover

- Objectives of a responsive, culturally sensitive policy.
- Techniques to research and create a responsive policy and program.
- How to validate features with constituents (employees and their partners, line managers, HR managers in country).
- How to write a user friendly manual that communicates to the entire expatriate body.
- How to implement a responsive policy.
- How to evaluate program effectiveness.
- Outsourcing as a policy administration option.

Imagine an employee coming home and telling his spouse that he has a wonderful opportunity for a job assignment in Spain. He waxes poetic about the job possibilities.

Finally his startled wife exclaims: "Spain? Isn't that in Europe? How are we going to get there? What are we going to do with the house? Where's Johnny going to go to school? Do they have Little League there? When's this going to happen? Are you going to be paid in dollars or other kind of money? What kind of homes do they have there? Can we bring the station wagon?"

Often the employee answers in one of two ways.

"Don't worry, honey. The company's taking care of everything."

Or

"I understand that as expatriates we're going to live like royalty."

Frequently, the first factual information a family receives about an international assignment comes from the company policy booklet. Good policies clearly define the company's compensation and deployment objectives so that employees who are affected by them understand the concepts underlying the plan. They must be comprehensive enough to address a wide array of needs and circumstances, and flexible enough to respond to the uniqueness of each destination and expatriate family. In other words, international relocation policies are complex.

As a result, international policies are more a set of guidelines and descriptions that require an accompanying letter of understanding (LOU) or a letter of agreement (LOA) to address a particular expatriate's needs. The LOU specifically spells out the agreement between the employee and the company. It also covers the compensation arrangement and the relocation policy features that apply to his or her move.

The very fact that expatriate assignments are almost always accompanied by a LOU implies that the provisions were individually negotiated. When partners and employees discuss their "packages," inevitably there are differences that leave expats wondering if they got a fair deal.

Their feeling is not unfounded when you consider the way typical companies approach this situation. One 10-year-old policy booklet that was an obvious leftover had penciled edits and revisions tagged on one-after-another. When asked if expatriates received a copy of the document, the global manager responded, "No way. That way they would know everything they're entitled to and negotiating with them would be impossible." It's small wonder, then, that most employees and partners believe that their expatriate policy provisions were individually negotiated.

The LOU speaks to an individual move, and the policy is often regarded as merely a set of guidelines. Usually spouses are not even aware that a policy has been applied to their move. They think the entire program is the result of a series of ongoing negotiations between the company and the employee.

As complex and individual as each assignment is, there will always be a LOU attached to a policy. The policy, however, must present a specific set of parameters so that each expatriate feels he or she is fairly treated.[1]

OBJECTIVES OF A POLICY

Why have a policy at all? Why not just negotiate each case individually? Maybe expatriate relocation is an activity that defies the "one-policy-for-all" method. The answer lies in three words: cost, control, and fairness. Companies require policies to meet these objectives. And expatriate relocation policies, because of the long duration of an assignment and the cost involved, must be defined under a policy that makes sense and can be administered fairly with relatively few exceptions.

Before discussing methods for developing a responsive, comprehensive expatriate policy, let's look at how policies in force today have been developed and the hazards that accompany them. A company's policy generally is developed over time, usually in a piecemeal fashion. A provision is added or deleted or revised, and the policy is adjusted. New laws take effect, and the policy adds a note or addendum. No wonder policies become convoluted and confusing.

Moreover, the policies are frequently developed by administrators who may only have secondhand knowledge of the expatriate experience. Policies also run the risk of subordinating the needs of the expatriates or the business function in favor of ease of administration. They are often complex "do-it-yourself kits" that require so much effort on the part of an expatriate that they become a job in themselves. Furthermore, programs are often administered by understaffed departments who have neither the time nor the knowledge to adequately support the questions arising from the "do-it-yourself" policies they administer. They also have little sympathy for the concerns that expats raise. This attitude on the part of administrators sometimes emerges in two ways: (1) "After all, these people are well-paid managers, getting a bunch of money for their assignment. Besides, they took the assignment as a great opportunity for their careers, so they should just stop complaining"; (2) "Can you imagine how difficult it has to be adjusting the entire family to a new culture. Children leaving friends, spouse unable to work in the new location. They've got an awful lot to deal with."

In *designing* a responsive policy, we need to listen to the concerns of expatriates and their families as well as the managers who send them on assignment. In *writing* a policy, we need to make it as clear and comprehensive as possible so that expatriates have a guide to understanding the process they will be going through. In *administering* the policy, we want to be as supportive as possible, recognizing that whatever effort and strife we save the expatriate will be returned to the company in greater productivity and assignment success. We often see that administration of policies is such a challenge that individual design features that business units may need are passed over in favor of simplicity and uniformity.

Indeed, one study conducted by the Society of Human Resource Management indicated that employees sometimes perceive support by the company as more important than financial incentives in expatriate assignments.[2] In other words, expatriates who need help with a problem may be better served through counselor assistance than by being given funds to solve the problem on their own. Over and over again, service proves to be more cost-effective than simply throwing money at a problem.

Oftentimes, companies don't recognize this fact. Imagine the surprise of Corwin Ellis[3]—chosen by his Scottish firm as the top candidate for an assignment to Japan—when the company turned down his request to send him and his wife for cross-cultural counseling because it was not a feature of the policy. Imagine further his amazement when his wife refused to go without the training and the company instead sweetened the deal by offering him an annual salary increase of $10,000! Stunned, the Ellises accepted the offer and simply paid the $3,000 fee out of the pay increase for pre-departure training and pocketed the rest.

The SHRM study also indicates that if expatriates feel slighted and perceive a lack of personal and family support, they are likely to leave the company after reentry. On the other hand, nonfinancial support at the appropriate times can ameliorate turnover and result in greater retention upon repatriation.[4]

The ability to effectively relocate should not be misconstrued as proof that an expatriate will be an effective manager in a foreign country, and it should not be used as a test for expatriate competence. Human resource consultants to major organizations hear all too often that "our managers are tough and can handle the challenge of relocation on their own—we expect that from them." How foolish and what a waste of precious time and energy! Expatriates should be concerned with understanding the business activity in a Farsi-speaking country, not trying to interpret a 200-page relocation manual written in English "administratese."

Outsourcing expatriate policy administration (discussed in detail later in this chapter) represents an opportunity to bring improved expatriate support and service to existing programs. Unfortunately, many organizations outsource their administrative activities without taking advantage of the opportunity to enhance the service levels of their programs. The primary outsourced service providers are tax and administrative organizations instead of HR organizations, which might be more prone to enhance service levels. In any event, once the outsourced mechanics have been transferred, the now freed-up HR managers can focus on the more subtle aspects of service and enhance the programs delivered by the outside providers.

The objective of this chapter is to familiarize readers with a process for designing, developing, and issuing a comprehensive policy. While a LOU will still be required—and many aspects will still be too complex for most expats to fully comprehend—at least the policy will address the fairness issue and limit the need for constant negotiation. After all, the expatriate is not the enemy. And the responsibility is to get them and keep them as productive as possible.

DEVELOPING A RESPONSIVE POLICY AND PROGRAM

RESPONSIVE POLICIES

- Enable employees to become productive as quickly as possible.

- Cover all reasonable costs associated with the assignment.

- Clearly communicate entitlements and limit the need for individual negotiations.

- Are flexible enough to enable adjustment to individual needs.

- Are competitive with the best practices, so that employees do not have to wonder about their company's wisdom.

- Help the company and the HR department meet global deployment objectives.

- Create no administrative nightmares for overextended HR departments.

Responsive policies do *not* need to be more expensive policies. Contrary to popular thinking, enhancements are often likely to save money by substituting intelligence for cash when solving problems. Policy changes require contemplation and attention, and they often produce well-considered alternatives that address the most serious expatriate concerns. These concerns cannot be solved by simply offering up greater allowances although that has been a favorite quick-fix used by companies to improve a situation.

The most costly policies are often the same ones that have the greatest need for an update. For example, companies often retain outdated allowances that might have been appropriate 10 years ago or that fail to take advantage of available tax savings that could be achieved with better planning.

Expatriate deployment policies are intended to outline all the relevant policy provisions and reimburse all reasonable expenses that are necessary to get an employee to accept an assignment and become productive as quickly as possible. The rationale for the entire exercise, which is sometimes forgotten in all of the administrative minutiae, is to accomplish a business mission. Policy features should not be interpreted as either generous or frugal, but in terms of what is necessary to achieve a business objective—what it takes to get the job done.

For example, expatriate housing in Hong Kong in the early 1990s became extraordinarily expensive; in many cases it was more lavish than that of the home country. As in many other locations, however, there is a limited middle ground of available alternatives, and the local housing market in Hong Kong would be inadequate for most Western nationals. In other words, it takes whatever it takes, and expatriate policies shouldn't be shortsighted and complicate the process for the expatriates. On the other hand, giving expatriates what they need does not mean that cost-effective options don't exist. In the case of housing, for instance, some companies—to reduce costs—are using flat housing allowances which, while allotting a certain amount of money for housing, empower expats to spend less and pocket the difference. (This isn't a viable tax option in all countries.) Such options still accomplish the necessary ends while introducing innovative cost-reduction opportunities. Chapter 7, Globalizing compensation examines various opportunities for similar program enhancements.

EFFECTIVE SUPPORT PROGRAMS
KEEP THE PROMISE OF THE POLICY

A successful policy needs to be accompanied by a comprehensive support program. We like to think of the policy as the promise, and the program as the method of keeping the promise. So, if the policy sets forth the company position about benefits and reimbursements, the program describes how they are accessed. Therefore, policy and program must complement each other. Otherwise, expats develop expectations that cannot be fulfilled.

For example, if the company decides to reimburse certain expenses, forms on which to file for those reimbursements should be easily accessible. Once submitted, the forms must be promptly processed so that expatriates don't have to wait and wonder. If the policy provides for a specific housing allowance and indicates that home-finding help is available, the delivery of those services must be provided in a globally consistent manner not subject to the vagaries of local HR managers' definitions of such assistance. Thus, once the company defines such a policy, it's important to either centralize controls and standards, or communicate those standards to the individuals responsible for implementing the policies.

DEVELOPING A RESPONSIVE POLICY AND PROGRAM
REQUIRES RESEARCH AND ANALYSIS

We have outlined a comprehensive process to define an optimum policy and program for organizations with existing policies. It includes a research and development phase, and an implementation phase. Slight modifications of this approach are useful for organizations undertaking their first effort in policy development.

Research and Development Phase

The research and development phase consists of benchmarking studies to get competitive analysis, polling constituents to define program objectives, and defining the current administrative process and costs incurred.

Polling Constituents

Interviews with Line and Program Managers   Since a "customer's" view is essential to evaluate the responsiveness and efficiency of the program, a series of management interviews must be undertaken. This would take place both in the home country and in other countries around the world. These interviews should be conducted with policy makers, line managers, and human resource professionals, including HR generalists and recruiters.

Management interviews help identify the strategic objectives of employee relocation, the corporate culture, what needs to be reflected in human resource and relocation practices, and how well managers feel the current program is achieving those objectives. Interviews also help to establish the objectives of the program and define the way the program is used, the exceptions required, and how well the current policies support the business mission.

Interviews with HR managers and people who are directly involved in the global relocation program help develop a complete picture of how well the strategic objective is supported throughout the organization. Interviews should cover virtually all aspects of how well the relocation program supports the organizations:

- Philosophy and corporate culture
- Management Planning Activities

The interviews should also cover perspective on:

- Problems with the existing program
- Needs
- Ideas and recommendations

The information obtained from these interviews is used in the next step, the Employee and Spouse Review.

Expatriate Employee and Spouse Review

The people most affected by the relocation process are the expatriates themselves. Candid input from people who have been moved by the company is essential to an understanding of how well the present program works. It is critically important as a means to identify areas that need change. To obtain this input, a company should employ: employee/spouse focus groups and expatriate surveys.

Employee/Spouse Focus Groups   Focus groups allow participants to speak about and explore issues of concern arising from the current process—what works well and what does not. The perspective of the employees and their partners or spouses enables practitioners to glean what is important to the recipients of the policy. Focus groups allow greater exchange and input than a questionnaire, providing a way to access ideas of which you might not have otherwise been aware. While valuable in and of themselves, focus groups also provide excellent input for a survey questionnaire.

Employee Surveys   The employee survey provides the most reliable and persuasive evidence available about the present global relocation program and how well it meets corporate objectives. The survey should be a customized and validated questionnaire. Every employee whose transfer has been completed within the past year should fill out a survey questionnaire. Because the instrument yields quantitative data, it is a much-needed ally when selling program changes to management.

The surveys are designed to:

- Identify and quantify specific expatriate needs.
- Pinpoint areas of possible improvement.
- Identify service differences by geographic destination.
- Point out geographic hot spots that may have escaped attention in other measurements.
- Reduce the guesswork associated with revisions.
- Overcome excessive influence by the vocal few among the expatriate population.

Surveys also provide an excellent communication vehicle between the company and its employees. They put the entire organization on notice that the company is concerned about what employees say and that the company is taking an active interest in the relocation and expatriation process. This subtle message can be amplified and used in a variety of additional communications to the employee population. Questionnaires explore such topics as:

Relocation policy	Postmove adjustment
Program implementation	Respondent demographics
Vendor services	Efficiency of the process
Spouse career issues	Employee opinions about services
Family issues	received
Schooling	How employees would like to have
Cost issues	services provided
Special problems	

Administrative/Process Analysis

Policy Analysis/Benchmarking   Benchmarking against competitive practice is exceptionally useful. Management is naturally interested in how the company's relocation policy compares with those used by other organizations. To collect these data, conduct a benchmark study comparing the salient features of policies and practices against companies within the same industry and with similar characteristics. Copies of international relocation policies should be obtained from competing or peer companies. It might also be beneficial to include at least one "excellent" company in this benchmarking study. "Excellent" companies are those not necessarily in the same industry, but which are consistently innovative and on the leading edge with their programs and policies.

Compile the results into a matrix delineated by policy features comparing each company (see the sample table below). A separate portion of the grid can include implementation approaches that are used, including which departments perform certain functions and which areas are provided by outside companies.

POLICY COMPARISON MATRIX				
Policy Provision	**Current Practice**	**Company A**	**Company B**	**Company C**
Sale of Automobiles	Reimburse loss (retail price vs. selling price) up to 20% of retail value, no maximum on dollars or number of cars.	$3,500 allowance per car sold, maximum 2 cars	Reimburse loss (retail price vs. selling price) up to 20% of retail value, maximum 2 cars	$1,000 allowance per car sold, maximum 2 cars; if car(s) are less than 1 year old, allowance is $2,500 per car

Work Flow Analysis/Process Mapping   To document the administrative and financial processes in place for the current global relocation program, interview all appropriate staff, including human resources, tax, legal, treasury, accounting, payroll, finance, and transportation.

Cost Analysis: Direct and Indirect   In addition to the comparative study, also identify and study the current relocation policy costs. You will use these costs as a baseline against which to measure any modifications. The costs of the current program should be identified during the work flow analysis and will include costs directly associated with policy provisions as well as the costs to administer the program.

Program Recommendations and Cost Estimates

Now your organization is in a position to consider various options, including innovative approaches. These could be in the form of changes and additions in the following areas:

- Policy
- Procedure
- Methodology
- Delivery systems
- Administration
- Vendor activities
- Communications

Cost Estimates

It is a good idea to support each recommendation in detail by providing the anticipated cost of each feature. This is accomplished by estimating the cost of the feature, adjusting it to family size, and multiplying it by anticipated usage to get an annual budget estimate. That budget estimate could then be compared to current company practice to illustrate the savings achieved or the additional cost of the feature.

Obtaining Buy-in

Since you've polled people in surveys and interviews to gain the insight for the recommendations, it is critical to consider a variety of approaches to launch these recommendations and obtain the buy-in of various constituents. Before the program is introduced, the effort is enhanced by conducting workshops and meetings to explain the new program and rationalize the changes.

WRITING USER-FRIENDLY POLICIES AND INTERNAL OPERATING PROCEDURES (IOP)

Based on the approved changes in the current program, you'll be able to generate new policies and internal operating procedures (IOPs). These include new employee handbooks and other methods of communication that will document the new policies and the manner in which they will be administered.

Different Policies for Different Kinds of Assignments

Companies typically have employees going on assignments of varied duration and assignees at different levels. Each type of assignment requires its own policies. Therefore, several different policies should be written, one for each of the specific constituents to whom they're directed. Expatriates shouldn't have to plod through material for which they are not eligible, or have to wonder why certain features don't apply to them. For example, there should be policies for long-term, short-term, permanent, and project-specific assignments.

Flexibility

Flexibility is often referred to as a necessity of an international relocation policy. It is certainly a prerequisite of the compensation portion of the policy, which is always individually designed. However, the relocation portion can retain its responsiveness to individual needs while being specific in its entitlements. After all, one of the objectives of a policy is to limit negotiation and individual tailoring of features.

Selection

Candidate selection has been addressed in Chapter 8, and it is not logically a part of the policy development process or the policy document itself. However, the subject is mentioned here because the expatriate policy may be the only corporate or management document that outlines the expatriation process. Selection is typically done by line managers based primarily on technical competencies. In many companies, people about to go on expatriate assignment have no idea of the challenges they will face or the unique skills they need to thrive in a foreign culture.

Therefore, the policy should include a short section on selection in order to empower expatriates to select/deselect themselves once they have learned more about the assignment. A paragraph on self-selection and the availability of selection counseling should be included in the policy introduction. (Obviously, the company should make it available, and the expatriate should be encouraged to take advantage of it.)

Remuneration

Discussions on remuneration, cost-of-living adjustments, housing, children's education, and other special allowances should be included in a separate document and be part of a separate discussion. Inasmuch as each of these arrangements is different from expatriate to expatriate and not all provisions apply, the inclusion of all the possible provisions in one policy make that document unnecessarily cumbersome. In most cases, those discussions will be completed and a LOU will be in process by the time the remainder of the relocation policy comes up for discussion.

However the information is presented, it is critical that it be well explained with text and examples. It will invariably need additional dialogue with an HR specialist in compensation and benefits. Chapter 7 contains sample worksheets and further discussion of compensation.

Relocation Features
The policy should contain as much detail about the relocation provisions as possible. For instance, it should specify the number of home-finding trips and the duration of each; the class of airline service for employee and family members; the expenses covered during these trips; interim living expenses, shipping and storage limitations; how to dispose of vehicles in the home country, furnishing and appliance allowances (this could be in the country-specific information); domestic home sale and property management provisions; vacation, family, and emergency leave provisions; a miscellaneous expense allowance; and other company-specific data.

Many organizations consider covering some of these expenses with a lump sum allocation. This empowering provision allows for employee flexibility and limits the amount of paperwork. To be effective the "lump sum" must, of course, be reasonable and adequate. Most compensation data suppliers, such as ECA Windham, have researched local business travel costs and can provide information on appropriate allowance levels for most locations in the world. The policy also should be as specific as possible in identifying destination home finding and settling-in resources. Contacts with those organizations should be established before the initial look-see or home-finding trip.

Helpful Information

It's important to keep in mind that the international relocation process is an unfamiliar experience for most people. As a result, including helpful hints on subjects ranging from what clothes to take to local electrical service will be appreciated by expatriates and be beneficial to them. A

FIGURE 6–1

Expatriate Relocation Time Line

Count Down

Do Immediately upon Accepting Assignment	Do 4–8 Weeks Prior to Departure	Do 2–4 Weeks Prior to Departure	Just Prior to Departure
Meet with relocation coordinator.	Finish required government forms.	Meet with movers for information on packing and shipping.	Confirm that leases are intact.
Schedule "look/see" get acquainted trip.	Complete health forms and physical examinations.	Be sure to obtain all immunizations.	Confirm that utilities are being connected.
Begin passport, visa, and work permit process.	Contact moving company.	Be sure all paperwork is moving ahead correctly.	Confirm that housing will be in "move-in" condition upon arrival.
Schedule cross-cultural orientation.	Identify things to ship.	"Goodbye" events with family and friends.	Be sure that all medications, prescriptions, hard-to-get family items are obtained.
Schedule language program.	Identify things to purchase.	Arrange to sell automobiles.	Notify friends and post office about address change.
Obtain tax cousel.	Complete necessary school enrollment forms.		Air ship items immediately necessary.
Talk with children.	Schedule meeting with tax advisor.		MOVING DAY!
Discuss property management and/or sale possibilities.	Consider and schedule events to say goodbye to family and friends.		
Identify home office mentors.	Arrange spouse counseling.		

schematic (see Figure 6–1) that shows the various tasks that must be completed within a certain time frame is also valuable.

Country-Specific Information

Country-specific program entitlements in a separate addendum with each policy booklet. That addendum contains the names and phone numbers of country HR managers as well as specific features that are applicable. Those features might include items like: automobile allowances, provisions for household help, appliances, as well as special visa and work permit requirements. It will also particularly useful if each policy manual contains a host country outline, providing the expatriate with important local information and phone numbers. Several such booklets are available in the marketplace, including ECA International's Country Profile for Expatriates.

Sequence the Policy to Reflect the Expatriate Process

Developing and communicating the policy provisions in the same chronological order as they are experienced by the expatriate makes it far easier for them to understand and absorb. Since there is so much for the expatriate family to do, in the pre-departure time frame, following a chronological sequence makes the possibly overwhelming venture manageable.

FIGURE   6–2

Sample Policy Table of Contents

Phase One: Predecision

Statement of Corporate Philosophy
Intent of the Policy
Spirit of the Program
Assistance Available
Self-selection counseling
Special Needs
Statement of Eligibility and Assignment Definitions
Introduction of World-wide Administrative Team
   What to expect of them and how to reach them
   Defines each step in a user-friendly diagram
An Overview of the Expatriation Process

Phase Two: Pre-departure

Immigration, visa, work permits
Tax impact of expatriate assignment

Initial Home-finding trip and school arrangements
Cross-cultural training
Language training
Health and physical examination
Home and automobile disposition
Storage provisions in the home country for items not shipped

Phase Three: Relocation

Home-country housing
Home-finding support
Shipment and storage of household goods
Health and safety
Personal finance
Temporary living expenses
Relocation allowances
Educational allowances
Automobile allowances

Phase Four: Settling-In

In-country settling-in support
Spouse and family support
Home leave and travel
Emergency leave and travel
Miscellaneous expense allowances—one-time and ongoing
Other special company benefits such as medical, etc.

Phase Five: Ongoing Support

Tax returns
Home leave
Family visits
Home-and host-mentoring programs
Emergencies
Periodic adjustments for currency fluctuations and inflation

Phase Six: Repatriation

Advice and counsel regarding personal pre-departure and post-arrival activities
Reimbursement forms and procedures

MAKING THE POLICY CULTURALLY SENSITIVE

A policy document must be responsive to several different constituents, including employees, managers (all global HR and line managers), and the entire expatriate family. In addition, a policy must also respond to the different needs and interests of HR managers in numerous international locations. Some of these managers will be on the receiving end of expatriate assignments and have a different set of concerns than managers on the sending side of the process. In any event, it is important not to skew the policy in favor of home-country expatriates, and to include similar benefits for assignees globally.

Futhermore, creating a single policy document that is meangful across various cultures is very difficult, and care must be taken to avoid jargon, colloquialisms, and legalese. Straightforward, concise language becomes all the more important because not all users will be home-country nationals.

IMPLEMENTING A RESPONSIVE POLICY

Leading-edge thinking among human resource professionals is defining HR management away from the service delivery arena into a core business strategic function where HR managers are partners with line managers. Few human resource activities have more detail associated with them than the administration of the international relocation process. Therefore, a method needs to be found that allows for efficient program administration without burying the human resource department. There are several approaches that can be used to achieve that end.

Regardless of whether a program is large or small, (an option that is discussed in detail below), it must take advantage of technological advances to make it more efficient and responsive to users. Policy administration has to be flexible and responsive enough to support the needs of the expatriates and family, yet consistent enough to make it manageable. It must also address the range of needs that business managers have to enable them to achieve the business objectives that prompted international deployment.

Some companies find it easier to implement an expatriate program using a centralized approach, while others prefer a completely decentralized effort. The centralized approach allows for a larger dedicated team of professionals specializing in this activity. Centralization may also achieve additional cost savings negotiated by more experienced consumers. However, centralization inevitably creates friction with business units that feel it is not responsive enough to their unique activities.

In any event, the implementation team needs to take a very supportive role with both the expatriates and the line managers. Neither are intimately familiar with the administration of expatriate programs, and they have a right to expect proactive support.

EVALUATING PROGRAM EFFECTIVENESS

However a program is administered, it is important to get ongoing feedback on the efficiency of the policy and the services utilized. It is also important to track exception requests. Both provide valuable insight into the kind of fine-tuning that needs to be done in the future and how well the program is working.

It is useful to conduct a program evaluation six months into the expatriate assignment (and at periodic intervals thereafter) to see how well the services achieved their objectives of facilitating adjustment and accelerating return to production. Interestingly, what will inevitably surface are reports of creative solutions that expatriates discovered on their own, hidden resources available in host countries that will be helpful to others, and a greater understanding of the expatriate experience. The box illustrates how one company, Allergan Pharmaceuticals, created a responsive expatriate policy.

SEARCH FOR BEST PRACTICES: ALLERGAN PHARMACEUTICALS—Creating Responsive Policies

Allergan is a $1 billion pharmaceutical firm with over 6,000 employees headquartered in Irvine, California. Approximately 56 percent of its revenues come from outside the United States, and 48 percent of its employees are outside the United States. The company is well known as an organization that is responsive to its employee community. In 1991, the company reorganized and simultaneously increased its expatriate population from 8 to 40. Then, in 1994, Allergan created a continuous improvement team whose goal was to address policy-related items in order to be more responsive to the expatriate community while assuring that the company followed competitive practices. The team consisted of the vice president of compensation and benefits, the director of international compensation and benefits, a regional VP who was a former expatriate, the VP of HR development, the VP of tax, the VP of worldwide manufacturing (who had several expats reporting to her), and the VP of financial planning.

Charged with evaluating and constructing new policies to better meet the needs of the expatriates as well as the company, the group had no intention of developing policies in a vacuum. It created a 74-item questionnaire covering all aspects of the move and ongoing administration and surveyed its expat population. Questions included: "Was your tax equalization calculated accurately?" "Has your family adjusted to the new community and country?" "Is the goods-and-services allowance fair?"

Overall, the team used the survey to focus on the areas that needed improvement and followed recommendations that were made to answer those concerns. In addition, the team sought outside information on competitive practices, which proved to save the company money. For example, after surveying other companies, Allergan discovered that a high percentage of companies in many countries used an efficient purchaser index for its cost-of-living allowance (COLA) whereas Allergan's COLAs were always straightforward allowances. The improvement team decided to change that part of the policy. Thus, in countries where 50 percent or 60 percent of the companies used efficient purchaser indexes, Allergan did likewise. (It allows a six-month period with a full allowance—paid in a lump sum—before going to the efficient purchaser index.) Because the team realized this would be perceived as a "take-away" from the current expat package, it exempted all current expatriates and started the plan with new expats. Furthermore, when it became apparent that the policy posed a hardship for those in Japan, the original full allowance was reinstated (even though over 60 percent of the companies they spoke with used a scaled-down allowance).

In a six-month process that included developing and analyzing the questionnaire, making recommendations to the HR management team, and communicating the new policy to the expats, the team kept focusing back on the results of the survey to be sure they'd adequately responded to the needs. In communicating to the expatriates, they explained clearly how the new policies were responsive to the areas that needed attention.

POLICY PROVISION CHANGES

Before: Physical examinations were not provided.
After: Predeparture physicals for all employees and dependents. Annual physical for employee and dependents assigned to developing countries.
Rationale: Employees felt at some risk when assigned to a developing country. Allergan's business is going more aggressively into these areas, and it would become an increasing concern.

Before: Spousal career transition wasn't addressed.

After: Recognize career transition by providing reimbursement of eligible expenses up to $1,500 per year to working spouses who are accompanying an expatriate employee.

Rationale: Working spouses were incurring expenses as a result of the expatriation of their spouse. This tool is an attempt to begin to address that issue.

Before: Familiarization visit was up to seven days including travel time.

After: Familiarization trip is seven days excluding travel time. Reimbursement for babysitting and pet boarding.

Rationale: The time allotted previously wasn't enough to complete community visits, search for housing, and conduct school hunting.

Before: Country orientation was previously given only as needed.

After: Included for all assignees and family members.

Rationale: The team concurred that there was a great need for a thorough orientation of expatriate employees and their families in order to help the expatriates succeed.

Before: Host country exceptions required the approval of a corporate compensation and benefits person.

After: The line manager with the assistance of the local HR and international compensation and benefits manager can approve additional expenses up to $5,000 over the course of the assignment.

Rationale: This plan allows for flexibility that becomes apparent—and applies to issues—in the host country that weren't covered by policies in the handbook. Furthermore, by including line and local HR managers in the decision, it continues matrix decision making in the matrixlike environment that characterizes Allergan and is also more responsive to the expatriate's needs.

Before: Tiered approach to goods and services based on salary grade.

After: All employees are on an efficient purchaser's index after the first six months.

Rationale: Tiered approach retained, but costs reduced.

Before: Repatriation was an extremely sensitive issue because of the unknowns expatriates faced upon reentry.

After: The repatriation section of the policy was rewritten, identifying roles and responsibilities. Most noteworthy, the goal was to develop a formalized expatriate team for each international assignee. The team includes the assignee's direct supervisor, the mentor (chosen before leaving on assignment), and human resource managers from the home and host countries. The team develops specific career and job-related objectives prior to the assignment with a tentative timeline. Each year, the team meets with the assignee in person or by teleconference to complete expatriate review forms. This team coordinates repatriation activity when the reentry date is selected. Usually, the repatriation target date is set about six months prior to departure, and the team begins to have individual and group meetings with functional department heads and local HR managers. As part of the process, the assignee is required to spend at least one full day networking in the home country office per year. This is designed to maintain visibility and strengthen communication ties. As a way to help all concerned with repatriation, Allergan also developed a 90-day special assignment. The team must make every effort to place an international assignee in a suitable position upon return, but if that is unavailable, the expatriate is offered a temporary 90-day special assignment. If, after that time, no position is available, the repatriated employee would be laid off.

Rationale: The team realized that this was possibly the most important item to be managing in their expatriate workforce. It remains a highly visible issue. To protect the company, however, an expatriate must receive a performance rating of at least "exceeds expectations" to continue the assignment. If this rating isn't met, the international assignee is immediately repatriated and reassigned. This minimizes performance issues at repatriation time. In other words, expatriates are going to be high performers.

Thus, going back to the model stated earlier in the chapter, Allergan *designed* a responsive policy by listening to the concerns of its expatriates as well as comparing it to competitive practice and receiving input from global managers. It *wrote* a clear, comprehensive policy to guide expatriates in understanding the process. Furthermore, in communicating the changes, managers were sensitive to the recipients and gave them time to digest the material. Allergan also conducted a follow-up survey to be sure expatriates felt the process was an improvement. Finally, the continuous improvement team was careful to create a policy that would be equitable to all, and fair to *administer* as well.

According to Jim Lofstrom, vice president of compensation and benefits, and Linda Cox, director of international compensation and benefits, Allergan's motivation for the survey and the implementation of the policies was threefold: (1) to enable expatriates to express their concerns, (2) to ensure more satisfied expatriates because the policies were responsive to their needs, and (3) to ensure that Allergan practiced competitive policies.

CULTURAL SENSITIVITY IN POLICY DEVELOPMENT, COMMUNICATION, AND IMPLEMENTATION

We have devoted a lot of attention to cultural sensitivity in this book, and we shouldn't leave this section without underscoring its importance in policy development and program administration.

For example, why do companies allow American expats to send their children to private school in Europe without having the same provisions apply to Europeans coming to the United States? In roundtables around the world, British, Dutch, and U.S. HR managers each indicated that inbound expatriates did not receive the same home-finding and settling-in support that they provided to home country expatriates. In other words, beware of ethnocentric policies.

Furthermore, if the policy document is intended for distribution around the world, be sensitive to the wording. Local colloquialisms, difficult-to-understand phrases, and technical abbreviations will lead to misunderstandings. If the document is going to be translated, watch for terms that don't translate well. For example *vision* in Portuguese translates into "dream" or "fantasy." You don't want the CEO's corporate vision to be perceived as a "corporate fantasy."

In general, be aware that there are myriad ways that cultural sensitivity comes into play in program administration and communication. For example, if you're administering a centralized program in the United States for people who live in Hong Kong, the difference in time zones means that the latter have to call the United States in the middle of the night. Keep in mind that an offer of help in some cultures can be construed as a loss of face or lack of confidence in management, and it will be never be used.

The paragraphs above illustrate clearly that the staff implementing a policy needs to participate in cultural awareness programs because they are dealing with people from several cultures who are going through a stressful period. They, more than others in the corporation, need to be sensitive to the way they deliver the company's message.

IS OUTSOURCING A SOLUTION?

More and more major corporations are asking about outsourcing their global relocation programs. Why? What has happened in the past few years to create such a groundswell of interest? We know that it is part of industry's endless quest to enhance productivity, but is it a harbinger of a fundamental change in human resource management or just a passing management fad? We suggest that it is the former, that today's complex business will require a completely different contribution from HR professionals. They will have to become strategic business partners in core activities and will no longer be the service providers they have historically been.

This transition of function is critical in a world where capital and technology are becoming increasingly fluid as they move across national borders and where the only sustainable competitive advantage companies can achieve will come from the contribution of people. The HR executive and line manager will have to know how to exploit and manage that potential advantage; if the human resource field doesn't provide that leadership and strategic direction, it will cease to exist.

Outsourcing may indeed be the first step in clearing the playing field of old obstacles and allowing for a *strategic* focus as opposed to the *administrative* focus that consumes so much time and energy.

What's more, is that the outsource providers will, in very short order, develop capabilities that will allow for the introduction of cost efficiencies and service enhancements into a field badly in need of new thinking to respond to the new challenges of a global village. Technology will be a major contributor to that improvement and will be made possible by the greater volume and wider exposure that these specialized outsource firms will have.

In the Global Outsourcing Survey, 1996, study conducted by Windham International, the National Foreign Trade Council and the Society of Human Resource Management on the subject of outsourcing, some startling findings surfaced.[5] Among them was the fact that while half of the respondents felt that outsourcing the administration of the expatriate function was an inevitable trend that would continue, over half of the respondents, felt it was a bad idea! The conflict over whether outsourcing is a solution or a new problem, has permeated the debate since the inception of the practice.

Companies have been outsourcing noncore business activities such as cafeteria management for decades. Human resource managers already outsource such tasks as tax, immigration and work permits, cost-of-living information, household goods moving, and home sales without even giving it a second thought. Will activities such as complete policy administration, vendor coordination, and other aspects of expatriate financial administration also fall into those noncore business categories?

Perhaps the increased interest in outsourcing is the result of a confluence of events that have made companies leaner in size and global in scope. Human resource managers are beginning to be responsible for both U.S. and international relocation. As a result, they must become knowledgeable in a wide variety of topics. These range from real estate transactions and U.S. tax law to international compensation packages. But acquiring this expertise is something else altogether.

WHY COMPANIES NOW CONSIDER OUTSOURCING

More Complex Role for HR Managers

It's no news that the role of the human resource manager responsible for developing and implementing global programs is infinitely more difficult than ever before. There has been an enormous increase in the number and complexity of international assignments—by location, by volume, and by emerging market destinations. These factors are further complicated by the intricacies of family issues and dual careers, by the importance of appropriate selection, and by the amount of money companies are spending and generating out of these international assignments.

Advance the Organization's Strategic Business Objectives

As restructuring continues to diminish head count and jobs have been eliminated, there are simply fewer people to handle tasks. Companies want their HR managers to focus on core competencies and strategic HR objectives rather than administrative detail. The more they're able to focus on the overall strategy of managing the function and developing a global workforce and the less they have to be involved in time-consuming administrative details, the better they can do their jobs.

Enhanced Levels of Expertise

All of the above says nothing of the complexity HR staffs face in staying abreast of new tax, social security, and local labor laws in an ever-increasing number of countries. Add to that the pressure they face to reduce expatriate costs in light of a weakening dollar and increased costs around the world. It becomes easy to understand why HR staffs want to get as much of the administrative responsibilities as possible off their desks and turn them over to an outsource agent.

Lower Cost

When companies use outside resources more efficiently, they ease the burden for these already overworked managers. Organizations also realize another advantage to outsourcing: They avoid the fixed, built-in overhead costs of in-house professionals dedicated to relocation activities regardless of the number of people being moved. Instead, when companies use outside providers, the cost is typically allocated on a per family basis as each one goes through the relocation program. That is, the cost of the outsourcing service is automatically tied to transfer volume and is therefore self-regulating.

Cost Effectiveness

Equally important is the duty of the outsourced organization to ensure that the client's program is operating cost effectively—without sacrificing service. This is especially critical in areas with high cost exposure, such as home sales and compensation. The administration of expense processing is also more efficient because the outsourced firm focuses specifically on developing systems to process relocation costs—a process that otherwise requires the part-time attention of various departments in the client's organization. These factors allow the client greater flexibility in managing the program, quicker response time to resolve issues, and the ability to demand a higher standard of performance than they can generally place on their internal organization.

Growing Trust in the Sophistication of Outsource Providers

Outsourcing becomes attainable for an organization when the processes related to the functions to be outsourced are considered "routine." A company must be convinced that a set of functions has reached the point where it can easily be systematized and implemented with minimal risk to the company. In addition, the new outsourced process must be evaluated and controlled through a rapid feedback loop to correct deficiencies quickly.

Under these circumstances, companies are suddenly in a position to outsource areas which previously were considered too complex or risky. The most stunning example of this is payroll. Considering the risks and importance of this function, one would never believe that it was suitable for outsourcing. Yet, over time this has become not only possible, but companies often have to justify why they don't outsource the payroll function.

Certainly, many of the benefits and advantages achieved by outsourcing can be accomplished by an intelligent reexamination of an internal program. Indeed, most companies already outsource some of their functions. But outsourcing an inefficient process will only add cost and confusion. Intelligent outsourcing allows for—and should be accompanied by—a comprehensive reexamination of the entire process. It requires that a custom-tailored solution be put in place.

The process doesn't end there. Like any new system, it needs a great deal of attention. There will undoubtedly be a need for midcourse corrections and there is no substitute for a strong, committed partnership between the company and its outsource supplier.

WHAT CAN BE OUTSOURCED?

Any aspect of the program which is not strategic in nature can be outsourced. Since global relocation covers such a wide range of activities that means a great deal can be turned over to professional service organizations. Companies frequently outsource part or all of their domestic or international relocation management and coordination. The most effective way to handle outsourced programs is to have a dedicated relocation team responsible for coordination, cost tracking, and expense reimbursement. This method more closely resembles a company's in-house program. As such, it allows for an easier transition and provides a greater sense of comfort to the company.

As Figure 6–3 shows, a comprehensive program that integrates all activities does more than just streamline the process. It actually makes the relocations more uniform and the company more responsive to the employees.

For example, the same outside provider that validates compensation and cost-of-living data could develop an initial compensation package according to company guidelines and save time that the company's international human resource staff currently spends. The same firm that

FIGURE   6–3

Centrally Coordinated Outsource Program

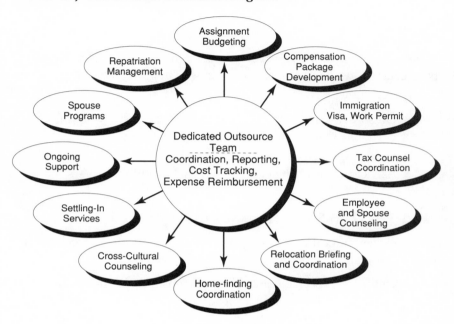

conducts cross-cultural training can also coordinate the destination home-finding and settling-in services. The company that provides property management or home sale services can also coordinate the household goods shipment. And the same organization also can coordinate many other activities and even review expense reports and make reimbursements.

Of course, with so much money and responsibility tied to one vendor organization, the company must minimize the risk involved in the relocation transaction. This includes internal control assurances and an understanding of how the outsourced vendor will actually provide the required services. The outsourced vendor will coordinate many functions which will, in turn, be outsourced. A clear understanding of how this is accomplished is vital to a successful outsourcing assignment.

Overall, outsourcing can integrate the entire process and benefit not only the human resource manager who is delivering the services, but also the employee and family because the services and information are *more consistent*. This saves the company staff a great deal of time and it makes the process easier for the family, which will have fewer people and companies to deal with.

RISKS

In the Global Outsourcing Survey[6], respondents indicated that there were three major downside risks of outsourcing. They were concerned about:

- Loss of control;
- Outsource firms being able to interpret the policy in terms of the corporate culture;
- How the policy works; and
- Expatriates receiving enough personal attention.

KEY FEATURES FOR THE SUCCESS OF OUTSOURCING

Here are a few important considerations to help ensure an excellent outsourced program:

- **Dedicated service team.** This team ensures that programs and services are delivered in a way that is consistent with the corporate philosophy and corporate culture.
- **Programs designed and tailored to fit the corporate culture.** Programs can't be designed around the capabilities of the service provider. Service providers have to take their competencies to fit the corporate need. It is important to find an organization that understands your corporate culture, that can do things in the style of the company, and that can present a seamless process.
- **Partnership between supplier and company.** This spirit of partnership and trust is very important because of the depth of the relationship. The service company shouldn't be perceived as simply a "vendor." It must be regarded as an integral part of the organization—empowered and entrusted to help deploy the company's most valued assets.
- **Dedication to quality, technical competence, and systems capability.** These attributes are essential before embarking on a preliminary discussion with an outsourcing agency. A basic requirement is that the company must be able to provide top-notch, quality services that are technically proficient.

NOTES

1. For a detailed example of a specific policy, see the National Foreign Trade Council's *Manual for Expatriate Compensation and Benefits* and the 1995 *Directory of International Human Resource Professionals*. Published by the National Foreign Trade Council, Inc., 1270 Avenue of the Americas, New York, NY 10020.
2. Society of Human Resource Management, 1992 survey.
3. Not his real name.
4. Society of Human Resource Management, 1992 survey.
5. The Global Outsourcing Survey, 1996, study conducted by Windham International, the National Foreign Trade Council and the Society of Human Resource Management, fall 1996.
6. Ibid.

CHAPTER

7

⑥ GLOBALIZING COMPENSATION*

This chapter will cover

- The philosophy of compensation for expatriates.
- How expatriate compensation programs are developed.
- The host-based versus home-based methods.
- When to use a hybrid or international approach.
- How culturally appropriate compensation plans are developed for local nationals.

Jon Andrews is vice president of international compensation at Globex Corporation, a growing midsize multinational. He worries a lot. Jon often feels he's performing a high-wire balancing act without the benefit of a safety net. His struggle is trying to maintain fairness while doing his best for the company and his expatriates.

On one hand, Jon faces the prospect of enormous expatriate costs that he must manage according to company policies in an era of intense global competition and cost-cutting while helping Globex fulfill its strategic business objectives. He views himself as a guardian of the expatriate program and must see that compensation sufficiently motivates and re-

---

*Contributing author to this chapter, Alan Chesters, is operations director of ECA International and member of the board of ECA Windham.

wards expatriates and local nationals while not allowing their needs to create a financial black hole.

On the other hand, Jon is struggling to maintain fairness and consistency while line managers are trying to cut individual deals—asking him to be flexible and somehow curtail the costs of the expatriates they need to have—at the same time expatriates are calling him with complaints and requests for greater remuneration. It's a tough challenge. For some expatriates he's using the balance sheet; for others he's calculating differential compensation to augment the host country program. All the while, his highwire act demands that he satisfy each constituency: design effective, creative programs that work for his company, come in with compensation packages to satisfy line managers, and develop compensation packages that address the needs of expatriates who struggle with the adequacy of their allowances.

Few activities in the expatriation process concern global business managers as much as compensation. Why? Because this is where the most visible, direct cost of the assignment lies. Typically, the cost of an assignment is three to five times the employee's annual salary. That multiple is made up of the salary, cost-of-living allowances, housing allowances, children's education and other unique reimbursable items, and of course taxes. Taking these expenses into consideration, an expatriate earning $100,000 a year in the United States can easily cost the company $1 million to $1.5 million on a typical three-year assignment. Quite a premium to be paying.

It's no wonder that this is the area that receives the most focus—and causes the most anxiety. The global manager is concerned if the compensation package is too much, corporate management watches the overall cost of the expatriate process, and the expatriate wonders if it's going to be enough.

Global business managers have nightmares about expatriates getting rich on their generous compensation packages. We've seen movies and heard stories about the exorbitant expatriate lifestyle—homes fit for kings, scores of servants, lavish expatriate clubs, and extraordinary entertainment activities. This colonialist scenario no longer exists. Indeed few things are further from the truth. The life of an expatriate is challenging, full of long work hours, and often lonely. At the same time, it is usually financially comfortable but rarely exorbitant.

As we move into the 21st century, however, an expatriate assignment is becoming a part of a normal business career and will be increasingly common as world business continues to become more global. Gone forever is the expatriate adventurer who was enticed by extraordinary financial gain to go on exploitive missions. This character is replaced by a serious executive who goes on assignment as part of business as usual. The attraction of "join the Navy and see the world" has declined; it's not only the military who have trouble attracting a mobile staff in the age of global leisure travel. However, some myths from the old days persist and still affect the expectations and prejudices about expatriate lifestyles. They cloud the reality.

Actually, the process of developing a compensation package is logical. It is a combination of facts pertaining to researched costs in the destination and a subjective, subtle tailoring to meet individual needs and circumstances. The most common goal of the compensation package is to assure that the expatriates' income is adjusted fairly to reflect the added costs they will encounter when they live in a foreign country. Care needs to be taken to avoid creating extraordinary windfalls for the expat while not creating hardships.

What is *fair*? How much is *enough*? What about the relationship between expatriate pay and that of the locals? And what about special premiums and allowances? In France, a car and driver may be excessive, whereas in Indonesia it is a prudent allowance. In some countries, it's inappropriate for a middle manager's family to do their own food shopping, and sometimes cultural expectations of the trappings of senior management dictate a lifestyle that would seem lavish in the home country. And at some locations, providing company-sponsored R&R is an absolute necessity. All this is further complicated by the fact that certain locations appear to be hardship assignments to some, and wonderful places to live for others.

So, we again ask, what is *fair*? This chapter goes from the most basic elements of structuring compensation and benefits programs for expatriates to the more complex issues of developing programs for host country employees. It also examines the ways in which culture and local laws impact attempts at establishing global compensation policies and practices.

Compensation is where everything converges. It is the confluence of all the streams of international business activity: cultural understanding, economic opportunities, local laws, and ways to motivate a workforce. All these come together to accomplish the original business impetus to go international. To use an American metaphor, it is "where the rubber meets the road," where we put into practical application all the related information and wisdom we have gathered.

Compensation is the ultimate motivator: How are you going to pay your expatriates in relation to their domestic counterparts and motivate them to accept an overseas assignment? How are you going to pay Malays in Malaysia, when you don't know what motivates them? How can you create global teams in India if you're paying different salaries to people who have the same positions—only because they originated from different countries? These thorny issues confront global managers every day.

PHILOSOPHY OF COMPENSATION

Compensation strategy is one of the most powerful weapons in the corporate armory for focusing the organization. It sends the strongest signals to members of the organization about expected attitudes and behaviors. Fred Herzberg demonstrated in his research that compensation can be completely dysfunctional if misaligned with corporate strategy and behavior.[1]

For example, you may wonder whether the collapse of Barings Bank initiated by one individual in Singapore would have occurred if the compensation strategy had not been totally skewed toward immediate profit results and against the long-term health of the organization. In contrast, as we shall see later, Shell Oil's approach to expatriate pay has done much to reinforce the internationalization of its management.

In the international arena, compensation is complicated by the interplay of the objectives of the corporation and the home and host country's culture. Therefore, compensation design needs to be an expression of corporate culture as moderated by local culture and local legislation. While bound by local laws, a successful global compensation program must be responsive to the deeper-seated effects of cultural attitudes. For example, cultural dimensions such as group dependence, time, and status will affect pay-for-performance compensation schemes and early job-completion bonuses.

To be effective globally, the successful organization capitalizes on flexibility and tailors its compensation program the same way that it tailors other business activities. It is vital to maintain core values to ensure that the messages communicated through the compensation plan conform to the corporate culture while being sensitive to local business imperatives. It does that through a flexible compensation delivery system that is culturally consistent with the corporation and achieves its business objective while conforming to the local culture.

Creating a global compensation structure involves two distinct activities. One is a responsive expatriate compensation program that enables the company to deploy human resources in response to business opportunities. The other is an effective program for compensating local nationals which is sensitive to both the local culture and is consistent with the corporate culture and its business objectives.

DEVELOPING EXPATRIATE COMPENSATION PROGRAMS

International assignments fall into three basic categories. Each has a specific business and economic justification. These categories are:

1. Fixed-term assignments.
   a. Short term—usually less than 12 months and focused on completing a particular task.
   b. Contract assignments—again focused on a particular task but of a longer duration.
2. Permanent transfers—expected to be indefinite and more appropriately perceived as a transfer.
3. Expatriate assignments—either a single or a series of assignments of two to three years with the intention of returning "home."

While these categories fall into the broad definition of expatriate assignments, each has a slightly different objective and can be supported by different compensation arrangements. The two-to-three-year expatriate assignment constitutes the main body of the general expatriate population. It is different from the other types of assignments because the employee is expected to return to the home country workforce, which makes it imperative to stay on a track that will enable a smooth and logical reentry process.

These expatriates are also the primary contributors to the organization's global resource pool of international management. Their compensation structure needs to ensure that this essential link to the organization's overall globalization will continue.

The compensation methodology a company chooses must meet a number of key requirements. It has to:

1. Fit the business strategy of the organization.
2. Be competitive in the appropriate marketplace.
3. Respond to the needs of the expat and the family.

COMPENSATION PLANS FOR FIXED-TERM ASSIGNMENTS

Compensation programs for fixed-term assignments fall into two categories: (1) the short, fixed-term assignment and (2) the long-term assignment for a particular contract.

A short-term assignment (less than one year) normally means that the employee retains home salary and benefits, with allowances or reimbursement for additional costs. For a long-term fixed contract, the employee will usually be placed on local salary and benefits with reimbursement of one-time moving costs.

Regardless of length, the organization needs to focus primarily on compensating the employee for mobility and flexibility, as well as establishing appropriate value for the position. Developing the package will become more complicated when families accompany the employee on short-term assignments or (as in the case of Americans) if double taxation difficulties arise.

COMPENSATION PLANS FOR LONG-TERM TRANSFERS

In the case of long-term transfers, which are more like permanent relocations, it is usually appropriate for the employee to be on the host country's salary and benefits structure. Because a relocation is involved, the company also will cover one-time relocation expenses. The major difficulty with these transfers arises in the area of long-term benefits, where the potential exists for an incompatibility between corporate and country social security and benefits structures. That incompatibility can often leave the employee with an unexpected gap in benefits provisions.

COMPENSATION PLANS FOR EXPATRIATE ASSIGNMENTS

The major complexities with the implementation of international compensation occur with the expatriate assignment. There are three approaches:

- Home based
- Host based
- Hybrid

All of these approaches assume that the employee will remain vested in home country social security (where possible), pension, and other retirement programs. Each method has its strengths and weaknesses, and each has its complexities. However, it is important to keep in mind that the underlying philosophy of an expatriate package is relatively simple. It's designed to allow the employee to go on international assignment, do the job, and return without any extraordinary loss or gain.

Complexity comes from balancing the inherent conflict between the three equities:

- Equity with the expatriates' peers at home.
- Equity with the local workforce.
- Equity with the expatriates' peers in the international workforce at the same location.

HOME-BASED COMPENSATION SYSTEM

The home-based compensation system, usually known as the *balance sheet,* is designed to facilitate mobility. Its premise is that the employer should preserve the employee's standard of living in the overseas location and determine, through premiums, the additional financial benefit of the assignment, if any. In this way, the organization controls the benefits the employee gains from mobility and facilitates moves from one international location to another. In addition, the system simplifies repatriation because it keeps the employee on a track consistent with peers at home.

The advantage of the home-based system, or balance sheet, is that it is designed to address both the expatriate's home-based obligations while covering the added costs incurred by living in another country. In brief, an expatriate package is determined by taking a home net income, adding or subtracting an allowance for daily cost-of-living differences, and supplementing this with optional mobility premiums determined by the company. The expatriate retains the ability to maintain home country commitments and is provided with the additional funds necessary to preserve his or her lifestyle in the host country. (See appendix describing balance sheet methodology.)

Determining Net Salary

The first step in this process is to determine a home gross salary. This may sound simple, but it can be complicated by the need to calculate the value of certain nonsalary-related benefits such as a company car and bonus calculations.

The next step is to deduct home tax, social security and any other regular, compulsory payments such as pension contributions. The decision here is whether to make these deductions on a hypothetical basis or to look at the employee's particular circumstances. While the latter will focus the package more closely to the realities of the expatriate's situation, it runs the risk of trespassing on what is traditionally considered the employee's private domain and is more complicated to administer. The former, by definition, will be advantageous to some while disadvantageous to others.

Protecting Cost-of-Living Differences

Having done that, we arrive at an appropriate net income. The next step is to establish how much of that net income the company will protect against cost-of-living differences. This can be an arbitrary amount, say 65 percent of net income, or it can be based on data provided by companies such as ECA Windham, which provide substantiated research on spending norms for each home country. Whichever way this sum is obtained, it is intended to represent expenditure for day-to-day living costs in the home location.

Optional Approaches to Cost-of-Living Protection

The next decision is what type of cost-of-living protection to provide. Traditionally, the protection has been based on an expatriate's home country lifestyle and the expatriate's lack of knowledge of the best places to shop in the new host location. As a result, these cost-of-living allowances often seemed high. In an effort to reduce expenses and make expatriates more efficient as local shoppers, new standards have been introduced which assume that expatriates will learn to shop more like the local population after they've lived in the host country for several months. Increasingly, organizations are providing protection only against differences within an international lifestyle and are assuming some competence on the part of expatriates at local purchasing. Some organizations will provide higher cost-of-living allowances for a limited period of time (typically three to six months) before switching to the less costly approach, which assumes that the expatriate knows where to shop.

Housing Allowances

Another crucial element in the expatriate compensation package is the housing allowance. Most companies research the cost of housing in the host country or obtain it from data providers. The company then determines appropriate accommodation levels depending on the expatriate's position in the company, income level, and family size. Often, a housing allowance is calculated on the differential between home and host country housing. This approach may be done on either a hypothetical or actual cost basis. Another approach is to provide a flat housing allowance.

Whether the organization provides company housing or pays a housing allowance, there is often some deduction for hypothetical home country housing. Increasingly, however, there is growing recognition of an expatriate's need to retain housing in the home country. Residents of Los Angeles or London may take an assignment in Kuala Lumpur, but they need to keep their housing at home because they are going to return—and if for no other reason, as a hedge against potential inflation, which might make housing unaffordable to them upon repatriation. As a result, the hypothetical deduction is not taken—this is particularly common among European and Asian firms—and programs have been developed to enable employees to manage their home country housing in their absence. (In Chapter 6, we examine options provided for selling home country property and property management.)

Because such a large portion of the expatriate population is comprised of families who have two wage earners in the home country but must live on one income in the host country, many companies use the housing allowance to recognize that home country housing is supported by two incomes. They realize that one of these salaries will be lost, so that purposely inflate the housing allowance figures or make special provisions to cover home country carrying costs during the tenure of the expatriate assignment.

Assignment Premiums

The next step is to determine appropriate premiums to be paid for the assignment. There are normally two types of premiums—the mobility premium, which is paid regardless of location, and the hardship premium, which is paid according to the perceived difficulty of the location. The mobility premium may be paid as a lump sum or as a regular monthly payment. It can be calculated as a flat sum or related to salary, but typically is calculated in the currency of the home salary. The hardship premium also is usually related to and calculated in the currency of the home country salary, but is nearly always a regular ongoing allowance and varies by location.

Criteria used to determine differences in the level of hardship premium are climate, cultural differences, geographic isolation, medical and social facilities, health and security risks, and availability of essential goods and services.

Bringing It All Together
The decisions about cost-of-living adjustments, housing allowances and deductions, and special premiums will be included in the adjusted net home salary; that is, a net home salary plus (or minus) allowances. In addition, the company also will need to provide payments to cover the cost of education and, where appropriate, the cost of domestic help, sports, and social club fees.

The next step is to determine the quotation currency and payment currency to be used. The distinction is deliberate. Payment currency will be a function principally of tax effectiveness and administrative convenience, but the decision of the currency to be used is important because it affects the degree of exchange-rate risk taken by the company or the employee. Quotation in home currency puts the level of compensation for local daily living costs at risk. Quotation in host country currency puts the home commitments at risk. The most sophisticated organizations will quote the local day-to-day living costs (local spendables) in local currency and the housing, savings, and premiums in the home currency.

Tax Treatment
However quoted or paid, the salary has to be grossed-up for local taxes. Gross-up refers to the amount of money the company provides the employee to offset additional taxes. Normally, the organization will protect the employee, so that only the original home salary tax burden remains unchanged. This is called *tax equalization*. Sometimes the organization will not recover a windfall if local taxes are lower (called *tax protection*), or will gross-up on a hypothetical basis instead of an individual basis.

Companies generally limit tax support to direct income earned by the employee and don't cover income earned from other sources such as private investment or spouse income.

In the case of U.S. citizens who are taxed on worldwide income, this total amount (salary plus allowances plus premiums plus local tax gross-ups) is subject to U.S. tax reporting, and additional gross-ups may be necessary (see Figure 7–1).

F I G U R E   7–1

Balance Sheet

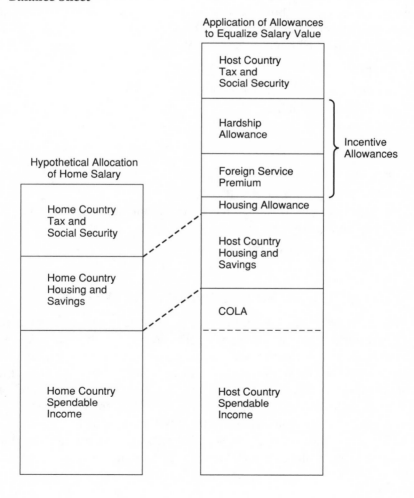

Summary of Home-Based Compensation System

The home-based or balance sheet approach covers actual cost-of-living differentials between the two locations, attempting to keep the employee equal with home country peers. However, one major caution is required: The balance sheet process maintains the distinction between expatriates and local nationals. It risks keeping expatriates in "ghettos" and maintaining a lifestyle that creates a barrier to their integration into the local culture. As a result, part of the value of the international living experience for the expatriate and the company is not optimized. By focusing so much on protecting against financial loss of the assignment, it overlooks some of the career and business gains that can be achieved. For example, it defines the assignment exclusively in monetary terms and overlooks the potential for career and personal growth.

Advantages

- Employee neither gains nor loses financially.
- Facilitates mobility.
- Eases repatriation.

Disadvantages

- Expensive.
- No link to the local pay structure.
- Expatriates of the same seniority from different origins will be paid differently.
- Administration can become complex.

HOST-BASED COMPENSATION SYSTEM

On the other hand, the *host-based* system calculates salary as if the expatriate is a local national. Obviously some additional allowances are included, such as one-time relocation costs, assistance for the employee to retain home country retirement and social security benefits, and other situation-specific items. This system provides a clear link to the local pay structures, delivers equivalent pay regardless of country of origin, and can be easier to administer than a home-based approach.

The disadvantages of the host-based system are that it is more difficult for an expatriate to understand the real buying power of the host country salary and what impact that will have on his or her standard of living. This of course will represent a barrier to mobility and restrict the organization's ability to deploy people as it needs. The host country compensation structure works only on an "upward escalator"—if local salary and standard of living improve the lifestyle of the expatriate. This also tends to make the host-based system very costly because it only really works well when the expatriate can improve both salary and standard of living.

On the other hand, it is an excellent way to get expatriates integrated into the local culture and removes many of the distinctions between expatriates and locals which often get in the way of effective teamwork. It also encourages expatriates to look at, and appreciate, the career implications of their expatriate assignments because it doesn't define it just as a financial equation. However, it does make it much more difficult to repatriate from higher standard-of-living locations.

This simplest of the compensation systems is also known as the *destination approach*. Two preconditions are required for the destination system to work at all: Organizations must have (1) an understanding of the local market and (2) a rigorous system for determining the weight of the job the expatriate is to undertake. The latter normally requires some form of job evaluation.

If these preconditions exist, establishing an appropriate salary and perks package is relatively simple. But the decisions do not stop there. First, the organization has to determine whether it is going to pay any premium solely for being an expatriate. This might take the form of a mobility payment or an ongoing additional allowance. Second, the company needs to determine whether it will pay for certain expenditures that the expatriate might incur specifically because he or she is not a local. For instance, there is usually a penalty to pay for late entry into a housing market, and an expatriate is by definition a late entrant. Equally important are items normally provided by the state to locals (e.g., education and health care), which may not be appropriate for expatriates. The organization has to decide whether, and to what degree, it is going to reimburse the expatriate in these areas.

Furthermore, the organization has to convince the expatriate that this assignment is a worthwhile experience. This is a question of relative revenues, costs, and exchange rates. The point to remember with host-based systems is that to encourage expatriates to be mobile, the destination must retain a premium over home salaries. Because the host-based system, by definition, works best when the expatriate earns more money in the host country, this overall approach is likely to be the least cost effective.

In any case, from the expatriate's perspective, regardless of methodology, the expatriate will see the package in two parts:

- The one enabling him to live locally.
- Those resources required to meet home country commitments (e.g., housing, savings, investments, home country taxes). By definition, these are more difficult to manage in a host-based system.

Tax Treatment.
This is very simple for most nationalities because of the absence of continuing home tax liability. In this situation, the expatriate under the host-based system needs to pay only host-country taxes on income earned in the host country. However, it is more complicated for Americans because the continuing home tax reporting responsibilities may result in additional tax burden above that incurred by the equivalent local employee. In these circumstances, the company will normally pick up the additional tax involved, thereby reducing the cost-effectiveness of the host-based approach.

Summary of Host-Based Compensation System

The host-based or destination approach treats expatriates as if they're local nationals to the extent that is possible. Certain allowances are still necessary to cover home country commitments and obligations.

Advantages

- Employees all operate on equivalent pay.
- The system is easy to administer.
- All employees, including expatriates are paid the same.

Disadvantages

- Complicates reentry.
- Most applicable when salary and living standards improve, thereby becoming expensive.
- Unprotected fluctuations in the exchange rate puts company and employee at additional risk.
- Certain host country benefits are not applicable to expatriates.

FIGURE 7–2

International Base Salary Comparison, 1996

In U.S. $

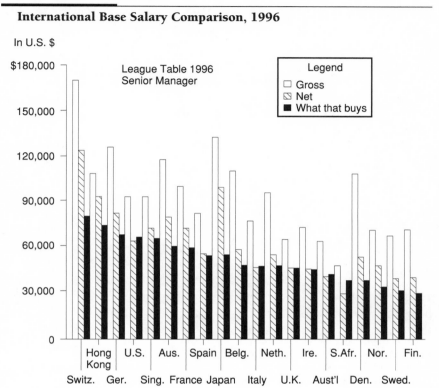

Figure 7–2 illustrates the salary levels for similar positions around the world, plus the effect of taxes and differing prices on those salaries. The white column shows gross salary; the second column is salary after taxes; and the third column equalizes those net salaries for relative cost of living.

HYBRID COMPENSATION SYSTEM

As we've seen, the balance sheet approach makes too great a distinction between nationalities, so you end up with different levels of cost-of-living allowances. While these may be statistically correct, people don't perceive them as equitable. On the other hand, with the host-based approach, the differences in standard of living between the host salary and home salary are so variable that it is sometimes difficult to get people to be mobile.

Therefore, organizations have introduced *hybrid* compensation systems that blend appropriate features from the home- and host-based approaches to respond to specific business challenges. These international hybrid systems are so diverse that cost-benefit analysis is difficult to measure. The purpose is to end up with an international expatriate workforce that, while not coming from one location, is paid as though it were. See Figure 7–3 for a comparison of the three compensation systems.

By definition, hybrid systems are unrelated to local markets so they provide no equity with local staff and are almost always complex to administer. However, organizations usually consider a hybrid option when managing relationships within the international cadre has become the paramount and overriding concern.

The hybrid system usually consists of some adjustment to the balance sheet to create equity between nationalities. Their use is often limited to small groups of executives who—either by status (the senior cadre of an organization) or by geography (a region or a headquarters location)—warrant different handling.

The simplest form of hybrid system is to pretend that all expatriates, regardless of country of origin, belong to one nationality (e.g., paying all foreign national expatriates as if they were Americans). This tends to be a highest common denominator approach to turn them into the

FIGURE   7–3

Key Features of Compensation Systems

Home-Based	Host-Based	Hybrid
▪ Consistent treatment of expatriates of same nationality	▪ Equity with local nationals	▪ All nationalities paid equitably
	▪ All nationalities paid same	
▪ Facilitates transfer from country to country	▪ Simple administration	▪ Facilitates transfer and "international management cadre"
▪ Link with home country structure/economy	▪ Variation in "value" by localities	▪ Some link to "home" structure/economy
▪ Different pay levels for different nationalities	▪ No link to home country structure/economy	▪ Complex administration
▪ No relationship to local employees	▪ Difficult to transfer to lower paying location	▪ No relationship to local employees
▪ Complex administration		

highest paid nationality you've got—so its use has been limited to companies headquartered in countries where high salaries are paid on an international comparative basis.

Other forms of hybrid systems involve applying identical cost-of-living allowances to all nationalities, uniform premiums, and—most commonly—uniform housing and other local allowances. The other decision points mentioned in the description of the balance sheet remain to be decided for hybrid systems, sometimes these are made more complex by the need to manage many different home environments within one system (e.g., taxes). See Figure 7–4 for an illustration of the workings of the hybrid system.

Figure 7–5 illustrates the worldwide approach to managing an international workforce adopted by Royal Dutch Shell, the international oil giant. All employees receive the same local spendable regardless of country of origin, and the same incentive and hardship premium based on a

FIGURE 7–4

Hybrid Basis

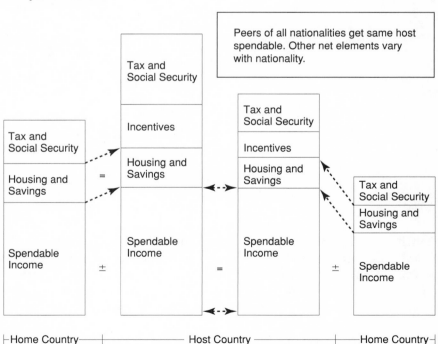

FIGURE 7–5

Shell System

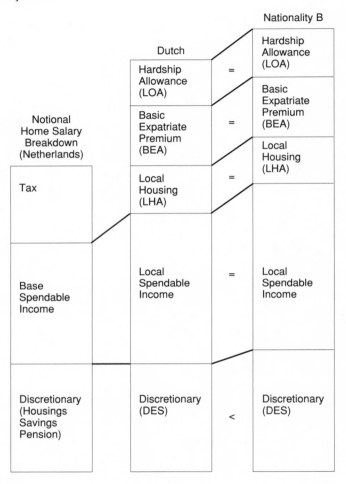

Dutch norm. Discretionary income (housing and savings) is related to the expatriate's home country standard of living, but differences are smoothed out so that no nationality is particularly favored or discriminated against. The system provides Shell with an international salary methodology that enables it to maintain an expatriate staff of as many as 6,000 staff at any one time.

Figure 7–6 illustrates a different variation on the hybrid approach adopted by another major multinational corporation, Unilever (also an

FIGURE   7–6

Unilever System

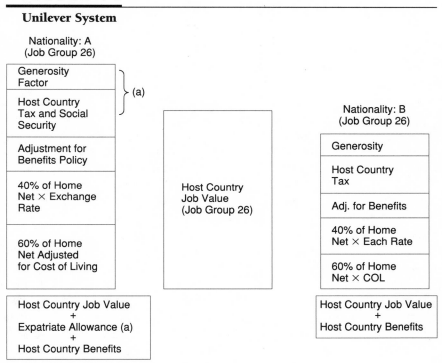

Nationality: A
(Job Group 26)

| Generosity Factor |
| Host Country Tax and Social Security |

} (a)

| Adjustment for Benefits Policy |
| 40% of Home Net × Exchange Rate |
| 60% of Home Net Adjusted for Cost of Living |

Host Country Job Value
+
Expatriate Allowance (a)
+
Host Country Benefits

Host Country Job Value
(Job Group 26)

Nationality: B
(Job Group 26)

| Generosity |
| Host Country Tax |
| Adj. for Benefits |
| 40% of Home Net × Each Rate |
| 60% of Home Net × COL |

Host Country Job Value
+
Host Country Benefits

Anglo-Dutch organization). The firm's aim is to identify the expatriate with the local employer he or she joins. It is a system best used in developed countries because competitive local salaries are possible in those locations. Thus, in the developed world, all expatriates appear to receive a local salary without additional local benefits. Behind the scenes, however, a balance sheet calculation is carried out that reflects differences in the standard of living and cost of living between the home and host locations. This is calculated on the basis of a standard employee at that job level (i.e., not the individual expatriate) and negative differences are compensated through a single allowance, which is normally paid outside the expatriate location.

Advantages of Hybrid System

- All expatriate nationalities are paid equitably.
- Assists transfers and development of an international management cadre.
- Some link to "home" salary structure and economy.

Disadvantages of Hybrid System

- Complicated administration.
- Sometimes difficult to communicate.
- No link to the local pay structure.

The Lump Sum Payment

In today's never-ending search for more efficient, better ways to do things, some companies are exploring the lump sum or *flexpat* approach. In its simplest form, this approach says that instead of trying to calculate and administer line-by-line allowances, expatriates are given a lump sum—annually or periodically—to use at their discretion to cover housing and market-basket items as well as other special hardship or location allowances.

Companies adopt the lump sum approach in an effort to control costs, eliminate discussion about adequacies of allowances, and empower employees to make decisions on their own. The major shortcoming of this approach is that it requires expatriates to agree to an amount of money whose adequacy they have no way of appreciating. While the lump sum approach may be easy to administer, it still requires periodic adjustments for inflation and exchange rates, and theoretically would have to be based on a balance sheet workup in its initial calculations.

The lump sum approach has been used successfully to reimburse specific relocation allowances, spouse program allowances, and travel expenses. It also works well in controlling costs related to destination housing. The application of lump sum payments to expatriate housing depends on the taxable status of the housing payment. In countries where the entire payment is taxable, the employee can spend as much or as little of the allowance as he or she wishes and pocket the remainder. In countries that offer a tax advantage to the company to pay for housing directly, the company could share with the employee the difference between the rent the company actually pays and the housing allowance.

Advantages of Lump Sum Payment

- Effective for items such as housing and relocation.
- Simplifies administration.

Disadvantages of Lump Sum Payment

- Asks employees to make a commitment for which they have inadequate knowledge.
- Requires ongoing administration.
- Saves money at employee's expense.

Finally, all the methods assume that people will remain within their home country retirement, pension and other long-term benefits plans. By their very nature, these plans are long term and should not be disturbed prematurely. The home and hybrid systems manage this very well in principle. However, the host system finds the concept more troublesome, particularly if local contributions to plans at home by the individual are less than what the equivalent local employee would pay. But the cost to the organization is even higher because expatriates do not receive the same favorable tax treatment as local members of the plan.

The foregoing summarizes the key points in determining an expatriate compensation approach and some of the issues involved in the decision. The final choice should follow the business purpose of the assignment and its relationship to the needs of the assignee.

WHEN IS EACH SYSTEM MOST EFFECTIVE?

To answer this question, let's review the three equities mentioned earlier in this chapter:

- Equity with the expatriates' peers at home.
- Equity with the local workforce.
- Equity with the expatriates' peers in the international location.

Let's add to the mix the organization's long-term goals for the expatriation program and the current status in the evolutionary process of the organization's internationalization. The choice between the options now becomes clearer.

There is an evolutionary process which makes different solutions appropriate for organizations at different stages of their growth. Initially, companies entering the international arena generally need to capitalize on their home country resources to support their globalization. In this context, whether compensation is developed for a manager who is opening a sales office or a software systems expert whose skills are unavailable outside the home country, the strategic objective will be to maintain relationships and parity between the expatriate and peers at home. For an organization at this level of development, the emphasis is on the company's expatriates in other locations. In either case, organizations will probably want to use the home-based balance sheet approach to expatriate compensation and maintain equity with peers at home.

The focus of the organization and the interests of the employee both benefit from the balance sheet approach, which enables employees to undertake expatriate assignments without financial threat while maintaining parity with peers around the world. Simultaneously, the organization maintains maximum mobility of its human resources, enabling it to continue its momentum toward globalization.

Once the organization is firmly established internationally, its employee mobility requirements evolve (see Figure 7–7). The primary concern in this phase is to support continuing technology transfer and to promote development opportunities. Now the business is typically centered around the local bottom line, and the organization wants to ensure that the expatriate is closely identified with the success of the local business. Consequently, the focus may shift to place greater emphasis on maintaining equity with local peers. In such situations, host-based or destination-based packages may be much more appropriate. Equally, if a principal motivation for the expatriation is career development, it is easier to "sell" an expatriate to a local manager if the visible costs of the expatriate are no greater than those of a local employee. In practice, of course, expatriates are always more expensive because in addition to relocation costs, premiums, housing, and other allowances need to be added.

As the organization evolves into a truly global business entity, the focus shifts again. The mobility equation becomes multifaceted. Expatriates are dispatched to fill a variety of needs, ranging from management

FIGURE   7–7

Aligning Policies with Business Need

- Business expansion
- Task requirement
- Technology transfer
- Management development
- Organization development

Home
↓
Local
↓
Expatriate

development to technology transfer, to accomplish a strategic business mission and to run or support local business operations. As a result, the focus returns to maintaining equity with peers in the home location, with the local workforce, and presumably with expatriates of different nationalities in the same location.

A number of compensation techniques can be used to manage this final equity. They range from the simplistic and costly approach of turning all expatriates into a single hypothetical nationality—which is always expensive—to a series of complex formulas that provide gradual shifts from a true home-based model to an international hybrid scheme.

The international hybrid approach attempts to achieve visible equity among the multinational expatriate workforce while not having to raise pay schedules to the highest common denominator.

Each of the three methodologies has intrinsic strengths and weaknesses. The choice between them depends on the business motivation of the organization, whether it is international mobility, local accountability, or organizational development. Regardless of the motivation, the choice must be made in light of the corporate culture and competitive practices in similar industries.

CURRENT PRESSURES IN COMPENSATION AND BENEFITS

Many of the principles discussed in this chapter are simple, even if their implementation is not. However, the increasing complexities introduced by rapidly changing organizational structures and societal business values are putting increasing pressures on the operation of an international compensation strategy.

Looking back 10 years, managing an international workforce would have focused on several scenarios:

1. *Centralization.* The development of global product lines supported a centralized international workforce management approach. The need to develop in-house expertise in the complex world of international compensation and benefits further encouraged centralization, and limitations in information flow kept the process centralized.

2. *A focus on career development.* The cost of international mobility and the need to extract value from the existing workforce meant that corporations placed great emphasis on management development and manpower planning. This investment was justified by the expected tenure of these employees since it would be amortized over the life of a career.

3. *Cost control.* A major concern of corporate management while establishing an international workforce was to control the costs of mobility. This despite the fact that at the time technological developments were sufficiently limited to ensure that hardly any corporation knew the actual total cost of its mobility programs.

4. *Consistency.* Organizations focused on major global product lines and on creating global consistency and conformity in their international human resource practices and policies.

In the past decade, the business world and society as a whole have evolved significantly and dramatic changes in the approach to managing an international workforce have occurred along with it. The implications of this strongly influence the context in which international compensation management is practiced. As a result, the forces at work today are in tension with those that prevailed a decade ago. (See Figure 7–8.)

1. *Decentralization.* Many organizations are decentralizing the control of business activity (the bottom line) to smaller business units. This is incompatible with centralization of the international human resource management process and results in major difficulties in maintaining single-policy approaches. However, the need for cost-effective international human resource management still requires the maintenance of centralized expertise. As a result, many organizations are looking to outsource elements of the process to obtain economies of scale and expertise while at the same time encouraging the decentralization of crucial decision making to local management.

2. *Self-development.* Increasingly corporations are unable to offer career-for-life understandings with key employees. Additionally, the wider access to information results in the placement of knowledge workers at the centers of power in organizations. Therefore, career development

FIGURE   7–8
<hr />

Tensions in Expatriate Management

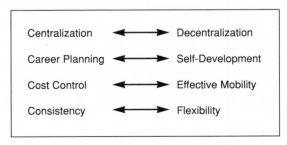

F I G U R E   7–9

The Potential for Cost Control

Business Purpose: A 30-month "task requirement" in Tokyo for a New York employee earning $100,000 annually between mid-1995 and late-1997/early-1998:

Traditional "Unplanned" Approach:
Departs July 1995, returns January 1998

Salary and Accommodation Costs

	1995	1996	1997	1998
Net U.S. income	$ 28,200	$ 67,600	$ 67,600	$ 5,640
COLA	43,620	104,600	104,600	8,720
Expatriate allowance	10,420	25,000	25,000	2,080
Housing allowance	22,900	55,000	55,000	4,580
Tax	62,900	151,000	151,000	28,600
Total	$168,040	$403,200	$403,200	$ 49,620
Grand Total				$1,024,060

Planned Approach:
Departs June 1995, returns December 1997 (to avoid 1998 residence tax). COLA determined using ECA Windham OECD international lifestyle index. Housing paid by the company. Expatriate allowance paid as lump sum in United States prior to departure and following return.

Salary and Accommodation Costs

	1995	1996	1997	1998
Net U.S. income	$ 33,800	$ 67,600	$ 67,600	—
COLA	37,650	75,300	75,300	—
Expatriate allowance	25,000	—	—	$ 25,000
Housing allowance	23,500	65,000	65,000	—
Tax	58,650	101,700	101,700	8,250
Total	$160,100	$299,600	$299,600	$ 33,250
Grand Total				$ 792,550
Savings				$ 231,510

processes are increasingly subject to forces beyond the organization's control; international human resource management must concentrate on the short-term self-development advantages of assignments in contrast to the historical emphasis on long-term planning and development.

3. *Effective mobility.* While controlling costs remains a priority for international human resource practitioners, there is a simultaneous and increasing need for global employee mobility. This requires careful attention on a case-by-case basis and adjustment as necessary to facilitate mobility while controlling costs. Figure 7–9 illustrates how effective scheduling of a repatriation can result in significant savings.

Another example, family pressures such as dual careers and children's education can result in decreased mobility, but the most effective response is not necessarily to throw money at the problem. Instead, individually tailored creative solutions that respond to the employees' needs may be the best answer.

4. *Flexibility*. The catch-phrase, "think global, act local," has replaced the world-product concept for international business. This mind-set change is reflected in international human resources practice. No longer is conformity to corporate policy the overriding objective. It has been replaced by flexible standards that meet the needs of particular circumstances while preserving corporate values. The challenge is to maintain the company approach to business while enabling local management (either geographically or by business sector) to deliver the profit targets in a flexible manner.

DEVELOPING CULTURALLY SENSITIVE COMPENSATION PLANS FOR LOCAL NATIONALS

We have seen that the approach to compensation design for expatriates may be affected by an organization's evolution and strategic business mission as well as by local compensation practices. While this is not simple, it pales in complexity compared with developing compensation structures for local nationals. Structuring national compensation programs is far more complicated because it is subject to the inconsistencies of national cultures and how those cultures complement or conflict with corporate business philosophies.

Local compensation systems are affected by both the corporate culture of the organization and the local culture of the host country. Compensation schemes that might be extremely effective in a home country location will fail if they violate local cultural values. Nevertheless, corporate cultures are very powerful and in some instances can override accepted local practices providing they do not violate the core values of a culture. Industries that tend to use individual reward and pay for performance as both a motivator and core compensation component worldwide risk the backfiring of their compensation strategies.

The effectiveness of using reward as a motivator is influenced by cultural attitudes about motivation. In group dependent societies, neither individual pay nor self-actualization are high in the society's hierarchy of needs. More powerful motivations are those centered on the fulfillment of group aspirations and potential. Incentive programs, such as an employee-of-the-month selection, are likely to cause embarrassment. Motivation needs to be based on rewards that recognize the group rather than the individual. Programs that are aimed at differentiating individual performances are likely to be far less welcome in these group dependent societies where fear of loss of face may turn a successful U.S. program into a demotivator. Such programs may be equally unwelcome in nurturing societies that attach greater importance to solidarity among colleagues, and individual prominence will be inclined to provoke resentment and jealousy.

Let's take a look at how national culture creates a bias in compensation design. U.S. corporations, for example, tend to structure programs that:

- Pay for performance measured in financial terms.
- Have a relatively short-term horizon.
- Differentiate pay by responsibility level within equivalent positions.
- Differentiate between job responsibilities.
- Encourage flexibility in benefit provision, allowing for individual choice.
- Have little emphasis on perquisites.

It is interesting to contrast this approach with the northern European approach, which will also pay for performance but concentrates less on individual differences and has a much more nurturing approach to benefits with strong, standardized state provisions. Those societies with hierarchical social structures (such as the U.K., Germany, France and Italy) emphasize recognizable perquisites, sometimes even beyond their intrinsic financial value.

In Japanese society, culture has a different effect again. Pay for performance is linked to the success of the entire company. It is unlikely that in a year that the organization loses money, the CEO is the only one to receive a bonus while the rest of the organization is being downsized. Furthermore, the Japanese have long-term horizons, differentiation is constrained by respect for age, and rewards operate around a built-in age escalator; benefit provision is completely inflexible; and while perquisites play a strong role in reward, they are typically much less ostentatious than in Europe.

When a U.S. organization looks at designing structures for local national organizations, it is important to identify which aspects of these culturally determined approaches fundamentally reflect the organizations' business culture and which are merely a reflection of the presence of a U.S. cultural norm.

For example, take the issue of reward at risk. Is the presence of a bonus system in the United States reflective of a precise relationship between the success of certain behaviors and the success and survival of the organization? Or is it simply a response to the cultural drive to differentiate between individuals? If it is the latter, will imposing such a system enhance or damage performance in a culture such as Japan where collective success is highly prized? If it is the former, can it be adapted to a society in the developing world where discretionary income may be very limited and the imposition of an at-risk strategy may make base salaries dangerously noncompetitive.

Similarly, differentiation may have unexpected effects quantitatively and qualitatively. Imposing U.S. norms such as a 20 percent salary progression for job levels may be entirely inappropriate in both directions—in Scandinavia where differentials are commonly smaller or southern Europe where they are frequently much larger. In addition, the progressive pay system typically used to differentiate between responsibility levels may be entirely inappropriate to a culture that traditionally rewards either age or length of service. In some cultures, the award of a new status level may have a greater impact; for example, the significant effect of being made *dirigenti* (senior management cadre) in Italy.

Similarly, many cultures have little appreciation of the oft-touted advantages of flexible benefits. These countries either mandate corporations to provide benefits or have a state-provided benefits structure that is more than adequate for the population. Flexible benefits—or any additional benefits—would have little value in such cultures. The addition of flexible benefits will either be rejected outright or accepted only as an unnecessary "add-on" to already sufficient provision.

Finally, it is dangerous to underestimate the importance of perquisites in many cultures. From the designated office or parking space in France to the overseas training course in Russia, these provisions may have a perceived value far in excess of their cost and at a level unappreciated in an aggressively egalitarian society such as the United States. Nevertheless, their absence will damage both competitiveness and productivity in the local environment.

In other words, the new global business manager needs to be just as adroit in understanding global human resource issues as in understanding domestic labor relations. That manager also needs to understand what impact local cultures will have on the acceptance of products and services. What works well in one society can cause a complete disaster in another.

It is also important to know how local compensation structures are calculated. Don't agree to pay an employee a monthly salary unless you know the number of months that constitute an annual salary. (Some countries calculate salaries on 13 or 14 months.) Furthermore, don't offer bonuses unless you are certain that they remain as bonuses. In Italy, bonuses can become part of the pay package and cannot be taken away. Moreover, make sure you understand if salaries are quoted in gross or net dollars. And if you agree to pay in dollars in a peso-based country, be sure that employees understand that if the dollar devalues compared with the peso, they're not protected.

It is also important to understand the impact of culture on national legislation—and through legislation—on company compensation strategies. For example, many corporations are trying to spread stock options across the globe. This can have unfortunate and unintended effects. In the Netherlands, options are taxed at the point of grant; in France they're taxed at the point of exercise; and in the United Kingdom at the point of sale. Thus your plan will be perceived very differently in each country. Indeed, if the employee is unfortunate to be granted options in the Netherlands, moves to France when he or she needs to exercise the options, and then to the United Kingdom to realize the profits, the benefits of the scheme will not be apparent. Conversely, the employee would be delighted to move in the opposite direction!

Regardless of cultural uniqueness, organizations should always consider those aspects of compensation design which they regard as fundamental to their own company culture. All cultures comprise a spectrum of individuals. Provided that all cultural norms are not disregarded, a nonconforming aspect—which is key to a strong corporate culture—will still attract a certain number of individuals in any culture. For example, the financial community has been quite successful carrying forward its U.S.-style pay-for-performance bonus system throughout Asia despite its contrariness to the national cultures which prize collective behavior and disdain individual rewards. The compensation structure is so key to the business practice that gaining acceptance of it was vital.

The key to business success is to be aware of the impact that your corporate culture and business practices will have in the local environment. A corporation's culture and values are vitally important to its success in the global arena. What is important is that those values have universal application and flexibility of interpretation in areas where they test the local cultures.

NOTE

1. F. Herzberg, B. Mausner, and B.B. Snyderman, *The Motivation to Work,* New York: Wiley, 1959.

8

⑥   SELECTING EXPATRIATE
FAMILIES

This chapter will cover

- How to build global awareness within your company, to better manage international opportunities.
- How to develop a globally astute workforce that appreciates the challenges of working in a foreign country.
- The qualities to look for in potential expatriates and their families—with special recognition of the working partner.
- Assessment processes and tools as well as training to enhance global business skills.
- What line managers need to know to be more effective.
- How to follow up after the selection process.
- The effect of repatriation on selection and overall success in the global arena.

Social change always lags behind technological advancement. Indeed, technological advancement creates social turmoil because it catapults society into a new era before people realize what is occurring. Consequently, the faster people realize what's happening and take advantage of the opportunities, the better the organization and community will function in the new environment.

You can see the way technology remade society when you examine the introduction of assembly-line production around 1900. The assembly line changed the way people worked, the way they related to each other, the availability of consumer goods, and the migratory patterns of people. It also accelerated the labor union movement and the way management and employees interacted. Similarly, today's technology of fax machines, E-mail, cable optics, interactive television, and even standard overnight delivery from any hamlet in the world, hurls humanity into a breakneck pace of life that alters everything. Things that a decade ago would have taken a week to accomplish (at a blistering pace), now take only minutes.

But society's growing addiction to speed and immediate gratification also creates enormous stress on individuals. Many people resist the change; others are simply confused by it. Obviously, individuals are more difficult to reengineer than products. They require education and time to adjust to change. Consequently, the organizations that are able to help their people adapt rapidly to the changes brought about by globalization and can maximize them for their own benefits, will realize enormous gains.

Earlier, we explained why the global village is already here, how much revenue is generated by global trade, and how education and technology have already revolutionized the way people think about the world and their place in it. Most of all, globalization has put us in daily contact with individuals in hundreds of countries who have different values and points of view. Cultural values and perspectives shape the way we define right and wrong, the way we relate to each other, what we think are good and bad manners, and the way we work. As millions of sojourners move out from their insular villages into the teeming global marketplace, they need the tools with which to succeed. We have the technology to get there, but can we develop the social intelligence to bridge the cultural chasm? Fortunately, social intelligence can be taught and the companies that have people who will learn it best—and learn it fast—will seize the preeminent position.

How do you get the organization ready for this new game? You have to educate everyone and raise the level of global awareness throughout the corporation. No one is exempt from the need to know because everyone will be part of the new global team—the receptionist who answers the phone and projects the image of a global organization, the engineers who create global products, and the CEO who develops the strategic vision to compete and win in the global marketplace.

LEARNING THE RULES

If, in fact, globalization is creating a whole new game, the first thing you need to do is to make sure that everyone knows the rules. Then you need to identify the players who will take the various positions on these new global teams. They are not the same players as those on our existing teams. They will need different and additional skills because in many instances they will be exploring new ground and defining new business opportunities. Where are they going to come from, and how will they be selected?

The Orbox scenario points out how important it is to select the right people for expatriate assignments and how devastating a poor choice can be to a company. Moreover, the failure was not only the employee's. Could James Simon have succeeded if he had gone through cross-cultural orientation as Reuben Jones did? Shouldn't Jonathan Orbox and the HR staff have prepared James for the assignment? In retrospect, with no cross-cultural background, James would have had to be a genius to surmount the enormous challenges he faced.

How a company identifies the special skills and recognizes them, and then selects and prepares potential expats is critically important. Once selected, they must be trained and their skills enhanced. These are the individuals who are most ready and capable to handle—and even lead—the change. As they develop, they will eventually become coaches.

The role of all leaders in this global business is to be sure that everyone knows the rules and is adequately trained to play the game. Leaders are those who ensure that the rest of the company understands globalization and its importance to the survival of the organization, appreciates cross-cultural impact, and understands the additional skills it needs to develop if it is going to play in this more sophisticated game.

This chapter is about globalizing a company, which begins with selection, moves through training, and then capitalizes on the growing skills of those who are already trained. It focuses on ways to institutionalize behaviors needed to succeed in the global game. A winning organization integrates such thinking into its collective consciousness, so that it permeates the corporate culture. At that point, it is ready to tackle enormous challenges and come out on top.

BUSINESS GLOBALIZATION CYCLE

Companies that use the Business Globalization Cycle (see Figure 8–1) find that the dividends are enormous. When a manager is needed quickly in Singapore, a pool of qualified candidates that can be tapped already exists. The candidate selected should still participate in a country-specific cross-cultural program together with other members of the family.

The Components of the Global Awareness Cycle

1. Introduce awareness programs to the total corporate body, so that employees think about the process before they consider becoming expatriates.
2. Identify the characteristics of a successful expatriate and high potential performers.
3. Identify individuals within the corporation who may fit the profile.
4. Create an effective repatriation process to enhance global awareness within the organization and provide a role model to potential expatriates.

GLOBAL AWARENESS TRAINING

Global awareness programs can last anywhere from one day to several weeks. All programs focus on providing participants with a complete understanding of how culture affects lives and creates a set of values, how cultures are different, and how some of those differences manifest themselves. The program focuses on developing intercultural fluency and a comprehensive appreciation of cultural differences. The objective is to enable participants to recognize cultural differences and develop general guidelines about how to modify behavior and address culturally based challenges appropriately.

In its most basic form, a global awareness program provides participants with greater cultural understanding and new skills for operating more effectively. It also helps participants understand the overall global

FIGURE 8-1

Business Globalization Cycle

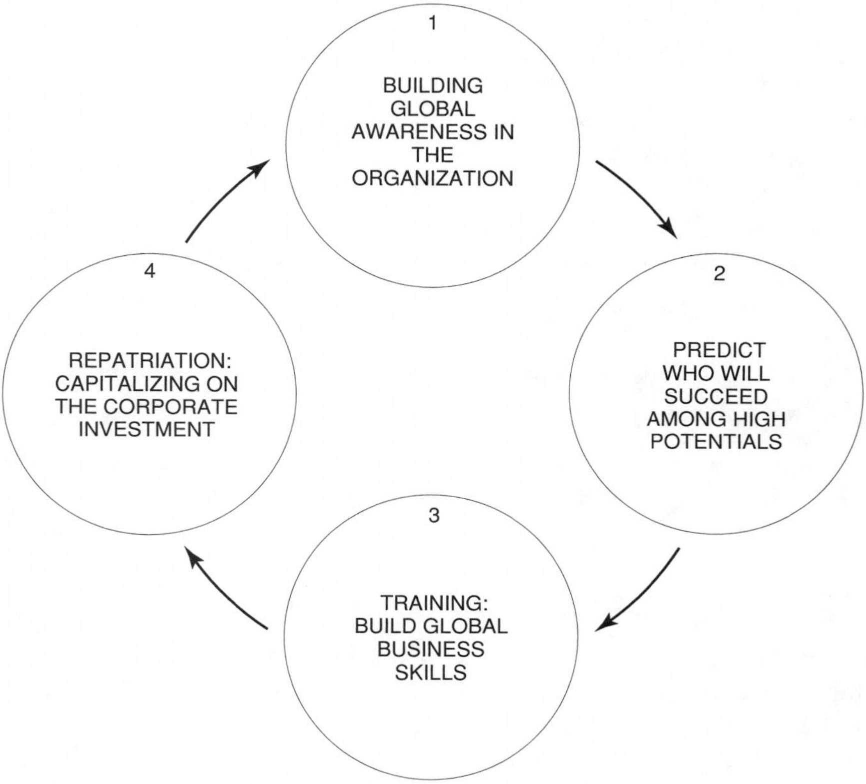

As Figure 8–1 shows, the Business Globalization Cycle is a comprehensive process that begins with an overall cultural awareness program (1), from which candidates are either identified or self-selected to further explore their career potential as expatriates. (2) This pool of potential expatriates then participates in an assessment process that identifies their potential strengths and weaknesses. This is followed by a series of individually designed global business skill programs for each employee. These programs focus on building the skills necessary to function in the global business arena. (3) Graduates of these programs make up the cadre of globally astute executives in a corporation, from whom the organization's potential expatriates are selected, as well as members of the organization's intercultural teams and managers of short-term assignments around the world. When the assignment is complete and a repatriation program is conducted (4), the repatriated employee and family can continue to support the company's continuing globalization effort by participating in ongoing global awareness programs. Part of the repatriation effort is intended to allow them to contribute their international expertise to the growing pool of knowledge in the corporation's global awareness program. At that point, the cycle is complete.

strategy and the importance and role of the global market in the growth
of the company. A typical program might instruct candidates how to:

- Appreciate cultural diversity.
- Recognize the impact of culture on business.
- Master global management skills.
- Understand how culture impacts business issues.
- Impart knowledge about challenges faced by business people
  around the world, including significant concerns and
  motivations of business people.
- Develop a framework for understanding cultural differences.
- Master strategies for cross-cultural problem-solving and
  negotiation skills.
- Learn decision-making strategies that work across cultures.
- Explore ways to build business relationships.

A more in-depth version would also focus on global leadership
skills, managing a multicultural workforce, and functioning on an intercultural team.

PREDICTING WHO WILL SUCCEED

Recent surveys indicate that finding potential expatriates is the single
biggest challenge facing international human resource executives. That
fact is compounded by the second biggest challenge facing managers: effective coordination with peers who have line responsibilities.[1] Therein
lies a great deal of the difficulty involved in selection. Expatriates need to
be adaptable and have interpersonal skills, but they also require technical
expertise to carry out their business missions effectively.

Finding candidates who possess these skills is as important a business challenge as locating capital for business development. A company
can thrive or fail depending on *whom* it has in *what* positions, and
whether these individuals—and their families—are suited to living and
working in another culture. For example, Jonathan Orbox, an astute en-
trepreneur, didn't even realize that he had a gold mine in Reuben Jones
and his family. Surprised by James Simon's failure, Orbox was equally
baffled by Reuben's success and the enormous benefits the Mexican operation brought the company. Through no brilliance of his own, Jonathan
selected a candidate who was globally astute to lead the firm. Not only

did Reuben have technical capabilities, but he also possessed a deep understanding of Mexican society based on innate sensitivity and years of study. Furthermore, Reuben understood enough of the hardships of expatriate life to include his family's well-being in the equation. Thus, the entire family was a good choice for the Orbox advance into Mexico.

James Simon, on the other hand, was chosen in much the same way that the overwhelming number of expatriates are. The reality in today's business environment is that almost 95 percent of all expatriate employees are selected by line managers for assignment based on their technical skills. In 47 percent of these cases, the decisions are validated with input from the company's human resources department. While many forward-looking companies now define specific criteria for expatriate success and factor it into the selection process, only a mere 7 percent use any formal assessment procedure.[2]

While technical competency is the primary selection criteria, international experience is considered less than one-third of the time and cultural adaptability is factored into less than 10 percent of all selections.[3] No wonder so many expatriate assignments fail. As James Simon illustrated, domestic competence doesn't automatically translate into international success. The attributes that make people a success in one culture may be the very things that cause them to fail in another—unless they have the ability to adapt their styles and translate their skills.

Technical competence is relatively easy to measure, and every organization has the existing tools in place to do so. However, measuring cultural adaptability is far more challenging because it is not based on prior performance. In addition, the psychological tools that could measure cultural adaptability aren't usually part of the corporate arsenal. Although prior domestic performance isn't a predictor of cultural adaptability, most people can be trained to function in another culture. Although no guarantee of success, it is an effective hedge against failure. While James Simon may never have become culturally astute—no matter how much training he had—many of the strategic errors he made could have been avoided had he better understood the impact of his decisions. James's error was not taking time to study Taiwan's culture; Jonathan's error was not assessing James and discovering his weaknesses. Because technical competencies can be measured, they are called "hard" skills, but competencies that are difficult to measure are termed "soft" skills. There is nothing "soft" or easy about predicting cultural adaptability, nor should you underestimate its impact on the successful business mission.

Whatever the reason for deploying expatriates or conducting international business—the transfer of technology, filling a job vacancy, opening new markets or starting new ventures, or building global business awareness in an organization—selecting and preparing the right candidate is critical. Think about it. It's impossible to transfer technology without a messenger who can speak effectively to the recipient. A culturally unsophisticated employee cannot undertake a job in another country effectively, and the ability to build global awareness is a two-way mission (the expatriate who goes on assignment, learns culture, and returns to the corporation to share knowledge) that requires a conduit who is adept at translating cultural messages. Not everyone has the abilities, skills, and demeanor to achieve corporate objectives and post outstanding results. You must find the people who are able to excel.

Because expatriates play such a key role in the globalization process, the pressure is intense to choose the right person for the job. Expatriates who possess technical skills but are not adept cross-culturally may actually cause more problems than those whose technical skills aren't as good. The manager who lacks technical skills will know when to ask for help, but a colleague who isn't skilled cross-culturally may not even be aware that there's a problem. The colleague continues to plow forward, wasting time and resources, while threatening to alienate those he or she comes into contact with.

WHAT IS FAILURE?

While the risk of improper selection forebodes failure, human resource managers and line managers can only guess at what failure rates really are. One of the reasons for this situation is that the organization has no operating definition for assignment failure. Obviously, early repatriation is not the only yardstick for gauging assignment failure. "Brownouts" (i.e., the walking wounded who don't repatriate early but do not complete the business mission anywhere near what they should be) and failure to meet business objectives, including the collapse of entire joint ventures, are other messy failures. While these failures are difficult to blame entirely on selection, undoubtedly selection is the first line of defense against these fiascoes.

There is no empirical measurement of failure. Many factors can lead to an early repatriation: another job opportunity, a spouse or family issue, or personal issues. In many cases, failed joint ventures are blamed on a variety of issues rather than the very real possibility that the wrong people were selected to manage the operation. Personal brownouts are often framed as family or medical issues when in fact they were entirely avoidable if the company had made the proper selection and provided adequate preparation. Equally consequential, few companies effectively evaluate completed assignments to determine their level of success or failure.

Surveys from Windham International and the National Foreign Trade Council indicate a failure rate under 10 percent,[4] while experiential and anecdotal information tend to support the notion that failure rates actually range from 30 to 40 percent. This supports earlier research, which cites failure rates of 20 to 40 percent.[5]

There's plenty at stake. Reyer A. Swaak of the National Foreign Trade Council estimates the dollars and cents of a poor staffing choice range from $200,000 to $1.3 million in identifiable costs.[6] The bottom line, however important, pales in comparison to what happens on the front lines of business. A single *faux pas* can ruin customer goodwill; ignorant remarks can devastate a firm's reputation, and an international fiasco can derail promising careers and demolish lucrative programs. Such costs are incalculable and jeopardize long-term business opportunities. While workers may know how to build a gas turbine faster, better, and cheaper than competitors, the company with the best technology and the best systems isn't necessarily the one that will flourish on the job. The one that can conduct business effectively in a multicultural environment will.

Furthermore, the enormous ripple effect of an inappropriate expatriate selection is virtually impossible to measure. It can affect the overall business mission and wreak havoc with potential revenues. Quantifiable or not, plenty of horror stories have been told about the collapse of major negotiations—along with the evaporation of multibillion dollar contracts—simply because the wrong person was sent on the assignment.

The importance of having the right person selected for a job is further reinforced by looking at international joint ventures. Remarkably, the popular press estimates that international joint ventures fail at a staggering rate of 40 to 75 percent. It doesn't take an industrial psychologist to figure out that such profound failure rates are at least partly due to expatriate managers who cannot adjust to local business practices. The manager who excelled in Omaha fails in Osaka very likely because the selection process is flawed. He or she wasn't given sufficient training to offset any cultural deficits so that the manager could be effective in the new situation.

This lack of insight isn't surprising if you consider that many of the global managers who choose expatriates have never lived out of the country themselves. Amazingly, only 14 percent of Americans are passport holders compared to a much greater number of Europeans.[7] It's analogous to asking someone who has never eaten Chinese food to choose the best Schezwan restaurant in the city. This person is operating without adequate knowledge.

What's a human resource professional charged with overseeing global staffing to do? Quite simply, screen candidates for technical capability, but also diagnose an individual's cultural adaptability and help shore up weaknesses with training. A thorough individual screening is essential and should include the spouse and family. Interviews should be structured and standardized to ensure consistency and eliminate potential legal problems. Too often, companies simply react to an immediate need overseas and hurriedly dispatch an unprepared employee to Bombay or Brussels. They gloss over interviewing and assessment, so that candidates end up with little or no understanding of the implications and subtleties of working in the international market. Quite simply, they wind up fighting fires instead of establishing an overall strategy and plan.

CHALLENGES TO EFFECTIVE SELECTION

The more you examine the global staffing problem, the more complex it becomes. Imagine a beleaguered HR manager mired in the administrative details of a job. He informs an equally busy line manager that the Japanese candidate who has distinguished himself as a team player in Tokyo is too passive and deferential to succeed in the aggressive corporate culture. To further complicate things, the corporate culture of the U.S. organization dictates that the best and the brightest be rewarded, and the Japanese candidate is just that. You can predict the line manager's reaction: The candidate will remain at the top of the list. This isn't the case because the line manager is stubborn, but because there is a dearth of qualified candidates who are culturally adept.

Even if we could introduce a selection instrument that could predict success, we'd still have to contend with the limited pool from which candidates can be selected.

Some of the challenges that make selection difficult include:

- Scarcity of qualified candidates.
- Spouse careers and other family issues.
- Legal limitations regarding testing procedures.
- Need to make rapid deployment decisions.

SCARCITY OF QUALIFIED CANDIDATES

One of the major underlying problems is the lack of personnel qualified to handle an overseas assignment. One enormous challenge is dealing with the growing demand for expatriates among companies that have no history or background in the global business arena. Of course, many corporations—the Shell Oils, IBMs, and Goldman Sachses of the world—are well known for their global positions. Anyone joining such an organization knows from Day One that an expatriate assignment may be in the cards. But there are plenty of firms where overseas assignments have only recently entered the equation. The idea of living outside one's native country is, quite literally, a foreign concept. That's especially true for small companies that are just beginning to forge global links. In many instances, employees must obtain passports and shots, and learn the lay of the new land. These individuals often have nobody to turn to within the company for information and support.

Moreover, in today's rapidly expanding global business environment, many organizations are sending expatriates to remote locales that have no history or tradition of accepting foreign nationals. Even when a company has a pool of talent to choose from, these locations can sometimes prove vexing, and even the most experienced or culturally adept individuals have a difficult time adapting.

SPOUSE CAREER AND OTHER FAMILY ISSUES

We not only have to deal with the employee's ability to adapt to another culture, but must now add another variable: the spouse and family. It has been documented by countless researchers that spouses are a critically important aspect of a successful expatriate experience.[8] Human resource managers around the world will tell you that the more eager and willing a partner is to accept an assignment, the more likely the employee will fulfill the business mission. Yet, only 37 percent of all companies involve the spouse in selection discussion.[9] In addition, two-income families (which constitute the majority of families in the candidate pool) present an additional problem. They may encounter visa and work permit problems on expatriate assignments, and therefore face the loss of the spouse's income and career opportunities.

Perhaps the most frequently mentioned obstacle for a dual-career family (discussed more fully in Chapter 10) is having one partner abandon a promising career to follow the other. Not only can such a move create resentment and anger, it can compromise the effectiveness of the entire assignment. But other issues exist as well: the impact on finances when a family must adjust to the reality of living off a single salary, the difficulty that children face trying to speak another language and coping with an entirely different set of social customs, and the loss of one's support system, including parents and friends. All these factors contribute to a narrowing field of potential candidates, making line managers edgy about selecting expatriates from an already meager list.

NEED TO MAKE RAPID DEPLOYMENT DECISIONS

The absence of time is one of the most frequently cited reasons for not providing vital services and programs. When a business requirement in Singapore demands that a manager be sent immediately, filling that opening as quickly as possible becomes the only objective. What happens in the real world is the candidate with the needed technical skills winds up en route to Singapore almost before the global HR manager knows that an opening exists. In order to be effective, selection must take place well in advance of an opening. The company must be prepared; it must have a process or mechanism in place to ensure that a pool of candidates are available at any given moment.

IDENTIFYING SUCCESSFUL GLOBAL MANAGERS

Michael Tucker of Tucker International has studied expatriate assignments since 1973. His research with thousands of expatriates identifies six basic characteristics that distinguish those who adapt well to a new society. They are *acceptance, knowledge, positive emotions, lifestyle, interaction,* and *communication.*

Characteristics for Adapting to a Culture

Acceptance   Successful expatriates accept the local culture and show respect for local customs and behaviors. They don't criticize or make light of the culture; they accept it as different from their own but entirely natural for those living and working there.

Knowledge   Expatriates express a genuine interest in the assignment country. They learn historical and current information and are able to engage in conversation with local people about subjects of mutual interest.

Positive Emotions   Successful intercultural adjustment leads to positive feelings of well-being. These feelings are associated in turn with a positive self-concept and attitudes about the country and its people.

Lifestyle   Expats who adjust well, lead an active lifestyle that is rewarding as well. They participate in many of the same activities they did back home but aren't averse to trying new endeavors.

Interaction   People who adjust well in the country of assignment, mingle with local nationals on the job as well as during their discretionary time. They make local friends who enhance their experience and support their new lifestyle.

Communication   Individuals make it a point to learn both verbal and nonverbal ways to communicate with people in the local community.

👁 👁 👁

The task facing managers who select expatriates is to find people who will exhibit these six characteristics. To accomplish the task, Tucker developed an assessment instrument called the Overseas Assignment Inventory (OAI), a tool that identifies and measures 14 predictors of success on a foreign assignment:

Overseas Assignment Inventory
  1. **Expectations**
     Anticipation about what it will be like to work and live in a foreign country is a major issue. Research shows that individuals who are realistic and sensitive to the benefits and the potential difficulties have a greater chance of success than those who have low expectations

and do not look forward to the opportunity. A person who expects to succeed and looks forward to the assignment in the new country—while aware of the challenges—is far more likely to adjust and adapt to the new surroundings.

2. **Open-Mindedness**

Open-minded individuals are receptive to different beliefs and ideas without feeling as if their own value system is being challenged or threatened. On the other hand, those with ethnocentric attitudes— the belief that their own country's way of doing things is inherently superior—will face difficulties in creating relationships and accomplishing many tasks.

3. **Respect for Other Beliefs**

The capacity to be nonjudgmental of other people's religious and political beliefs is crucial in a foreign environment. Expatriates who respect and show interest in the beliefs of other cultures are more likely to establish meaningful intercultural relationships. Successful managers are those who are neither openly conversant about their own convictions nor critical about the convictions of others.

4. **Trust in People**

Faith and trust in other people are essential. Meaningful personal and professional relationships are more likely to develop if expatriate managers convey and encourage mutual trust among co-workers and business associates.

5. **Tolerance**

Effectively adapting to a foreign environment requires an ability to interact with, or live closely to, people who may have fundamentally different habits and lifestyles from one's own. It also can mean withstanding living conditions and surroundings that are different or less comfortable than what they have been accustomed to.

6. **Locus of Control**

This measures the extent to which people believe they control the process and outcome of their life events. Individuals who believe they can, to some extent, control, shape, or direct the course of their lives are likely to exert more effort to make things work. Those who believe that things happen because of luck or fate often wind up feeling helpless when confronted by new and changing life situations.

7. **Flexibility**

The ability to consider alternative approaches and points of view is crucial. This translates into a willingness to receive and accept feedback from others, and to realize that there is more than one valid way to approach and solve a problem. Flexibility is particularly important for expatriates who work as negotiators, work in joint ventures, or interact with a multicultural staff.

8. **Patience**

Managers must understand that a "sense of time" means different things in different cultures or they may find themselves paralyzed by frustration from unexpected delays. Managers must remain patient when business protocol demands a seemingly lengthy decision-making process or way of doing business.

9. **Social Adaptability**

This predictor pinpoints the ability to socialize comfortably with new people in unfamiliar social situations and to accept—and be accepted by—new groups of friends and acquaintances. Someone who feels comfortable only in a small, intimate group or feels intimidated by social or professional gatherings is likely to have more trouble adapting.

10. **Initiative**

By measuring the extent to which individuals are willing to take charge in a new or challenging situation, it's possible to predict their success. Successful expatriates are self-starters. They take charge and do not sit back and expect someone else to take care of them. Individuals who take the initiative not only trust the accuracy of their own judgments, but also are not afraid to accept the judgments and methods of others when new situations require different solutions.

11. **Risk Taking**

This predictor measures an individual's willingness to take risks, accept change, and meet challenges. Life in another country demands that people deal with many new things. A willingness to experiment makes the adjustment much easier.

12. **Sense of Humor**

A good sense of humor is one of the most important—and overlooked—aspects of effective intercultural adjustment. This dimension looks at the capacity to bring humor into difficult or stressful situations. The ability to laugh and learn from one's own mistakes often helps to ease tensions and facilitates communication. Expatriates who take themselves too seriously often have difficulty coping with the confusing and challenging aspects of international living, whether it's learning a new language or how to order in restaurants.

13. **Interpersonal Interest**
    Experience has shown repeatedly that strong people skills—in this case, cross-cultural people skills—are critical to an expatriate's success and effectiveness. Expatriates who are sincerely interested in, accepting of, and concerned for others have a great advantage in adjusting to another culture compared with those who are aloof and prefer to be alone.
14. **Spouse Communication**
    This measures the extent and quality of communication between couples. Experience shows that when communication is open and constructive, the relationship is often enhanced by the expatriate experience. However, the unique stresses of a new life in another country can be difficult and damaging to troubled relationships.

How Does the OAI Work?
Both candidates and their spouses complete the OAI questionnaire. The OAI yields a profile for each person such as the one shown in Figure 8–2.

CANDIDATE FOR ASSIGNMENT TO MALAYSIA— HIGH RISK

The sample OAI profile spotlights a candidate being considered for assignment in Malaysia (see Figure 8–3). Although the candidate displays strengths in the areas of expectations, open-mindedness, tolerance, locus of control, initiative, and risk taking, the areas of concern—trust in people, flexibility, patience, social adaptability, sense of humor, and interpersonal interest—lead one to conclude that this is a high-risk assessment of the candidate. The multicultural situation in Malaysia can be confusing, with Malay, Chinese, and Indian cultures all represented. However, social/interpersonal skills are critical for establishing relationships with members of all three cultures. This candidate is below the norm in these skills. Trust in people, social adaptability, and interpersonal interest are key characteristics in this case.

The low score on flexibility would almost certainly predict difficulties adapting to the multitude of opinions presented during business dealings and the growing pride in Malaysian capability. One cannot force one's own ideas on others and be very successful in Malaysia. Lack of patience is also a concern here because it was the lowest score on this can-

FIGURE   8–2

Overseas Assignment Inventory Profile

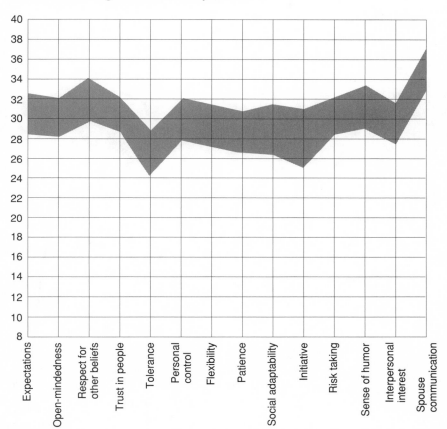

The shaded band shows the average range based on the scores of thousands of corporate employees and their spouses who completed the OAI before their international assignments. Each person's score is shown as indicated in Figures 8–3 and 8–4. Any score above the shaded band represents a strength, and any score that falls below the average represents an area of concern.

didate's profile. Not only is a high level of patience required when dealing with others in Malaysia, but it's essential to cope with frustrating delays that result from the problems of rapid growth and the associated infrastructure.

All of these concerns might be overcome if this candidate had a strong sense of humor. However, his below-average score on this scale

FIGURE 8–3

Overseas Assignment Inventory Profile

Candidate for Malaysia

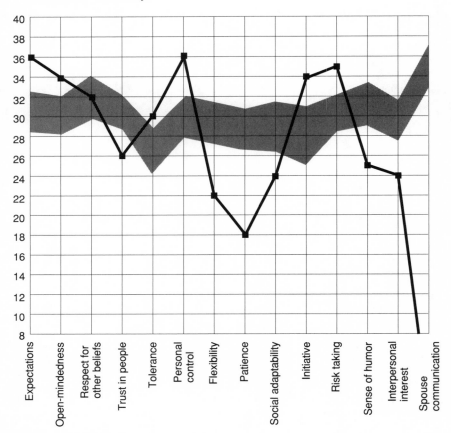

Source: Tucker International, LLC.

means that he takes himself too seriously and probably would not be able to use humor in stressful situations.

CANDIDATE FOR ASSIGNMENT TO SAUDI ARABIA— LOW RISK

The candidate considered for assignment to Saudi Arabia is likely to be a low risk for successful adjustment because the strengths shown in the OAI—open-mindedness, respect for others' beliefs, tolerance, and sense of humor—are critical for adjusting to the Saudi culture (see Figure 8–4).

Open-mindedness   Saudi Arabia presents many situations that are strikingly different to expatriates: censorship, the restricted role of women, and extreme forms of criminal punishment, to name a few. A high level of open-mindedness, and a nonethnocentric attitude are essential when facing these differences.

Respect for Other Beliefs   A nonproselytizing attitude and approach is a must for expatriate life in the kingdom, where Islam is the only religion allowed.

Tolerance   Although living conditions have greatly improved in Saudi Arabia, many physical challenges remain in the Saudi environment. A high tolerance for conditions that are different from what this candidate is accustomed to will serve him or her well in adapting to life and work.

Sense of Humor   Most people who have lived in Saudi Arabia cite the importance of maintaining a sense of humor. Many things happen daily that can be debilitating if people aren't able to laugh at themselves.

These strengths would outweigh the areas of concern in this profile—personal control, initiative, and risk taking—for this country and culture. This candidate would represent a low-to-medium risk.

BEHAVIORAL INTERVIEWING

Because the OAI is a self-response instrument, the scores on the OAI scales need to be checked to verify their accuracy. The most reliable way of verifying an OAI profile is through the Behavioral Interview Technique. Linking the OAI with behavioral interviewing is a powerful way to get a complete picture of a candidate's areas of concern.

The main premise of behavioral interviewing is that past behavior is the best predictor of future actions. For example, if the OAI profile indicates that a candidate is low on *patience,* then the type of situations or people that have tested his or her patience in the past need to be explored. It's essential to find out how this person has handled those situations. This often may be as simple as asking a candidate to describe how

Overseas Assignment Inventory Profile

Candidate for Saudi Arabia

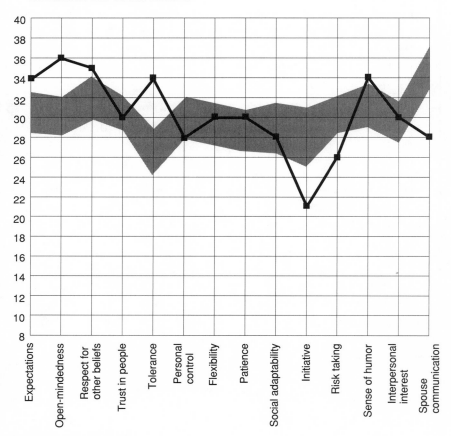

Source: Tucker International, LLC.

he or she reacted when someone kept them waiting for a meeting or took a long time to articulate and "get to the point" of an idea.

Using this technique with the OAI allows assessors to increase their objectivity by focusing on life experiences that are relevant to expatriate success. Asking hypothetical questions yields only hypothetical answers and is not highly reliable. In contrast, behavioral interviewing minimizes an interviewer's reliance on gut feelings or biases and reduces the tendency to make snap judgments about people.

PROFILE OF A SUCCESSFUL EXPATRIATE

Windham International has identified the following additional features of a successful expatriate:

- Strong marriage.
- Supportive spouse who is not "sacrificing" career or interests.
- Flexible lifestyle and possessions.
- Transferable hobbies and outside interests.
- Financially stable.
- Recognizes the value of an expatriate assignment.
- Feels that assignment is career enhancing (even if not with the same firm).
- Willing to learn the language.
- Feels that it's a good and fair deal.
- Enthusiastic and wants the assignment.
- Feels qualified and prepared.
- Able to establish interpersonal relationships.
- Possesses cross-cultural competencies.
- Demonstrated ability to deal with stress.
- Good communication skills.
- Comfortable dealing with ambiguity.
- Nonjudgmental.
- Curious and adventurous.

PROFILE OF A SUCCESSFUL EXPATRIATE FAMILY

- Small family.
- Young children.
- Adaptable to different lifestyles.
- No dependents left behind.
- Good health.
- Healthy parents left in home country.
- Children doing well in school.
- No ongoing medical care required.
- Enthusiastic about change.
- Family supportive of the assignment.
- Positive family attitude toward the adventure.
- Spouse willing to accompany employee on assignment.

TRAINING: BUILDING GLOBAL SKILLS

Finding a solution means recognizing the problem. It isn't good enough to tell an expatriate, "You know you don't have very much of a sense of humor" or "You're constantly going to be upsetting people in Asia because you're too direct." Or telling the expatriate to read a humorous book or watch a good comedy isn't going to change his or her personality. The person can accept or deny that information. It's far more useful to train an individual to recognize a weakness and then learn to make changes.

Based on the outcome of the OAI or other assessment procedures, skill-building programs are developed to capitalize on individual strengths and to recognize the areas that could present cultural challenges. They also can develop strategies to manage them. With the OAI output, companies are able to tailor training to fit the employee's strengths and weaknesses. Training is not simply telling someone what to do. It's giving them the fundamental tools to make changes; it is modifying behavior. Training recognizes that it is very difficult for people to change but builds on the potential they have to adjust behavior to specific situations. In other words, by understanding our own behavioral predilections, we can learn how to interact with other culturally based behaviors and adjust accordingly. For example, someone who is informal and overtly friendly is well served to discover those attributes and use them in other cultural settings, when appropriate. Knowing this means that an expatriate can play down traits and tendencies when they are not culturally appropriate.

The purpose of the advanced cultural awareness training is twofold. One is to develop core competencies; the second is to develop a pool of expatriates.

Building Core Global Competencies

Advanced cultural awareness training can take different forms. The primary objective of the training is to develop a cadre of globally astute managers who can help the organization accomplish its global mission in numerous ways. Indeed, some of these employees will become candidates for expatriate assignment; others will take their global business skills into a marketing or product design function; still others might join intercultural teams or conduct negotiations in China or Argentina. What is important is that, with these new skills, an organization is developing managers who can carry out the business mission of a global organization. Make no mistake, these skills are nothing less than a fundamental requirement.

During the coming decades, global management skills will become the underlying framework for all corporate business and management. Understanding how to shift between cultures and adjust behavior intuitively will be essential if a company is to ensure success and realize gains from its core business mission and competencies. The skill-building training described here is an imperative for any organization that's intent on becoming or remaining a formidable player.

Identifying a Pool of Potential Expatriates

Theoretically, at least, a company using these techniques could develop a group of employees who are well suited to live and work in Asia and another group that's well adapted to South America. Alas, the practical reality of running a business intercedes and makes such a scenario unlikely. What is more likely to happen is the greater awareness growing out of a strategic approach to global deployment can solve many problems before they ever develop. When an opportunity arises and someone is told that there's a possible assignment in China, the employee can say, "Look, I've gone through the entire cultural awareness program and my personal profile focuses better with Latin America, but I'll go. It doesn't mean that I don't want to go. I feel that I would do much better in Saudi Arabia."

To be sure, succeeding in a foreign environment means acquiring a level of "social intelligence"—learning the rules so to speak. Then, using that knowledge as a stepping-stone, one must deal with the more challenging issue of unlearning old habits while figuring out how to adapt and control deep-seated behaviors. That's an important point, because it's at the heart of the definition of what a global manager is. Quite simply, he or she reads the signals when facing a new situation—just as a globally astute executive would look at how people dress in an office to get some sense of the importance of the role hierarchy plays in the organization. Or take a look at whether doors remain open or shut to gain hints into how the organization or culture values "space." Then, he or she is able to adjust behavior accordingly. The manager might say to herself, This is a society that has greater respect for space and privacy. I shouldn't go barging into someone's office even if the door is open. I should retain a sense of formality.

Of course, it's impossible to read such a signal without being in tune with the culture. A manager might say to himself, Even though I may be somewhat undisciplined in the United States and walk into the middle of a conversation, I had better not do that in a "thick-door" society. Once this manager has begun to understand this reality and act accordingly, he or she will be better equipped to manage, sell products, and build relationships.

REPATRIATION: CAPITALIZING ON THE CORPORATE INVESTMENT AND INSTITUTIONALIZING GLOBAL BEST PRACTICES

Repatriated employees play a crucial role in the globalization process. First, they add invaluable knowledge to the global wisdom of a company as a result of their international experiences. They continue to broaden the scope of global vision and general global awareness within the corporation by sharing their experiences, both triumphs and failures. Second, they serve as role models and mentors for others who may consider expatriate assignments.

To succeed, repatriation programs must address the expatriate's need to return to the home country with minimal emotional turmoil. Reentry to the home country can be traumatic, and many experts agree that it requires as much cultural adaptation as the initial international move. Not only is the expatriate and family returning to an environment that is quite different from the one they left, but they don't expect it to be altered. In addition, their friends and family may not share their excited retellings of experiences and may even give the expatriates the feeling that they are being pretentious and arrogant. Furthermore, good repatriation programs also recognize that expats are an important asset to the business because of their accumulated knowledge and experience. What better and more visible role model could future expats have than someone who has been in the trenches and returned—having done the job successfully? If the organization recognizes and values the contribution, it sends out a profoundly different message than a firm where employees return to no job, are passed over for promotion, or are slotted into a dead-end position. In such a scenario, workers inevitably depart the organization to enhance their careers and capitalize on their expatriate experience elsewhere. And they create a brain drain in the process.

The way returning expatriates are treated in an organization sends out strong, clear signals to others considering taking on such assignments. Keeping in mind that the talent pool for potential expats is not great even in the largest and most successful global companies, retaining the wisdom of returning employees and institutionalizing it is critical for the message it sends to future expats.

Unfortunately, few subjects receive as much lip service—or as little action—as repatriation. The fact is that companies are remarkably blasé about the defection rates among repatriated employees. Studies indicate that as many as 20 to 30 percent of expats leave the firm within the first two years of reentry,[10] and authoritative anecdotal data puts it as high as 40 percent.

In spite of home leave and periodic business trips there is a re-entry culture shock that occurs. Here are some of the challenges that repatriated employees face:

Personal reasons:

- The expatriate has changed a lot as a result of the experience.
- Home looks different—both in reality and from a subjective perspective.

- Friends are different.
- Children need to find new friends and fit into a "home" community that feels very strange.
- The spouse often wants to re-enter a work environment.
- They have to live on a salary without additional allowances.

Job-related reasons:

- The job back home generally has reduced responsibility and control.
- There are more approval levels and less autonomy.
- Friends and fellow employees think that expatriates are bragging when they discuss their experience.
- The expatriate experience is not adequately valued by the company and employees feel underutilized and underappreciated.

Some companies also invite their returning assignees to present their experiences abroad to the larger employee population. Visible recognition of the experience encourages other members of the organization to be open to expatriate career opportunities. When returning expatriates receive the same or better career opportunities within the organization, it greatly reduces the odds that they'll find other employers more enticing. Without question, a high-attrition rate has profound repercussions.

INSTITUTIONALIZING GLOBAL WISDOM

As Figure 8–5 on Monsanto Company indicates, there is great value in using repatriated employees for an organization's global awareness program. They bring life and real experiences to the training. They bring a very real human connection on both a personal and professional level. Their adventures validate the value of a global assignment and allow new global managers to gain a deeper understanding of the international marketplace.

WHAT LINE MANAGERS NEED TO KNOW

As a rule, line managers make selection decisions, which means that they must be better prepared to recognize the characteristics of a successful

FIGURE   8–5

SEARCH FOR BEST PRACTICES: MONSANTO COMPANY

Monsanto Company is a food, chemical, and pharmaceutical company with over 28,500 employees and annual revenues of approximately $9 billion. The company has approximately 100 employees on global development assignment. It has adopted a comprehensive repatriation process that actually begins before the assignment is accepted. It was created with the idea that all the pieces of the assignment process work together.

Monsanto's program consists of:

- A philosophical framework that repatriation is a critical aspect of the global development assignment.

- Reacculturation sessions for employees occur two months after repatriation and help smooth the culture shock of reentry as well as recognize and assimilate their learning. This meeting focuses on the family as well as the business, creating the opportunity for the employee and spouse to share their knowledge and feel that their contribution is recognized.

- Debriefings occur a month later (approximately three months after repatriation) with several key colleagues and managers. This is to help expatriates demonstrate their new knowledge and to infuse that knowledge into the company and help further globalization.

- Debriefings are facilitated by a cross-cultural trainer who makes sure the sessions cover key points about the assignment and the global experience.

- Monsanto believes that development links the process together. It includes a global development plan created at the beginning of the assignment where the assignee and supervisor are held jointly accountable for the assignee's acquisition and transference of knowledge. Upon repatriation, utilization and validation of knowledge reduces the attrition rate, provides return on investment, and furthers globalization.

expatriate (see Figure 8–6). Moreover, in many instances line managers are also responsible for evaluating the performance of expatriates while they are on assignment and frequently for their reentry and repatriation decisions. In other words, it behooves line managers to learn as much as

FIGURE 8–6

WHAT LINE MANAGERS SHOULD CONSIDER WHEN SELECTING CANDIDATES

- Health of family.
- Age and health of parents.
- Spouses employment or career status.
- Age and grade in school of children; availability of space in the right schools.
- Personal flexibility.
- Open-mindedness.
- Social intelligence.
- Previous international experience.
- Familiarity with foreign language.
- Family cultural background.

FIGURE 8–7

WHAT LINE MANAGERS SHOULD KNOW ABOUT PRE-DEPARTURE TRAINING: CULTURE AND LANGUAGE

1. Importance of culture to the success of the business mission.
2. Allowing time for assignments to overlap.
3. Importance of relationships in destination country.
4. What are realistic timelines, and are timelines themselves meaningful?
5. Characteristics of leadership in the destination culture.
6. How business meetings are conducted and what they are intended to achieve.
7. Importance of titles and trappings of authority.
8. Negotiation techniques in the host country.
9. Political and legal structures of host country.
10. Role of gifts and other social niceties.

possible about the demands of each phase of the expatriate process (see Figure 8–7).

Line managers need to effectively communicate the challenges facing the expatriate and develop ways to better support the expatriate while on assignment (see Figure 8–8). The goal is to make the experience successful for the employee and the company while setting the stage for a successful repatriation.

FIGURE   8–8

WHAT LINE MANAGERS NEED TO KNOW ABOUT INTERNATIONAL ASSIGNMENTS

1. Line managers should know something about the country or countries to which they're sending expatriates.
2. They should know about the specific job function and assignment objectives.
3. Managers should learn about the process of cross-cultural adjustment.
4. They want to have a general knowledge of cultural dimensions and how people in different cultures have distinct ways of looking at life.
5. Managers need to identify skills and personality/family profiles that lead to success.
6. They must recognize potential problem areas.
7. Line managers should utilize developmental assignments.

NOTES

1. Windham International and the National Foreign Trade Council, *Global Relocation Trends 1995 Survey Report.*
2. Ibid.
3. Windham International and the National Foreign Trade Council, *Global Relocation Trends 1994 Survey Report.*
4. Ibid.
5. Rosalie L. Tung, "Selection and Training of Personnel for Overseas Assignments." *Columbia Journal of World Business,* 1981, pp. 68–78, based on statistics in E.R. Henry, "What Business Can Learn from Peace Corps Selection and Training," *Personnel* 41 (July–Aug., 1965).
6. Based on an NFTC/SRI survey in Reyer A. Swaak, "Expatriate Failures: Too Many, Too Much Cost, Too Little Planning." *Compensation & Benefits Review,* Nov.–Dec., 1995, pp. 47–55.
7. Figures from the U.S. Department of State, 1995.
8. J. Stewart Black, Hal B. Gregersen, and Mark E. Mendenhall. *Global Assignments: Successfully Expatriating and Repatriating International Managers* (San Francisco: Jossey-Bass, 1992; J. Stewart Black,

and Hal B. Gregersen. "The Other Half of the Picture: Antecedents of Spouse Cross-Cultural Adjustment." *Journal of International Business Studies,* Third Quarter, 1991, pp. 461–77; Michael G. Harvey, "The Executive Family: An Overlooked Variable in International Assignments," *Columbia Journal of World Business,* Spring 1985, pp. 84–91; Mark Mendenhall, and Gary Oddou. "The Dimensions of Expatriate Acculturation: A Review." *Academy of Management Review,* 10, no. 1 (1985), pp. 39–47; Marian Stoltz-Loike. "Work and Family Considerations in International Relocation." *Journal of International Compensation & Benefits,* July/Aug. 1993, pp. 31–35; Rosalie L. Tung, "Expatriate Assignments: Enhancing Success and Minimizing Failure," *EXECUTIVE,* no. 2 (1987), pp. 117–26.

9. Windham International and the National Foreign Trade Council, *Global Relocation Trends 1995 Survey Report.*

10. Windham International and the National Foreign Trade Council, *Global Relocation Trends 1994 Survey Report.*

CHAPTER

9

ⓖ **PREPARING EMPLOYEES AND FAMILIES FOR EXPATRIATE ASSIGNMENTS**[1]

This chapter will cover

- The impact of the family on the success of expatriate assignment.
- The challenge families face when on assignment.
- The cycle of cultural adjustment.
- How to prepare and support expatriate families.
- Recommendations for effective programs.

So, you've found your international assignee. He's eager, culturally sensitive, and brimming with ideas. Armed with briefcase, passport, and action plan in hand, he's ready to bound down the airport corridor and board the plane to Barcelona, Beijing, or Buenos Aires. But wait . . . he has a family.

Documented again and again, the expatriate family profoundly affects the success of an international assignment. More than any other single factor, the family impacts success or failure to such a great extent that assignment success is *contingent* upon the spouse and children's ability to adjust to the new culture.[2]

> what occurs or does not occur in the family affects performance and success on the job. This theory is magnified in the international setting where the distinct line between home and work becomes blurred. An

international assignment places a great deal of stress on the family and
how that stress is resolved may make the difference between a gratifying
and exciting assignment that enhances the executive's ability to make decisions, manage people, and be innovate, and a painful, fragmented one that
can create a depressed, tense, unproductive, and preoccupied executive."[3]

FAMILY ADJUSTMENT: A GROWING BUSINESS CONCERN

Families are no longer thought of as so much excess baggage. The days of
the dutiful wife and kids obediently following an employee anywhere in
the world are long over. Companies are recognizing that the family's well-
being is a hard business issue, pivotal to meeting corporate goals. Indeed,
the family must be integrated into the corporate mind-set, the same way
cost-of-living allowances (COLAs) and salaries are.

Moreover, spouse and family issues are a growing challenge to international assignments. On one hand, companies need greater employee
mobility and are beginning to expect international experience from their
senior staff; on the other hand, the number of dual-career couples is on
the rise, and these families are already struggling to balance their current
work-family demands along with their personal goals. As these needs
collide, the search for solutions grows more pressing.

Even with these current challenges, the number of expatriate families is unprecedented. For example, looking at the United States alone:

- In 1996, an estimated 350,000 Americans were working outside
  the United States.
- Eighty-eight percent of expats were male and 65 percent were accompanied by their spouses or partners.
- Of these families, 67 percent have at least one child with them;
  80 percent are under 12 years old.
- Over 65 percent of all married couples with children were dual-
  earning families in 1994 (up 9 percent in 10 years).[4]

It's not surprising that companies describe family adjustment to foreign cultures as one of the most critical challenges to expatriation.
They've discovered that the expatriate's adjustment is only part of the
equation. The family must be happy, too. Moreover, statistics indicate
that the vast majority of assignment refusals are tied to family issues (see
Figure 9–1).

F I G U R E   9–1

Expatriate Assignment Refusal/Resistance

**When asked to identify the most common reasons for candidates
turning down assignments, spouse career concerns (48%), assignment
location (32%), family issues (29%), and concerns about children
(27%) were the leading reasons. Respondents indicated that almost
9% of their expatriates accept but do not complete assignments. The
reasons for refusal/resistance can also be the reasons for failure, but
these have not been clearly quantified.**

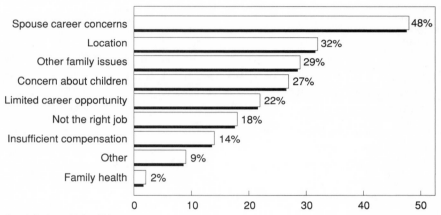

Respondents provided multiple answers.
Global Relocation Trends 1995 Survey by Windham International/National Foreign Trade Council

UNHAPPY FAMILIES ARE COSTLY

It is difficult to overestimate the complexity of life and challenges expatriate families face. Relocating one's home ranks among the top five most stressful life experiences, so it is little wonder that when families pull up stakes and move halfway around the world, the company that sends them faces enormous consequences and risks. As a result, the company, employee, and family enter a relationship like none they have had before, one in which the corporation becomes involved in the details of the expat's everyday life—where they live, what they purchase, and where the children attend school.

Surely, the family is where all the distinct elements of the expatriate policy—and package—coalesce and come to life. The careful COLA calculations take tangible form when the expatriate begins to purchase the first bars of soap and bottles of soda. Housing allowances metamorphose from scribbled numbers on a tablet to actual rooms with or without closets and spaces for the children to play. Investments in cross-cultural counseling pay off handsomely as family members adapt more easily to the ups and downs of the new culture.

This corporate-expatriate-family triangle benefits the organization as well as the expatriates because the family is a crucial source of stability and support for the international assignee. If well-adjusted, family members offer respite and predictability to each other as they steer through the labyrinth of new demands in an unfamiliar society. Family members share similar perceptions of the world and have the same cultural biases to frame their existence and give meaning to their lives.[5] In other words, they don't have to interpret each other's body language or hidden meanings because they've grown up in the same culture and navigate by the same compass. They carry their home culture with them into the new environment where it serves as a safe harbor while they're tossed about and trying to get on an even keel and make sense of their new world.

FAMILIES DEPEND ON THE COMPANY

In essence, international assignments create a special alliance between the company and the expatriate family. Mildred M. McCoy, a Research Professor of Psychology at the University of Hong Kong, who raised children as an expatriate, writes that because international relocation uproots the entire family unit, not just the individual employee, family members believe the company should be far more responsible for their well-being and happiness overseas than they would ever consider it should be at home.[6] This dependence creates additional demands on the corporation and global managers to create responsive policies and communicate them clearly so the practices will work in the real world.

In the home country, an employee who has a child with an educational or medical problem would never expect the company to get involved. However, on assignment, these problems loom large because the employee may not know who else to turn to for advice and support. Akin to a wellness program that buoys the employee's physical and mental well-being, global managers may be called on to help solve family problems that are only peripherally related to the business. They do so because these problems affect the employee's job performance.

Consider the Australian attorney living in Japan. She had to fly to

Bangkok to conclude a delicate contract negotiation the morning after her five-year-old son had suffered a fall that resulted in a deep facial cut. The boy was all right and the father was available to consult a plastic surgeon and care for the boy, but the mother could hardly concentrate on her work. She knew he was safe, but she was distraught and distracted because she didn't know how her husband would find the best plastic surgeon without the support network of friends and colleagues. In desperation, she called her expatriate manager who agreed to help the family locate the necessary medical assistance. His advice to her? Focus on consummating the contract negotiation and he would help with the rest.

Companies develop responsive programs because it makes good business sense. With assignments costing three to five times the expatriate's annual salary, and poor staffing decisions costing anywhere from $200,000 to $1.3 million per assignment in *identifiable costs* such as compensation, training, and relocation, it has become increasingly expensive to send a family overseas.[7] A mistake takes it's toll. Yet, it's not just the money. The social and psychological consequences of a mistake can disrupt the overseas location, damage potential business, and set adrift a project that the employee failed to handle. The ensuing chaos for that employee and his family creates immeasurable damage. It damages a promising career.

SEARCH FOR BEST PRACTICES: EASTMAN CHEMICAL—Successful Expatriates—Selection and Preparation Pay Off

Mary Beth Hallen opens the door of her spacious two-story home in The Hague. She invites you inside as if she's always lived there and introduces you to her husband Gary and her two sons, Edward (11) and Benjamin (8). Is it true that this expatriate family has spent only seven months here? You'd hardly know at first glance. Ben sits at a desk doing homework; Edward watches a videotape. There's the scent of dinner being prepared. Everything is clicking.

Neither magic nor luck have helped the Hallens adapt. They know they're in the Netherlands to fulfill business objectives. Why are they different from the people in many other stories you hear? No children with behavior problems who struggle at school, no angry wife who harangues her husband and believes the company doesn't give them enough.

The Hallens epitomize the ultimate expatriate family. Now, on a second assignment, their adjustment would make any global manager breathe a deep sigh of relief. This couple is resourceful, outgoing, and adventurous, and able to navigate the family through the rough spots of expatriation—a family capable of supporting the employee in his corporate mission.

Talk with the Hallens and you realize they're partners in the experience. Gary is the employee, but Mary Beth has encyclopedic knowledge about their surroundings and how to make their lives work. Affable and assertive, she chats about local customs and the daily routine. She'll explain about proper etiquette—that it's important to ask a Dutch plumber or handyman to partake of tea before he starts his job. And she'll display her deep cultural knowledge. But it's not simple, and the Hallens have learned to make the best of the expatriate experience.

Gary admits that he hasn't been home for Thanksgiving since the family first became expatriates in 1991—and it kills him to miss such a big family event; that he travels 50 percent of the time; that he is worried sick about his family's adjustment and his boys' lack of friends, especially when they were on their first assignment. Ask him, and he'll tell you that his wife is the one who faced the biggest adjustment, especially when they were isolated on their previous assignment in Switzerland. Ask, and he'll tell you that she's the one who keeps the family going.

It didn't just happen. It took hard work and partnership with their company, Eastman Chemical. The company considers the family when it makes selection decisions. It then helped the Hallens anticipate and prepare for the transition, offered them help when they arrived, and continued support throughout the assignment.

The company selected Gary carefully, knowing that all the Hallens eagerly wanted an international stint. This is typical for Eastman, which talks with the family before the relocation and gives them the chance to consider the assignment. It also allows plenty of time to prepare for the move. Notified in March that they would make the move to Europe in August, the Hallens spent the ensuing five months in preparation. They had days of in-depth briefings with different company specialists who helped them understand the details of their new life: taxes, compensation, benefits. Cross-cultural orientation, a househunting/get-acquainted trip hosted by the Swiss HR manager, and two weeks of immersion language training got them started.

Pre-departure preparation is only part of the picture, however. Eastman's overall philosophy creates a strong bond with new expatriate families and continues to provide an outstretched hand throughout the assignment. For example, in addition to the more basic briefings and provisions, the Hallens relied on their local HR manager to help them make sense of the world when they were in Switzerland. She was the one they contacted for cultural guidance when Gary received a call from the police explaining that there had been a citizen's complaint because he had broken the law by waiting in his car for 20 minutes on a residential street while his son finished playing soccer.

The company's matrix organization encourages this support. Regional managers—both HR and line—take great interest in individual expatriates. Furthermore, the company recognizes the importance of cultural sensitivity and adaptation by providing cultural training in the host country approximately three months after arrival. This allows expatriates the opportunity to talk about issues with each other and realize they're not alone.

Source: Parts of this case study are adapted from Charlene Marmer Solomon, "CEO Mom: The Tie That Binds a Global Family," *Personnel Journal*, Mar. 1996.

SEARCH FOR BEST PRACTICES: EASTMAN CHEMICAL—Key Program Features*

1. Considers family when making selection decisions.
2. Talks with family before relocation; gives them time to consider the assignment.
3. Helps prepare family for the transition.
   Allows plenty of time to prepare for move.
   Provides family with in-depth briefings and information from different company specialists.
   Recognizes the importance of culture by offering cross-cultural orientation.
   Offers immersion language training.
4. Supplies a "look-see" trip focused on family's needs to obtain comfortable housing and appropriate schooling for children. Assists with local person who helps expatriate and spouse learn basic logistics of the destination.
5. Continues support for and interest in the assignment.
   Cross-cultural training courses take place in host countries (where possible) approximately six to eight weeks after expatriate settles in. Group courses offer support among expatriates.
   Language training is available where necessary (e.g., employees in The Hague may not need it, but employees in Rotterdam might because they interact with more local people who do not speak English.)

Perks, such as company mail pouch in which families can send and receive mail and other small packages, including videotapes, in a timely manner.

A lump-sum payment to wage-earner spouses who are giving up incomes in order to recognize their contribution to the assignment (not income replacement).

Stateside counseling service that expatriates can access via telephone link-up.

6. Eastman's overall philosophy creates a strong bond between employee and company. Staff of International HR division at Kingsport, Tennessee, headquarters, as well as local/regional HR staff play a key role in maintaining a connection with the expatriate and having a sense that the family—and assignment—is going well.

---

* Where possible

ADJUSTMENT CHALLENGES FAMILIES FACE

CULTURAL ISSUES

Anyone who embarks on an international assignment enters the cycle of cultural adaptation. It is this natural progression through predictable phases that allows expatriates to eventually fit in physically, emotionally, and intellectually with some degree of comfort. To be sure, when expatriates and their families move to a new environment, they are confronted by a different set of lifestyle and workplace norms and their reaction typically goes through several stages.

What was commonly known as "culture shock," is actually part of the process of adaptation that occurs when individuals feel that coping with the unfamiliar has exhausted their level of patience and tolerance. Culture shock manifests itself in various ways—depression, increased hostility toward local customs and people, and decreased interest in new activities, including language studies and cultural activities. In this environment, people tend to associate with fellow expatriates, eat foods from home, and surround themselves with activities that remind them of home, such as watching American movies).

Lennie Copeland and Lewis Griggs put it this way:

> Culture shock is the result of stress overload, stress caused by the barrage of hundreds of jarring and disorienting incidents, many so subtle

we hardly notice and many so disturbing that we may feel seriously threatened. To function in the world depends on our ability to read hundreds of signs, respond to subtle cues and to behave according to countless explicit and implicit rules. At home we know how to read street signs, we know how to use the telephone, or how much to tip. We pick up signals when it is time to end a meeting or leave a party, or change a subject. Much of what we do is automatic, requiring little thought or effort."[8]

However, this simply isn't the case when we relocate to another culture.

EXPATRIATE ADAPTION CYCLE
(FIG. 9–2)

The Expatriate Adaptation Cycle takes about one year (of course it can take more or less time depending upon the family, the country, and the work-and-family challenges). This Expatriate Adjustment Cycle chart acknowledges the interrelationship of all the events that the expatriate family is involved in. It begins well before the family arrives at the new destination, and illustrates the euphoric impact of the recognition that accompanies most new assignments. That sense of enthusiasm is further fueled by the discussion about compensation and other allowances. It recognizes the importance of the entire expatriate support structure from selection to relocation, all the way through to cultural adaptation.

Phase 1—Pre-move phase—approximately two-to-four months. During this period of time, the combination of positive feelings resulting from recognition of employee competence that motivated the employee's selection, and excitement of the new adventure generates an overall positive feeling of well-being and enthusiasm. This is a period of increased pro-

F I G U R E   9–2

Expatriate Adaption Cycle

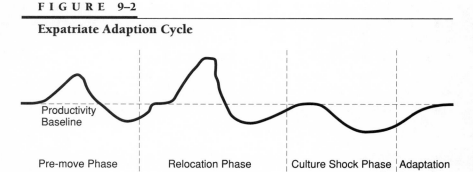

Productivity Baseline

Pre-move Phase · Relocation Phase · Culture Shock Phase · Adaptation

ductivity. This initial sense of well-being is enhanced by the salary increase and special allowances, as well as the increased recognition. The positive feelings are followed by the realization the assignment means the separation from friends, family and colleagues. At this point, the individuals begin to think about the difficulties of adjusting to the new environment.

Phase 2—Relocation phase—two-to-four months. During this phase, the employee and family experience the positive sense of excitement and hyperactivity of entering a new environment with its new discoveries. This is followed by realizing the full impact of leaving family and friends and familiar comfortable surroundings. They begin to feel the challenge that they will be facing, and after the initial excitement settles, they realize that they are alone in a strange new place.

Phase 3—First adaptation phase—two to four months. During this phase the expatriate family starts to adjust to the new location. The family starts making new friends and business contacts and daily life seems to begin to establish a pattern and stability. They begin engaging in activities within the new location.

Phase 4—Culture shock phase—two to four months.
Then, culture shock sets in. This is the period when the expatriate family begins to feel the weight of constantly confronting new, challenging, different experiences every day. The cumulative force creates a sense of isolation and fatigue that brings on the phenomenon commonly referred to as "culture shock." Culture shock is followed by a slow recovery period, when the family adjusts to the new culture and life begins to return to "normal." During this time the family begins to enjoy the new culture and the employee really returns to consistent pre-move productivity level once again.

Obviously, individuals go through these stages at different times of their international assignment, and may actually cycle back through stages. As different family members pass through the cycle, they affect each other both positively and negatively. Yet, most agree that the "honeymoon phase" is over after six months.[9]

Why can culture shock be so severe and devastating to a family? J. Stewart Black, Hal B. Gregersen, and Mark E. Mendenhall explain that individuals need predictability in their lives to maintain their sense of equilibrium so they can cope with their surroundings. Daily routines allow individuals to feel adept and competent because they navigate them with ease:

People establish a routine to obtain a certain level of predictability in life . . . Routines also provide an important means of preserving and maintaining one's ego and self-image. Living and working in new cultures generally disrupts established routines. The more routines disrupted, the more severely a given routine is altered, and the more a disrupted routine is critical, the greater the time and mental energy required to cope and the greater the frustration, anger and anxiety associated with culture shock.

Most important, however, is the fact that disruption of routines is generally accompanied by situations that challenge an individual's confidence, ego, and self-esteem. Threats to these sensitive areas cause the strongest reactions associated with culture shock—depression, anger, denial, and even hatred. In principle, then, factors that increase disruption and uncertainty tend to inhibit cross-cultural adjustment, while factors that reduce disruption and uncertainty tend to facilitate cross-cultural adjustment.[10]

It stands to reason, that the more you can alleviate surprises and create greater predictability through training and information, the more you are able to lessen the severe effects of culture shock. Cross-cultural counseling, get-acquainted visits, and transition support—settling into the destination, language, and business training—aid this process.

PERSONAL ISSUES

At the same time cultural adjustment is beginning in the new society, individual family members carry a suitcase full of their unique concerns and problems to the new location as well.[11] For example:

Children
- Have educational and extracurricular needs.
- Grapple with issues of self-esteem, independence in a strange environment, and frequent loss of friends who come and go with regularity.
- Become "third culture kids," a term used to describe these global youngsters who develop a hybrid of cultures—a mixture of their culture of origin and that of the destination, seasoned with the idiosyncrasies developed by the international community in which they live.

Spouses

- Face the challenges of setting up a home in a strange environment while giving up their support networks at the very time they need support the most.
- Confront the new society every day, wondering why the stores are closed on Mondays, why there's no hot water from noon to one o'clock, and why the neighbor acts cold and aloof.
- Function frequently as single parents because of the expatriate's intense travel schedule.
- Dual-career spouses also cope with loss of income and status in the larger world.

Expatriates

- Enter a new job with increased visibility and responsibility.
- Meet new people daily and make decisions while needing to demonstrate their creativity and insight.
- Travel extensively.
- Communicate across cultures (sometimes using a different language).
- Increased financial pressure if spouse's income is discontinued.
- Work is more intense because often they move into jobs without the same support infrastructure they depended on in the home country. Everything from administrative and secretarial support to reservations services for travel arrangements are in their own hands. In addition, there is often the absence of analytical specialists that executives have come to rely upon.

Other Family Members

- Elderly parents may be ill. Even if they're healthy, the greater distance strains the relationship and complicated logistics make it difficult on the expatriate family.
- Older children who remain home because of college or jobs still need their family whether or not they are on the same continent.

All of the above factors are interrelated and create a larger unit: the relationship between family members, or the *family system*. The bedrock of the unit is the marriage, which also undergoes significant changes during the international assignment.

Changes in the Marriage

- Communication between partners is different. Time for leisurely dinners in the home country is frequently replaced by short snatches of information exchanged between business meetings. Thus, while communication is even more critical than it was at home, it is at a premium because of the scarcity of time.

- Greater dependence on the working partner to meet the social needs of the nonworking spouse. When the expatriate returns home from work, tired from a full day of interaction and decision making, the spouse who has been out of the workplace and away from the usual network of friends and family is often eager to talk and craves recognition. This is especially true at the beginning of the assignment.

- Changing roles, because of the expatriate's travel or busy work schedule, create the need for partners to transform ways they've approached situations in the past. For example, the wife may feel burdened by additional parenting responsibilities, but the husband also has to feel comfortable relinquishing some control over child rearing. This heaps additional stress onto an already volatile situation.

FAMILY CYCLE ISSUES

The work of Virginia Satir, Jay Haley and other noted family theorists and therapists, describe the family as an integrated system.[12] When one part of the system encounters problems, the entire system suffers. Depending on the severity of the problem, the system, like an automobile, may simply malfunction (like a flat tire) or may not function altogether (like a dead battery). In other words, when you send an employee, his or her partner, and children on a foreign assignment, you have multiple, unpredictable variables, all interrelated and affecting each other. An awareness of possible malfunctions allows managers to anticipate and perform preventive maintenance whenever possible.

So far, we've looked at the cultural and personal variables. Now, consider the stage of life.

Families pass through a life cycle just as individuals do. Each phase carries with it distinct characteristics that influence the person's reactions to the world at that time. Although each family is unique (two-parent, single-parent, blended) and progresses through each phase at its own tempo, the framework provides clues about what is happening in a family unit when you're sending them on assignment. Certain stages have less risk than others.[13] That's not to say that managers need to postpone assignments, but that they should be forewarned of the risks so they can take preemptive action.

The Family Life Cycle Stages

1. **Married couples.** People marry, separate from their families of origin, and begin to see themselves as a household: husband and wife.
2. **First children.** The birth of their first child transforms them into mother and father.
3. **Childbearing years.** Families with preschool and school-aged children.
4. **Childbearing years.** Each new baby not only adds another person but forces the family to change.
5. **Families with teens.** Children age 13 to 20.
6. **Families as launching centers.** Families mature and the relationships develop; the parents' relationship may change. As the family gets older, the children begin to move out and start their own families, repeating the cycle.
7. **Middle age.**
8. **Aging family members.** Retirement.

Companies need not postpone international moves, but expatriate managers can use this information as a clue to what a family's level of risk actually is. During each phase, the family has specific characteristics, and each family member has entirely different needs as expatriates.

- *Babies, toddlers, and preschoolers.* Parents are the most important aspect of life to children of this age. Their outside friends and connections are usually insignificant, except in the case of close extended family members and beloved caretakers. Children this age are fairly portable and tend to pose little complication to the relocation. However, child care considerations are important. Without reliable, quality help at the new location, the loss of support will likely weigh heavily on the expat spouse who will

FIGURE 9-3

Family Life Cycle: Stages

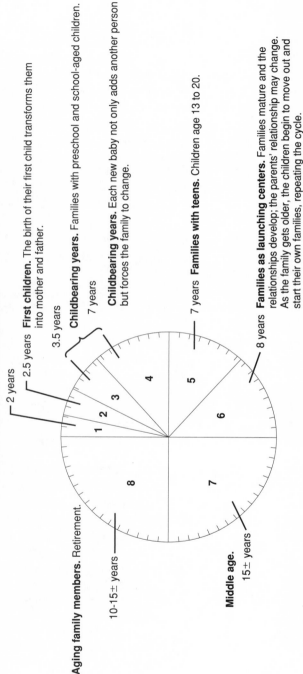

Married couples. People marry, separate from their families of origin, and begin to see themselves as a household: husband and wife.

2 years

2.5 years **First children.** The birth of their first child transforms them into mother and father.

3.5 years

Childbearing years. Families with preschool and school-aged children.

7 years

Childbearing years. Each new baby not only adds another person but forces the family to change.

7 years **Families with teens.** Children age 13 to 20.

8 years **Families as launching centers.** Families mature and the relationships develop; the parents' relationship may change. As the family gets older, the children begin to move out and start their own families, repeating the cycle.

Middle age.

15± years

10-15± years

Aging family members. Retirement.

Source: Adapted from *Marriage and Family Development* [5th ed] by Evelyn Mills Duvall copyright 1957, 1962, 1967, 1971, 1977 by J. B. Lippincott Company. p 15. Based on data from the U.S. Bureau of Census and from the National Center for Health Statistics, Washington, D.C.

The eight stages represented in the chart originate with E.M. Duvall. Notice that half of the couple's life is spent with children; half is spent after the children leave home. Typically, it's during that first half that international assignments occur. Moreover, there is a seven-year span during which the family has teenagers, the most difficult time for children to relocate.

E.M. Duvall, *Marriage and Family Development* (5th edition), 1977, Lippincott. Description of life cycle chart is adapted from Goldenberg, Irene and Herbert Goldenberg, *Family Therapy: an Overview*, 1980, Brooks/Cole Publishing Company, page 15.

become sole caretaker.[14] It's no small problem because the availability of quality caregivers varies widely.

- *School-age children.* Once children enter school, they suffer most
  from the loss of their friends and the predictability of their routine. Children this age are usually unable to anticipate life in the
  abstract and will have trouble visualizing their new life. The
  biggest challenge for parents with these children is, of course,
  schooling. (Parents are best off when children arrive just immediately before school starts.) At this age, children are continuing to
  form their self-image and develop a sense of self-esteem, and the
  friendships and success they realize at school are fundamental to
  their development.[15]

- *Teenagers.* This is the most volatile time developmentally. Most
  adolescents do not want to embark on international assignments
  because they frequently resent leaving friends, even for short vacations.[16] Why is this important? After the spouse's adjustment,
  teenagers pose the greatest risk to undermining an expatriate assignment. If teenagers are unhappy, their behavior can threaten
  family life, which in turn threatens the stability of the employee's
  daily work life. The end result: lower productivity. Helping
  teenagers adjust is a good idea, and can prove highly cost effective. Indeed, such foresight pays dividends later on. That means
  seeking their input for pre-departure decisions and arrangements, cross-cultural counseling, and language training, providing them with names of other teenagers in the destination country or of those who have recently returned, and finding teen peer
  groups and community organizations that might offer social or
  recreational events.[17]

Businesses (like other groups that send international representa-
tives, including the military and foreign service) tend to see the person as
a worker, but not within the context of the family. That's precisely why
global managers need to understand and appreciate the family's experience, the family life cycle, and the challenges that a particular family
faces at a particular time. That's why preparation for the assignment is
critical and why sophisticated relocation services and sustained contact
with an expatriate manager is so important. The end result: the company
saves money because it experiences fewer early repatriations; its employees are more productive more quickly; and there is less stress on the

WAYS TO MAKE THE TRANSITION EASIER

Because the family is crucial to job success, smart companies avert long-term crises by helping families prepare and adapt. Strategies include familiarization trips, pre-departure briefings, language and cross-cultural counseling, settling-in and relocation services, and continued active interest in the expatriates' lives, whether it's through a referral network or consultants who act as a clearinghouse or resource/crisis management service. Other specifics include:

1. Bringing the partner into the selection process. Listen to his or her input and concerns.
2. Providing as much information as possible about the country, community, and company.
3. Offering pre-departure cross-cultural counseling to the entire family.
4. Providing language training and time for language acquisition.
5. Helping the partner and family identify community members who will be possible resources.
6. Considering company policies about the accompanying spouse. How will these policies further the business objectives and help ensure assignment success?
7. Offering professional help with settling into the new location.
8. Providing information about local resources and community networks that employee and family can access.

global HR manager because the family is adapting well and not calling with constant complaints or trouble.

CHILDREN'S ISSUES

Anyone will tell you that unhappy children spell disaster on assignment. At the very least, they can generate a high level of anxiety and stress while creating formidable barriers to adjustment and productivity. At worst, children—especially teens—can become angry and behave badly, thus sending the family packing.

Consider the 1994 caning of Michael Fay in Singapore. The boy, who was attending the Singapore American School, pleaded guilty to spray-painting cars and possessing stolen street signs. He was slapped with a $2,200 fine, sentenced to four months in prison and six strokes with a thick rattan cane. Fay's father was CEO of an automotive supply company in Dayton, Ohio, and the boy was accompanying his mother and stepfather, who was working for a multinational firm in Singapore. Beyond humiliation, the event escalated into an international incident. Obviously, the families were bombarded by the press, had to endure ongoing scrutiny, and were forced to deal with the agony of their son's incarceration in a Singapore jail. Certainly, no company would want to be associated with this scene.

Of course, children don't have to misbehave in such a public way to create a headache. They can be equally destructive in more private settings. One 11-year-old boy in Hong Kong attended a party where his father was entertaining major clients—managing directors of multinational corporations. To everyone's horror, the boy was not only sullen, but openly angry. When the group congratulated each other on the fine job they'd recently completed and what a good attorney the father was, the boy screamed, "You may think he's a good person, but he's not. He's terrible and he's ruining our family." The boy stood upright, frozen, daring anyone to say something in return. Humiliated and furious, the mother whisked the boy out of the room. The effect: a major blow to the credibility of the father and complete embarrassment for the law firm.

Children on assignment don't have a monopoly on bad behavior. Many are simply experiencing the same ups and downs as any kid growing up in his or her native country. Most children adapt well and behave appropriately in public, but the family's highly visible status in the expatriate business community means that a child's actions may reflect more directly upon the company than at home. Surprisingly, although children have a profound impact on the assignment, not much research has been done on expatriate children and teenagers. The research that has been done shows that preparation before the assignment and support during it help children overcome the obstacles they face. The more support children receive, the more likely they are to adjust well. Expatriate children need supportive parents who invest time and effort—parents who are willing to explain the reason for the relocation and provide information about the new country they'll be living in. This cross-cultural counseling is essential to everyone's well-being.

> When children remain overwhelmed and feel burdened by the tasks of adjustment, they often are unhappy and exert pressure on their parents to discontinue the expatriate assignment."[18]

Several factors affect children: their age (as mentioned above), the developmental tasks they're encountering, their school experience, and the country they're moving to.

Clearly the overseas experience has its share of blessings. Children experience these advantages:

- Become more international in their perspective.
- Learn to appreciate diversity.
- Develop bilingual or polylingual skills.
- Realize that their home country isn't the only place in the world.
- Develop mature and polished social skills because they're expected to be more sociable throughout their childhood and make acquaintances with many people.
- Become "third culture kids," developing sensitivity to others and creating a hybrid of cultures.

Schooling

The number one worry—and most immediate consideration—for parents is education. Most companies cover the cost of private school tuition and incidentals at an international or American school or a boarding school. Some also provide for air travel to visit children attending college.

But cost is not the only anxiety. Parents need to consider:

- Academically gifted children.
- Special musical or athletic abilities.
- Learning disabilities.
- Extremely shy and timid youngsters who are concerned about the change in academic environments.
- Extracurricular activities.
- Boarding school options.

■ Preschoolers who are ready for nursery school even though the company doesn't provide for it.

School Placement Agencies

These organizations present an array of options for each child based on need, availability, cost, proximity, and so forth. They evaluate each child as an individual rather than as an afterthought to the relocation. If children are appropriately placed in schools, they're resilient and usually adapt well. They begin their routines and start to make friends. These agencies assess children with special needs and help parents where there may be limited opportunities. In addition, American junior and senior high school students also need the PSAT, SAT, and AP exams. The school placement organizations may help make special arrangements for children to take them or they can advise parents of options.

Global managers can advocate professional help in finding schooling. At the very least, they should be ready to provide reading material on international education. They should know something about the locations in which International schools *aren't* available and boarding school may be a necessity. That could affect the family's decision to take on the assignment.

Child Development

Parents are the most important factor in a child's life. They certainly have the strongest influence. If they feel confident about the relocation and take time to explain it to the kids—and if they spend time with their children after the move and are sensitive to their feelings—youngsters stand a much greater chance of adapting successfully. Children are forced to cope with many developmental issues during their expatriation. If they don't conquer each hurdle as it arises, the entire family can trip and fall.

1. *Potential problem:* Children are less able to anticipate the changes that await them in the new society and may worry about relocation simply because it represents the unknown.
   Solution: Cross-cultural counseling that educates them about the location and encourages them to ask questions about the experience.[19]
2. *Potential problem:* Loneliness, isolation, and a feeling of losing control over their lives. Profound loneliness and insecurity about being tossed into a

completely new situation. Good friends also help children learn to develop intimacy.[20]

Solution: Parents can help youngsters by providing them with concrete information about the experience to come. They can accomplish this by providing data about a youngster's new school and new community. Because school will be the focal point of activities, global managers should suggest that parents make contact with individuals in the school so children can begin a correspondence with kids in the same grade, if possible. Encourage parents to arrive at the location just before the school year begins and avoid dropping in midsemester. Also, it's advisable to avoid moving to a new locale during long school vacations when other children will be traveling.

3. *Potential problem:* Lack of a peer group means greater dependency on parents. One of the important areas of developmental problems arising with mobile children is achieving separation from parents. Because children are so much more dependent on family members as they move into another environment, particularly a country with another language, they often don't make the developmental progress of moving to peers for their social sustenance. Kay Branaman Eakin Ph.D., who relocated families for the U.S. Department of State, suggests that the anxiety level is exacerbated if the relocation takes place when it is normal for the child to move away from dependence on parents. Indeed, it can become a major issue at two crucial times: during early childhood, when preschoolers begin to rely on other adults, and over the teenage years, when asserting and testing independence is the primary developmental step. Moreover, many of these youngsters cannot drive cars at 16, aren't able to get part-time jobs, or engage in volunteer work after school simply because these opportunities aren't available in many countries. All of this can affect a teen's behavior and self-image.

   Solution: Make global managers aware of the risk factors involved in expatriating teens. In addition to involving teenagers in the relocation process, it is helpful for parents to have a list of resources if problems arise.

4. *Potential problem:* Lack of friends in adolescence can be damaging because peers help a youngster develop a sense of independence and self-image. Eleanor Haller-Jorden, managing director of the Paradigm Group in Zurich, Switzerland, notes that teenagers have a much harder time adjusting to international relocation than small children. They are at a critical stage in terms of forming peer group connections, so when they are pulled away from the security of their peers, their sense of identity can suffer.

   Solution: Teen peer groups provide the kind of support expatriate youngsters need. Managers can investigate the possibilities or simply

provide information to parents about the helpfulness of peer group
networks of expatriate children. At that point, parents can ask their
settling-in counselor for specific resources.

5. *Potential problem:* Many children enjoy greater freedom in the assignment
   country because they have easy access to public transportation and the
   assignment location is a much safer environment than the home country.
   Thus, they're able to be more physically mobile. Drinking alcohol is not
   uncommon and a greater availability of drugs and pornography isn't
   unusual. Both parents tend to be busy and often provide less supervision
   than they might in the home country. Although global parenting styles
   differ, adults tend to be more permissive.
   Solution: Global managers can warn parents that child-rearing styles differ
   and offer guidance on how to adapt to that country. They can also provide
   lists of resources and access to information in the destination. Books and
   parenting groups can provide assistance for individuals attempting to raise
   expatriate children.

6. *Problem:* Living in a transient community and always saying goodbye.
   Living in a transient community allows children to make fast friends, but
   kids who live in a community where people come and go must deal with
   loss. They make friendships and then lose them when the children move.
   It's only normal that the sense of loss begins to have a cumulative effect.
   There's a point at which children discover it's painful to lose friends, and
   their natural instinct is self-protection. This can be equally traumatic for
   younger children who invest a lot of emotion in child care providers and
   caretakers.
   Solution: Managers should alert parents to this potential problem and have
   them encourage children to express their hurt and disappointment.
   Moreover, parents should play an active role in helping youngsters
   maintain long-distance friendships. It's not at all uncommon for expatriate
   children to have friends the world over and even visit some of them from
   time to time. Without a sense of continuity, these children may begin to
   crawl into a shell and avoid friendships because they believe it's only going
   to end in pain.

7. *Problem:* Reentry. Practitioners and researchers concur that repatriation
   represents the most difficult phase of the entire process. At this time,
   children confront the changes they have made and how their homeland
   has changed while they were gone. Just as adults face a gamut of reactions
   upon their return—jealousy about the exciting lifestyle, a mild disinterest
   in their stories of adventures, the attitude that they are no longer special—
   so do children. Frequently, when they return to school and talk about their
   life experiences with other kids, they are thought of as arrogant or
   pompous.

But there's also the fact that they are simply out of step. They don't have a clue what the current fashions and popular trends are. This scenario may be uncomfortable for their parents, but children don't have the long-term perspective to understand that the situation will pass, nor do they have the patience to weather it particularly well. Eakin says these children never become single-culture (unicultural) people again. Parents cannot understand this because most of them have passed through their developmental periods in their home environment. But the child endures an enormous period of change, growth and development while he or she is living in another society. Quite simply, the child is a changed person.

Solution: The global manager's role is significant, yet simple. By acknowledging that children are part of the expatriate equation and have their own reactions to the experience, managers can sensitize parents and offer them some primary information and resources. They can encourage parents to read, form affiliations, and communicate with their children. Because the spouse and children have a tremendous influence on the outcome of the assignment, anything that managers can do to help them adjust quickly is a beneficial step.

Sustaining an adequate level of satisfaction throughout the assignment falls primarily to the family members, but global managers can lend a hand by showing a continued interest and making sure that expatriates' families aren't left adrift overseas. The following story relates the experience of Medtronic, Inc., in helping expatriate families adjust.

SEARCH FOR BEST PRACTICES: MEDTRONIC, INC.— Flexible Policies Help Family Adjust

Minneapolis-based Medtronic, Inc. makes heart pacemakers and other therapeutic medical devices. With 10,000 employees and 25 to 30 expatriates—mostly from the United States—the firm generates 44 percent of its revenues overseas.

Company policies recognize the strategic importance of family members. Despite limited numbers of qualified people to send on assignment, it chooses candidates irrespective of their family status. However, the company is well aware that the majority of failed expatriate assignments occur because of family issues. Medtronic's philosophy? By eliminating issues and stress from the lives of expatriates, there's a greater chance that family members will be happy with the assignment. That translates into the entire workforce viewing a foreign assignment as a positive and productive experience.

Built into their policies is the recognition that families face different challenges and situations, depending on where they are in the family life cycle (see Figure 9–3). Global managers are especially aware that teenagers pose a higher risk to the assignment and must be afforded more than just lip service.

The company actively encourages preteens and teenagers to participate in cross-cultural orientation programs with their parents. Medtronic's Flexible Reimbursement Account provides a 50 percent reimbursement—up to $6,000 per year—for miscellaneous expenses related to preschool or day care. That's atop a regular education fund for kindergarten through grade 12. The expense fund can also be used for additional telephone calls home, flying grandparents to see the expatriates, even buying new curtains. The intent: The company recognizes that expatriates have additional needs abroad. But, as beneficiaries of money, expats clearly must share the expense.

Moreover, Medtronic attempts to help dual-career families. In the past, the company worked with the spouse's employer to land a position in the same country. And it attempts to alter the timing of an expat's assignment—speed it up or slow it down—to accommodate the spouse's career. Finally, it helps with work-related legalities, such as acquiring visas and paying union dues.

KEY PROGRAM FEATURES

In addition to the typical goods-and-services differential, shipment of goods, foreign housing, etc., Medtronic offers:

- Flexible Reimbursement Account.
- Pre-departure cultural orientation to expatriate, spouse, and children, if appropriate.
- Automobile (plus special lease rates if a second car is desired for spouse).
- Language training prior to and during the assignment.
- Settling-in services to assist expats in finding their way to the bank, the grocery store, and the other activities of daily life.
- On-the-ground, in-country follow-ups by a third-party provider

(usually the cultural orientation firm) to be sure that the expatriate family is doing well.

The company has set goals to improve responsiveness:

- A comprehensive assessment of cultural adaptability for the entire family before the assignment to identify red flags.
- Establishing closer ties with the expatriates throughout the duration of the assignment; talking with them at specific intervals.
- At the same time, creating a network of global managers at other companies to determine what is state of the art.
- Measuring the effectiveness of current services. For example, how useful are settling-in services, cultural counseling, pre-departure training? Asking families what seemed to be missing.

GLOBAL PROGRAMS ADDRESS EXPATRIATE NEEDS

GLOBAL RELOCATION PARTNERSHIP (GRP)

Expatriates have similar basic needs, no matter where they are deployed. However, they face varying levels of complexity and difficulty addressing those needs in different countries. That people speak English in Hong Kong doesn't mean that the process of finding suitable living arrangements is similar to finding a home in Houston. And finding a pharmacist who speaks English in Seoul, Bangkok, or Jakarta can be a daunting task. However complex these issues are, they pale in significance to the more extreme problems that occur when people are alone in a foreign environment. An expatriate family may not want to consult a company colleague or local business manager concerning chronic depression and alcoholism or the relentless distress of children failing at school or acting delinquent. Instead, the family may suffer in silence because it doesn't want to jeopardize career opportunities by admitting problems to a manager. The reality is that an expatriate family is far more likely to speak with an independent third party.

Today, global networks are forming to meet many of these expatriate and family needs, ranging from finding a home and settling-in support to ongoing access to emergency care and a variety of counseling and support services. For example, the Global Relocation Partnership (GRP) is a network of independent international relocation companies that support these expatriate needs.[21]

Networks like the GRP provide a broad range of services. *Cross-cultural counseling* is country, company, and job specific, and addresses the family's practical needs related to living and working in a new location. *Spouse counseling programs* help the partner formulate plans so that he or she can adapt most effectively to the expatriate assignment. *Destination support programs,* specifically home finding and settling-in services, minimize the distractions and upheaval related to international relocation. *Repatriation programs* can be started in the host country and be continued at home.

PROGRAMS THAT PREPARE EXPATRIATES AND THEIR FAMILIES[22]

If international relocation is going to fully succeed, expatriates need to participate in some form of cross-cultural training prior to departure and require settling-in support on arrival (see Figure 9–4). Pre-departure cross-cultural programs are designed to enhance intercultural understanding and prepare a family to be effective in a new environment. They do this by pairing prospective expatriate families with individuals who have lived and worked in the destination country. Families that participate in such programs develop a reasonable set of expectations and are prepared to get the most out of the intercultural living experience. Cross-cultural programs can take place either in the home country on a pre-departure basis or in the destination country after arrival. Obviously, a family that's involved in these programs prior to departure is able to anticipate and prepare for some of the experiences they'll be facing. They can thus avoid errors and frustrations that will inevitably occur.

Cross-cultural programs do more than teach. They communicate the value of experience and create a dialogue between the expatriate and individuals who have lived in the host country. In this way, individuals can contrast lifestyles and share their own experiences. Moreover, a dialogue with people who have recently returned from living in the host country arms the family with practical knowledge about how to live happily and successfully in a new environment.

Cross-Cultural Preparation

Cross-cultural preparation is highly valued among survey respondents. Of the companies that provide cross-cultural programs, 90 percent rated it as having great or high value. Only 10 percent indicated that it had medium or little value.

Value of Cross-Cultural Preparation

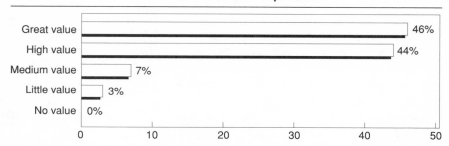

Most companies (62 percent) provide some type of cross-cultural preparation. Thirty-two percent of companies offer programs to all family members, 27 percent to the employee and spouse, and 3 percent to expatriates only. The number of programs for both expatriate and spouse has increased, and the number of programs for "expatriates only" has fallen from 8 percent in 1993 and 4 percent in 1994. This is a positive trend, but a discouraging 38 percent of companies offer no preparation.

Cross-Cultural Preparation Availability

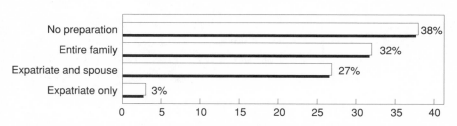

Companies that offer cross-cultural preparation programs make them available to most expatriates, but these programs are underutilized. Only 57 percent of the companies that offer cross-cultural preparation estimate that most of the eligible expatriates participate in them.

Participation in Cross-Cultural Programs by Eligible Employees

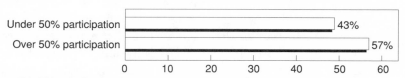

Source: Global Relocation Trends 1995 survey, Windham International and National Foreign Trade Council.

Settling-in programs are most effective when integrated with the cross-cultural preparation. They begin with the family's first home-finding trip and continue through the settling-in support after the family has arrived in the host country.

1. Cross-Cultural Preparation and Counseling

Cross-cultural programs are vitally important for preparing expatriates and their families for their experience in the new country. They also help establish reasonable expectations. The best of these programs are conducted by professionals and are tailored to an individual family, company, and destination. They range in length from one to five days and even longer when integrated with a language program. Cross-cultural programs usually incorporate cultural theory along with a discussion of the differences between the home and destination culture. Transferees have an opportunity to learn about daily living in the host country from individuals who have recently returned from that country.

For example, although learning cultural theory and history is important, it's difficult to contemplate those issues until you're comfortable and confident that you know what homes look like, how to navigate through a food store or to order in a restaurant, and how to use public transportation. An array of other seemingly mundane issues, such as knowing the kinds of clothes the family needs to bring and where you'll get them cleaned, suddenly become critical. Children want to know what they'll watch on television, what kinds of sports are available, whether kids go on dates, and what kind of clothes their peers wear. Even executives receive a boost from talking with a colleague who has held a comparable position in the host country. All are able to glean information and learn from their experiences.

Although generic programs also exist along with excellent videotapes and books—many provide important insights into adjusting to overseas life—they are no substitute for a personalized program. However valuable, they simply cannot address the specific needs of expatriates, nor can they keep up with the daily changes in the destination country. These programs are, by definition, not tailored to the special needs of the family and sometimes they tend to heighten the anxiety that people feel in anticipation of their assignment. Furthermore, the programs do not provide an expatriate with coaching about how to adjust to the cultural realities they will face. Moreover, learning about culture requires a degree of self-reflection—something that allows a person to understand their cultural biases and behavioral predilections. A customized cross-cultural program can accomplish this goal.

Cross-cultural programs can take place in the home country or destination country. Although individual programs for each family are most effective, cross-cultural group workshops are an option when a group of families move from one location to another.

A typical cross-cultural program includes the following components:

1. Learn the basic facts of the assigned country—history, religion, political structure, current events, and more—to make it possible to understand the values and beliefs of that culture. For instance, American perceptions about the importance of the individual are deeply rooted in the nation's historical origins. People came to America from Europe to pursue individual freedom.

2. Evaluate how *your* culture affects *your* perceptions of right and wrong, good and bad, manners, values, dress, and customs. At this point, it becomes clear that you are a cultural being and that affects the window through which you see the world. Appreciating the extent to which culture has affected you is a vital prerequisite to cultural adaptability. For example, is being prompt a universal sign of good manners?

3. Learn about other cultures once you understand how your culture has shaped you and your view of the world. This part of a cross-cultural counseling session focuses on how cultures differ in the home and host country. For example, is it good manners to call neighbors by their first name in Germany, even though it is expected in the United States?

4. Develop a personal cultural profile which indicates your position relative to your national culture. For example, although individuals who come from the same society have the same cultural tendencies, their behaviors are not identical and may fall into a range that fits the national cultural norm. Your place on that range will say a great deal about what you have to do to develop an effective behavior to adapt to the new culture.

Think back to the Orbox Telecommunications story. James Simon and Reuben Jones are both Americans. However, Reuben is much more relationship oriented than James, and James is much more transactional by nature and able to do business without developing personal associations.

5. Modify behavior. Because it's exceptionally difficult for people to change their attitudes, it's easier to learn how to alter behavior to adapt to another culture. This is called "gapping behavior." Gapping is the difference between how the individual would currently handle a situation and what he or she would have to do to be equally effective in a new culture.

6. Apply these lessons to the situations that the expatriate will face at work, at home, and in the community at large. Obviously, a dual-career family will have different concerns than an unmarried businessperson. And working partners will have their own unique concerns that will be addressed by customized cross-cultural programs. Individuals practice situational tactics and examples to be sure they know how to apply the learning.

7. Develop additional program modules for special circumstances: Regional managers, spouses seeking to develop their careers while on assignment, managers who will supervise local nationals or are charged with integrating international teams will need modules specifically augmented to meet those objectives. A cross-cultural program must be tailored to accommodate the concerns of all these constituencies, for whom tailoring a program is vital. With the help of a counselor, everyone can anticipate and develop coping strategies.

FIGURE 9–5

Benefits of Cross-Cultural Counseling

- Enhances success rate for expatriate assignments.
- Assures success of business mission by preparing employees to work effectively with colleagues from a different culture.
- Lowers relocation costs by reducing wasted time, eliminating costly errors, avoiding abuses, and making better use of money already spent.
- Lessens anxiety for employee and family and reduces management distraction.
- Accelerates return to levels of productivity before the move and reduces risk of assignment failure.
- Provides cross-cultural orientation programs and eases family assimilation with "on-the-ground" support system.

FIGURE   9–6

Cross-Cultural Counseling Process

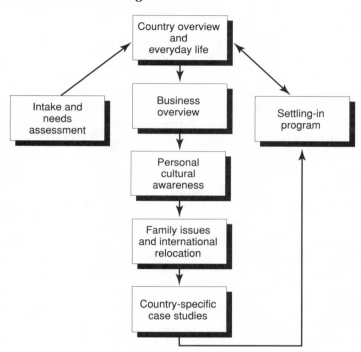

2. Taking That First Look:
The Pre-assignment Home-Finding Visit

Never underestimate the importance of providing home-finding/settling-in support. Think about how unwise it is to expect expatriates and their families to tough-it-out and find their own real estate brokers when they get to the new country. It's unreasonable to expect them to translate housing prices. You must remember that you're sending people to do a job, not test their survival skills or prove how resilient they are to adversity and challenge.

Most companies allow expatriate candidates an initial look-see visit which also serves as a home-finding trip. It is in everyone's best interest that the trip is well planned and highly structured. The old saying that you only get one chance to make a first impression is particularly applicable in this case. Strange places can either be alluring and quaint or downright scary and strange, depending on how well prepared a family is for the initial viewing. There's also no question that the individual who introduces them to the location has a great deal of influence over that impression.

In reality, however, the process begins before the family boards the plane. The first step of any successful program is to conduct a confidential needs assessment interview. During this time, a counselor discusses individual family and spouse issues, schooling, and medical concerns. The counselor also identifies housing needs and arranges for appropriate destination information to be sent to the expatriate, so that the usefulness of the home-finding trip is maximized.

To ensure that the familiarization/home-finding trip is successful, it is important to remove as many obstacles and headaches as possible. That means being met at the hotel by the a host-country counselor; a person who is familiar with the family's situation and has prepared an itinerary responsive to the family's unique needs. This is particularly helpful in reducing the anxiety level of the expatriate family. Knowing that such an introduction has been arranged and that they won't have to fend for themselves in such a challenging environment, paints a positive picture from the start for the family.

During the trip, the counselor will introduce the family to the new community, help select appropriate schools, identify community resources, and select an appropriate neighborhood to conduct a home-finding search. To simplify the home-finding search and take maximum advantage of the time available, the counselor must screen properties beforehand for viewing and eliminate inappropriate ones. The counselors should also provide negotiation assistance and guide the expatriate through the entire leasing procedure. Upon completion of the lease, the counselor typically makes arrangements for utilities, improvements, and deliveries that will need to be completed prior to the family's arrival. In some countries, full rent for a two-year assignment is payable in advance. In countries where there's no phone when you move in, there probably won't be one when you move out two years later. Expatriates need to be aware of the realities and prepare for the eventualities.

3. Settling-In and Ongoing Assistance

Finally, the expatriate family has a place to live and has completed a cross-cultural training program. Now they're faced with the daunting task of building a lifestyle in a new country. They need help and support in establishing this new lifestyle. That's what settling-in support is all about. Expatriates and their families need assistance to adjust to the daily routine of life abroad. The details and frustrations of day-to-day life can be endless: setting up bank accounts, dealing with bureaucracies, learning about healthcare facilities, discovering where to market, understanding the transportation system, and on and on.

In addition to the up-front support a family requires to establish a functional household, it's a comfort—and sometimes a lifesaver—to have access to the counselor's knowledge base of the host country for the duration of the assignment. Some companies build in ongoing sessions every 3, 6, or 12 months as a follow-up routine.

F I G U R E   9–7

Home-Finding and Settling-In Process

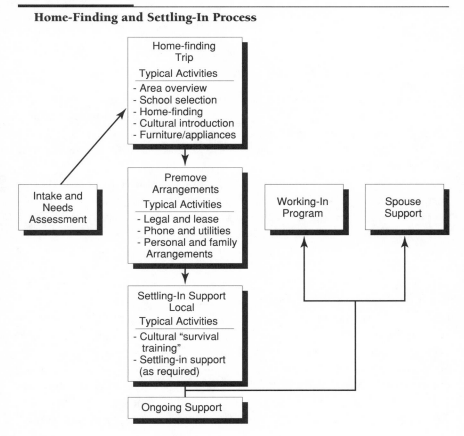

FIGURE 9–8

Settling-in Programs

- Individualized programs tailored to each family.
- Reduces anxiety and provides a positive first impression.
- Area familiarization: community and housing selection.
- School selection and arrangements.
- Cultural "survival training" for employee and spouse.
- Banking and other local arrangements.
- Support with auto purchase, driver's licenses, social security cards, local registration and documentation, utilities, hookups, furnishings, etc.
- Continuing family support for the duration of the assignment: Issues of daily living, healthcare and other recommendations.
- Healthcare.

4. Ongoing Intercultural Training

A few days of pre-departure cross-cultural training will not fully prepare individuals for every business eventuality they're likely to encounter. New challenges occur frequently and require a cultural translation if corporate business objectives are to be met. Ongoing access to intercultural coaching is vital.

Consider that an expatriate on assignment has taken his best shot at communicating to workers in that country how important it is to respond to faxes from the United States. Still, the problem remains, so it is clear that the problem may be something other than people's ability to understand the manager's words. The misunderstanding may arise from a different set of cultural priorities.

Likewise, resistance to reorganizing the work flow may be motivated by something other than stubbornness on the part of host-country employees. Or the at-home spouse may be having difficulty keeping household help or finding local service people who will finish the work they've begun. These kinds of challenges could be best addressed with access to ongoing intercultural training—formal or informal. While other expatriates provide many hints, too often their comments simply reinforce cultural stereotypes or increase the odds that an expatriate will adopt someone else's poor advice. That, of course, can spawn a legacy of errors and mistakes that are passed on from one generation of expatriates to another.

Formal, ongoing programs have the benefit of being professionally structured so they're efficient and meet specific expatriate issues instead of being haphazard, anecdotal information that may or may not work. Group workshops or individual sessions typically include:

- Business etiquette, office culture, and the practical aspects of interacting successfully in the new workplace.
- Managing a negotiation.
- Local laws and company policy.
- Managing in the new cultural environment.
- Introducing change in the host country.
- Coaching on specific management challenges.

FIGURE   9–9

Working-In Program Process

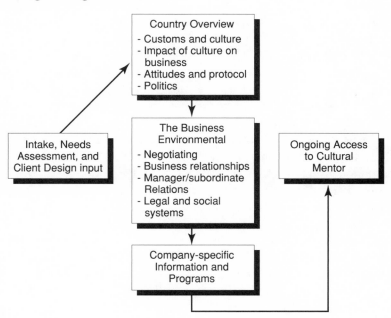

5. Ongoing Support

Formal employee assistance programs (EAPs) available in the United States are difficult to find internationally. While it's easy to recognize how important and valuable such programs can be, alternative support services must be identified.

Even after expatriates have settled into the new community, it's likely they will need a lawyer, a medical specialist, or a counselor. A child may be having trouble in school, might need special educational help, or have medical difficulties arise.

Companies need to make arrangements to ensure that these types of ongoing services are available to their assignees in the host country. Unfortunately, employees often fail to turn to their corporate HR managers or peers for this type of help because they may believe their difficulties are too private to involve the company. Therefore, it's important to offer the resources of professional service providers who are reliable before the need arises.

6. Repatriation Support

Repatriation is a far more complex subject than merely arranging for the physical return of the expatriate family. Capitalizing on the skill and experience of repatriating employees is an enormous challenge, one that any global company faces. The defection rate among repatriating employees is growing and it is an increasingly disturbing problem for global managers and their companies. The successful reintegration of employees returning from expatriate assignments is crucial because potential expatriates weigh such factors when they initially consider the career impact of an assignment and whether to take the assignment in the first place.

Indeed, overall career planning serves as the basis for any effective repatriation program (see Figure 9–9). Ideally, an individual will find a position waiting upon return, one that will build upon that individual's international experience. Such programs also must take into account that the return home is often more difficult than the expatriation for the individual family members. A family embarks on a foreign assignment fully expecting an adjustment, but no amount of preparation prepares them for the shock of reentry where nothing looks the same, nothing feels the same, the familiar is somehow strange, and good friends are no longer interested in the things that seem important to the expatriate family.

Therefore, an effective program begins with counseling for families several months before they return. This activity helps them prepare mentally for the challenges of reentry. It continues with appropriate levels of home-finding and settling-in support back home along with additional counseling to help the family adapt. Not only are such programs important for the repatriated employee, but also they make good business sense for the company. If one of the primary challenges facing a global corporation is finding suitable talent—cited by 74 percent of organizations in a 1995 survey[23]—then keeping repatriated employees positive about the international experience and communicating that to others employees is a vital step toward a solution.

F I G U R E   9–9

Career Planning

Almost half (48 percent) of companies conduct some formal career planning with expatriates prior to the assignment. Regrettably, 44 percent of companies do not formally address career planning with expatriates.

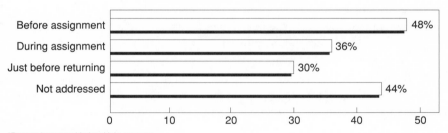

How Career Planning Is Addressed*

*Respondents provided multiple answers.

HOW MANAGERS CAN HELP THE FAMILY

- Keep in mind that an overseas assignment creates a special situation between the company on the one hand and the spouse and family on the other. Managing that relationship successfully requires patience and an appreciation of the expatriate experience as well as the objectives of the corporation and how the employee fits into those goals.

- Review your policies. Do they give the family a chance for success? Does the policy allow for experts to educate outgoing individuals in culture and language? Does it provide for assistance when the family reaches the destination and throughout the assignment? Evaluate the repatriation program in the context of the family's reentry.

- Make family members aware of who is available to answer questions. Identify the specific people for questions about compensation, relocation, and psychology. If your company doesn't use an educational consultant, at least be able to provide educational information.

- Encourage families to spend time on pre-transfer preparation of their children. When parents select the international school, suggest they take videos and photographs, and obtain school literature. Load the children with information.

- Try to connect families who have been in the location with new ones relocating. If kids can talk with others who have been there, they can ask questions like, "What do the kids wear?" "Do they have a prom, a debate team, a football team?" Don't underestimate the value of these simple connections.

- Involve youngsters in the planning phase. This will prove even more helpful for older children who may resent leaving home in the first place. Cross-cultural counseling for children pays big dividends.

- Consider an employee assistance program, either internationally or by phone.

- Have your antennae working. Understand that some depression and griping is normal in the adaptation process, but be sure it doesn't go on too long. Sometimes excessive demands for the company to cover expenses is a way of covering up resentment. On the other hand, a person who says that everything is perfect is waving a red flag.

- Teen peer group networks of expatriate children are a tremendous resource of information and insights. See if the third-party settling-in service can help with obtaining information about those types of community services.

- Provide a suggested reading list for parents. For example, alert them to the fact that their children may form strong attachments to caregivers in the destination country. Those housekeepers, nannies, and child care providers should be chosen as carefully as they would be in the home country.

- Make sure that community networks are available if a family has trouble. Suggest these resources at the outset before any problems arise.

- Children need to identify with their own cultural and national identity. Suggest that parents subscribe to many U.S. (or home country) magazines that keep the family up to date on popular culture. Suggest they find a way to have friends send videos of popular television programs or radio shows.

HELP YOUR EXPATRIATES:
Six Keys to Managing Their Career

1. Don't rely on the company to do it.
2. Identify a mentor before leaving on assignment.
3. Stay current with what's going on in the company.
4. Keep skills up to date.
5. Make people in the home office aware of what you're accomplishing in the field.
6. Visit the home office as frequently as possible.

NOTES

1. Parts of this chapter are adapted from *Personnel Journal*, March, 1995, "CEO Mom: The Tie that Binds a Global Family," by Charlene Marmer Solomon.

2. Global Relocation Trends 1995 Survey by Windham International and NFTC; Michael G. Harvey, "The Executive Family: An Overlooked Variable in International Assignments," *Columbia Journal of World Business*, Spring 1985, pp. 84–92; Michael S. Schell, and Marian Stoltz-Loike, "Importance of Cultural Preparation to International Business Success," *Journal of International Compensation & Benefits* 2, no. 4 (Jan./Feb. 1994), pp 47–52.

3. Michael Harvey, "The Executive Family: An Overlooked Variable in International Assignments." *Columbia Journal of World Business*, Spring 1985, pp. 84–91.

4. Figures from Rick Swaak, based on discussions with the U.S. Department of State; Windham International and the National Trade Council, Global Relocation Trends 1995 Survey; Bureau of Labor Statistics.

5. Mildred M. McCoy. "The Successful Expatriate Family," *Euro-Asia Business Review* 5, no. 2 (Apr. 1986), pp 5–10; and Harvey, "The Executive Family," pp 84–92.

6. McCoy, pp, 5–10.

7. Reyer A. Swaak, "Expatriate Failures: Too Many, Too Much Cost, Too Little Planning." *Compensation & Benefits Review*, Nov.–Dec. 1995, pp. 47–55.

8. From Lennie Copeland and Lewis Griggs, *Going International: How to Make Friends and Deal Effectively in the Global Marketplace* (New York: Random House, 1985).

9. Ibid.

10. J. Stewart Black, Hal B. Gregersen, and Mark E. Mendenhall. *Global Assignments: Successfully Expatriating and Repatriating International Managers* (San Francisco: Jossey-Bass, 1992), p. 48.

11. For a fuller discussion of these theories, see Marian Stoltz-Loike, *Dual Career Couples: New Perspectives in Counseling*, American Association for Counseling and Development, 1992).

12. Ibid.

13. Irene Goldenberg and Herbert Goldenberg, *Family Therapy: an Overview*, (Brooks/Cole 1980), pp. 13–27.

14. Karen Curnow, McCluskey, *Notes form a Traveling Childhood: Readings for Internationally Mobile Parents and Children*, Foreign Service Youth Foundation, 1994, pp. 14–16.

15. Ibid.

16. Ibid.

17. Charlene Marmer Solomon, "Work/Family's Failing Grade: Why Today's Initiatives Aren't Enough," *Personnel Journal*, May 1994, pp. 72–87.

18. Corinna T. de Leon and Diana McPartlin, "Adjustment of Expatriate Children," in *Expatriate Management: New Ideas for International Business*, Jan Selmer, ed. (Quorum Books, 1995), pp. 197–214.

19. Ibid., p. 201.

20. Ibid., p. 202.

21. The Global Relocation Partnership is a network of companies in 60 countries that provide destination support for expatriates and their families.

22. Parts of this section were adapted from Michael S. Schell and Marian Stoltz-Loike. "Importance of Cultural Preparation to International Business Success," *Journal of International Compensation & Benefits* 2, no. 4 (Jan.–Feb. 1994), pp. 47–52.

23. Global Relocation Trends 1995 Survey.

CHAPTER

10

⑥ **MANAGING EXPATRIATE PARTNERS AND THE DUAL-CAREER DILEMMA:**

The Pivotal Role of the Spouse and Partner[1]

This chapter will cover

- Challenges that spouses and partners encounter.
- Conflicts that dual-career partners face.
- Recommendations to assist spouses and partners.
- Case histories of programs that work.

To the outside observer, even to friends and acquaintances, Carol Lynne[2] looked fine. But she remembers the day problems began: a small luncheon with six other expat wives. As they sat around the table, introducing themselves, every woman gave her name, then her husband's title, then the company. Nothing else.

This was not Carol Lynne's way of doing things. A financial analyst herself who worked 60-hour weeks, she'd left a thriving career in New York when her husband was offered an international opportunity in Tokyo. Although she wanted to continue working, she quickly discovered the legalities of acquiring a new job internationally were almost insurmountable.

After helping her family settle into school and work, establishing the household, and getting into the rhythm of the new city, Carol Lynne realized she needed something more to occupy her time. At first she was happy to explore and meet other expat wives. But as the days went by, she began to feel the eroding of her identity; her self-image was so connected

213

with her work (which no one seemed to care about) that she didn't quite feel herself. Her self-esteem began to suffer and she found herself becoming less confident and a little angry. First, the introduction at the luncheon, then cocktail parties in which people talked about work and paid only passing interest to her ideas, then an encounter with a colleague of her husband who said all she needed was a "good cry." She started to go back to bed in the morning after she'd send the kids off to school. She began complaining to her husband that they hadn't received the same generous benefits package some of his colleagues had.

And then her friend from New York came to visit. Brimming with news of the office goings-on and delivering gossip about chums, her friend told Carol Lynne that she had received a well-deserved promotion. Filled with envy and sorrow at what she had left behind, Carol Lynne became increasingly annoyed with her situation. Why should all the focus be on Jack's career? On his work? Why was he the only one with a paycheck? She knew she could always have her old job back at home, and she began to feel like she was wasting time and wasting away while Jack (and her friends at home) were in high gear. She began to harangue Jack about returning early to the States.

One morning, when she found it particularly hard to face the day, Carol Lynne called home and spoke to her sister who encouraged her. She decided to take the kids at school break and go home. She would talk to Jack that evening but, ultimately, he would just have to fend for himself. She began to plan how to go about packing up the household she'd just established.

Carol Lynne isn't unique. Her tale is repeated in various guises by expatriate spouses around the world. She may be a stockbroker who, while able to trade on a foreign exchange, is prevented from doing so because she cannot obtain a work permit. Maybe she's an architect who cannot work because local customs prohibit women from working. Maybe she doesn't leave a career, but an active social life and a network of community activities. Increasingly, *she* is a *he*—as the number of male "trailing spouses" increases each year.

No matter what the reason or the gender, after the scramble to help their family settle in settles down, spouses confront an emptiness based on their own lack of routine, lack of network, and lack of a job. They must create a new life, often with a frequently absent partner and regularly without the prospect of employment for themselves. They face isolation, loss of identity, and diminished self-esteem. This occurs not only because they've relinquished their career (or at least paid employment), but also because they encounter stress every day in the new environment—stress that makes them question whether they can do anything competently anymore.

The dilemma of expatriate partners, particularly dual-career spouses, is a difficult one for global business, which is in large part dependent on the mobility of its managers. Furthermore, this problem isn't going away anytime soon. Statistics indicate that the problem is growing. The Bureau of Labor Statistics (BLS) points out that in 1995, over 65 percent of all married couples with children were dual-earner families, up 9 percent in 10 years.[3] Currently, women comprise 46 percent of the U.S. labor force. The number of married women in the workforce rose from 51 percent in 1981 to over 58 percent in 1991, and by the year 2000, the Department of Labor predicts that 80 percent of all marriages will be dual career.[4]

While the BLS points to population trends in general, the impact of dual-career and other spouse concerns on international deployment is reinforced by The Relocation Trends 1995 survey which indicates that spouse career concerns are the most common reason (48 percent) for turning down assignments.[5] Whether that statistic accurately represents reality or that employees are playing the "spouse card" to mask other concerns about the assignment, it is reinforced by experience.

As noted authority Reyer (Rick) A. Swaak puts it:

> In our haste to restructure or reengineer our organizations and to shed head count, we have paid little attention to the forecasting of our critical key management needs and the identification of talent with specific emphasis on required competencies. We have squandered talent who could have been utilized to fill *high-impact* positions overseas. Very few companies anticipated the emergence of new opportunities in faraway places and the need for special individuals with unique combinations of skills, knowhow and behavioral characteristics to make things happen around the globe.
>
> Without a well-defined program, which should be aligned with the business plan, the decision to use or not to use the best talent may be influenced by such factors as expediency, urgency, and other crisis-oriented considerations. If that talent turns down the offer to move to an overseas destination for dual-career or family reasons, often the second-or third-choice candidate gets the assignment, not the best candidate.
>
> Expatriates are now treated as cost-sensitive investments—that is, their cost of compensation must not exceed their economic value to the corporation. For that reason, companies are compelled to select only the very

best from a relatively small pool of available talent. In the meantime, with the increased emphasis on judicious and purposeful selection of the *right* candidates, companies are now also responding to the needs and requirements of the contemporary family, which more often than not consists of two working professionals. We can no longer ignore the very special wants and wishes of the family.[6]

Furthermore, the challenge not only rears its head during selection of candidates (when many turn down assignments because of the spouse's career), but it also affects the success of the assignment and, later, the ability of spouses and families to successfully repatriate. Global managers will tell you that the partner or spouse's career is becoming an increasing impediment to overseas relocations. The problem is more far reaching than the mind-set of the partner. There are other important concerns, such as potential loss of necessary income to cover existing expenses and replicate lifestyle, and the impact on the partner's career resulting from an absence from the workforce for a few years. These are becoming such important issues that some organizations are beginning to consider redefining the length of assignments so they're much shorter (and thus, less disruptive). Some are even willing to consider the alternative of international commuter marriages.

An increasing number of expatriates are women. Not only are their numbers in upper management growing, which leads to the inevitable opportunity for international assignment, but several theories are being put forward which indicate that women are better suited to be expatriates than men.[7] Women—because of societal expectations—tend to be more relationship focused, more group oriented, and therefore they more nearly mirror the rest of the world culturally. Whether you accept the reality of the increased numbers indicated in surveys or the assumptions about the preference of women as expats, the inevitable result is that more accompanying partners will be men. By virtue of their socialization in Western societies, men will be less tolerant of the passive role of the trailing spouse in an expatriate assignment. As this occurs with greater frequency, dual-career issues are likely to become increasingly complex.

Irrefutably, this is a growing issue which has no easy answers. But if expatriation continues to play the important role in global business that it does today, it is one for which we will have to find effective resolutions.

THE EXPATRIATE SPOUSE: BEGINNING EXPERIENCES

Pamela Drobnyk, executive director of FOCUS Information Services shares her experience:

When people enter a new environment, coming to grips with the loss of the familiar is the first crisis they face. They realize that everything is changed. All their support system is gone, and they simply can't find anything that looks familiar. This even happens in the U.K.

I remember when I first arrived here in London 13 years ago. I walked into a delicatessen and didn't know what to order. Even the bread looked different. You ask yourself, What's the difference? But how was I to know that they called the buns *baps,* and if you don't know what a *bap* is, you're in trouble.

Once I mustered up the courage, I ordered a ham and cheese with lettuce and tomato and the guy shouted at me, "Why can't you just say salad like you're supposed to?"

The first time I wrote a U.K. check, I couldn't figure out where to write the amount. How embarrassing! And the woman behind the counter couldn't believe that I'd made such a silly mistake. I felt I couldn't do anything right; I couldn't even order a sandwich right anymore. This loss of control of even the most mundane of tasks can make you feel so helpless. And even the simplest tasks take three and four times longer than they took before.

You suddenly feel like a child who's completely lost and helpless, you're in a place that is new, and you're trailing along with your spouse (agreeing that you'll give up your profession for a period of time) and you start to question who you are.

Then, there's the isolation. The phone never rings. Everyone you meet becomes potential new friends. It's an odd feeling to be weighing up everyone you meet. Gone are the days when you thought you had too many friends and wouldn't go out of your way to meet someone new because of your overcommitted life. There is no one to ask even the simplest of questions—you're all on your own!

One day my old pals from home phoned. They were having lunch together and they got on extension phones all over the house. They wanted to know all about my new life and the adventures I was having. I explained to them I hadn't been to Paris yet because I was still trying to cope with the clothes dryer from hell. They said with disappointment that I was obviously focusing on the wrong things.

It's then that you realize that you've even lost the support system from home because they don't understand you anymore.

If taken in human resource terms, the spouse or partner is in charge of the relocation and, because he or she plays such a pivotal role, needs to be involved in the entire process. Issues such as compensation, allowances, training, education, communication with the community, even wellness and EAP (when necessary) generally are in the spouse's domain for implementation. Moreover, spouses are the ones who interface with the new community and confront cultural differences immediately—and often. At the same time the expatriate employee has to learn the job and handle enormous pressure, the spouse has to manage the family organization and build a cohesive, well-functioning team of spouse and children, and has scant support while doing so. Moreover, the spouse or partner often functions solo because of the employee's travel and intense work schedule. There's no disputing that expatriates in many parts of the world carry a much heavier work burden due to the absence of support staff and increased job responsibility and scope.

Much has been made of the spouse's adjustment because he or she is either leaving a job or a community where the spouse's role is fairly well defined and comes to a new location where the task is to create a new community, build a new social network, and support the expatriate employee in work and children in their endeavors.[8] If the spouse can make the adjustment, the family will regain its equilibrium and be happy and thrive; if he or she enters a crisis phase and can't emerge from it, the whole relocation is likely to implode.

OBSTACLES PARTNERS ENCOUNTER

Consequently, if global managers want to help the "Carol Lynnes" (and the assignments they're on), they need to design practices to help them find meaningful ways to spend their time during international assignments. As daunting as the challenge may seem, companies and global managers know it's critical to tackle these issues. In some cases, this may mean helping partners find employment or navigating through a maze of foreign immigration technicalities; in other cases, it means helping them contact organizations to find out about volunteer work and educational opportunities; in still others, it means simply connecting spouses with a worthwhile network of peers. No easy task with no one-size-fits-all solutions. Nevertheless, global managers must face this problem, head-on, and attempt to tackle some of these myriad issues with innovative approaches.

What are some of the obstacles spouses or partners encounter in their quest to find meaningful work, paid or unpaid?

- *Immigration regulations that bar foreigners from working.* The complexity of obtaining work permits varies from country to country. With very few exceptions, such as the United Kingdom where spouse work permits are tied to the employee's, it is never easy. Exacerbating this already difficult situation is significant unemployment in Europe and parts of Asia as well as resistance to immigration in the United States and other parts of the world.

- *Language.* Even though English is considered the global language of business, it is not the national language of the entire world. Moreover, while there might be opportunities for people with English language skills in the direct business activity, the inability to communicate with co-workers and the local population results in a significant barrier to success even if a work permit can be obtained.

- *Lack of transferable skills to meaningful available work.* Nowhere is this more visible than finding people with medical degrees acting as laboratory assistants in countries where those degrees are not recognized.

- *Scarcity of volunteer opportunities.* Volunteerism is not a global phenomenon. Many countries lack an infrastructure that can accept well-intentioned volunteers.

- *Cultural barriers that don't allow women to perform certain jobs.* This is particularly true in Muslim states where women have little access to life outside of the compound.

- *Lack of knowledge about educational opportunities.* Some locations have few opportunities to further education except through correspondence courses which, while addressing the educational need, don't provide access to personal interaction.

- *Management resistance.* Managers in many countries are reluctant to help expatriates master certain necessary skills because of the limited duration of the assignment. Although partners may have the general job skills, they need some degree of education to master specific skills for the specific job, but they cannot find businesses willing to invest the time to train them.

SOLUTIONS TO THE DUAL-CAREER DILEMMA

The spouse and dual-career dilemma may be a difficult one, but it is not impossible to solve. Large and small companies are trying to help spouses or partners in many ways: helping them identify transferable skills that will assist in their adaptation in the destination, encouraging career development discussions before relocation, telling them about volunteer and educational opportunities that will further their careers, counseling them about possibilities such as taking a leave of absence and returning to the job for specified periods of time during the assignment, providing long-term career counseling and development support, providing names of local spouse centers and counseling facilities, and exploring collaborations with other global firms for job possibilities.

To be sure, it is not simple. Indeed, it may be one of the thorniest aspects of expatriation. People don't think solutions exist, but they do. However, the problems don't lend themselves to crisp, hard solutions that can be easily solved with money or policy changes. The solutions often look different from traditional problem-solving situations managers encounter. The situation requires an arsenal of other alternatives and creative approaches. The needs of the accompanying spouse must be adequately addressed or there may be no assignment at all. Even though it may seem as if the problem remains largely untouched, some companies in the United States and Europe are employing a wide range of alternatives to address this problem. Shell International and Hewlett-Packard Company (as well as Medtronic Inc. and Monsanto Company) take a two-pronged approach. First, they help the spouse overcome cultural and emotional hurdles and the loneliness of a new location by offering cross-cultural counseling and connecting them with a network of spouses in the host community; second, they offer a variety of options to begin to address the dual-career dilemma.

Eleanor Haller-Jorden, Ph.D., managing director of Zurich-based Paradigm Group, is an authority and frequent lecturer on this topic. An expatriate herself, Haller-Jorden says companies can provide a variety of simple services that address the problem directly. For example, they can consolidate data, creating a clearinghouse of information and resources, or set up a conference room and phone line for spouses or a small room to serve as a resource library with materials on the local community. They also can create a directory of expatriates, especially those who would be willing to speak with newly arrived expatriates. Firms that want to become more actively involved can create a job hotline in which project-based jobs are available or they can create a consortium of companies and pool resources in a specific location or within an industry and create a job bank. Moreover, they can always help with acquiring work permits and offering career counseling. Finally, companies should take stock of what they're currently offering and get feedback from expatriates. It is crucial to find out what is useful and what is not.

Whether male or female, individuals who leave careers to accompany their spouses or partners on international assignment face many of the same difficulties. Let's examine a few of them.

1. *Potential problem.* Whether the partner accepts the assignment.
Solution. Include the spouse from the very beginning in all preassignment interviews and meetings, and all discussions about compensation and benefits. The spouse is likely to be the person in charge of implementing the move and overseeing financial arrangements prior to and during the relocation. These discussions should be in depth and the HR counselor is well advised to take time to answer all questions and salve most concerns.

2. *Potential problem.* Loss of support group. This is a considerable problem for any accompanying partner. Simply put, the partner does not have a ready-made community as does the employed expatriate.
Solution. Caution: Don't underestimate the critical importance of helping the partner reestablish a community. As soon as possible, provide the family with the names of contacts in the host location. Community networks, women's clubs, expatriate groups (such as FOCUS), religious organizations, and educational facilities are extraordinarily helpful. If expatriates are heading for locations with few other international assignees, consider contacting settling-in services or relocation firms in the host country (such as the Global Relocation Partnership) for assistance. Consider repatriated employees as resources for pre-departure preparation.

3. *Potential problem.* Loss of self-esteem. This difficulty stems from both the change in the cultural environment, which makes even the most mundane activity a challenge, and the lack of support system. A supportive community helps to buffer the feelings of ineptness that occur in a new environment. Therefore, preparation for the shock of transition as well as addressing and ameliorating the cause, help tremendously.
Solution. Cross-cultural orientation is a good first step. This introduces the expatriate family to the new culture and, equally important, prepares them for the inevitable adventure of culture shock. A good cross-cultural training experience also will help individuals defend against the natural inclination toward ethnocentricity and isolation during the adaptation period.

The second step is to propose possibilities to the partner that will address the issue of isolation: community networks, educational opportunities, personal fulfillment (e.g., hobbies and other growth activities), and volunteer possibilities. Because the acceptance of volunteer activities vary from country to country, the global manager must be prepared to suggest possibilities. Not surprisingly, one of the most important ways to address this issue is for the company to openly—and repeatedly— recognize the contribution of the spouse or partner to the success of the expatriate assignment. This costs little and requires only that businesses find ways to communicate this fact to the expatriate, the family, and the employee population.

4. *Potential problem.* Interruption of career track.

Solution. Given the right set of circumstances, this specified period of time in a lifetime career can be turned into an opportunity for additional education and career enhancement. For this to happen, the company must offer certain alternatives, and the global manager who meets with the potential expatriate and partner must frame the experience in that way. It is important to begin with long-term career counseling and educational advice. Counselors can help expatriate partners identify transferable skills and look at an array of possibilities such as starting their own business, enhancing portable careers, and identifying additional educational requirements such as learning a foreign language, that might help with future employment. Some companies have established career development and learning centers that serve as a clearinghouse for information on local employment and other international career-related opportunities. Companies also can assist with reimbursement for educational and travel expenses to attend career-related conferences outside the host location.

5. *Potential problem.* Loss of income. This income may be crucial to the family's well-being. It may be necessary for mortgage payments or for the support of other family members such as college-age children or elderly parents.

Solution. Many organizations realize this is an important long-term consideration to a family. It is best not to attempt to avoid the issue but to discuss it in a straightforward manner and to attempt to find solutions. Some companies provide a percentage of the lost income during the first year; others provide lump sum payments annually—not as income replacement— for career or personal growth and enhancement. Others provide additional allowances to cover home-country obligations such as housing, which may have been based on two-incomes. In addition to serving as recognition of the spouse's efforts and sacrifices, the logic behind this financial arrangement is that this is an investment in future opportunities.

6. *Potential problem.* Finding employment for spouse or partner.

Solution. In some destinations, it is possible for the spouse to attain employment. In these cases, the company may provide help with culturally appropriate résumé preparation and providing avenues to help with the job search. Companies regularly provide assistance with visa and work permits.

Furthermore, some organizations will actively seek employment opportunities within their company through intercompany career networking or create a network with other companies whereby they exchange employees as needed. Financial reimbursement also can be in the form of payment for employment agency fees and association dues.

The lack of an organized global job bank is a major drawback. Initial efforts by some global organizations as well as a few multinational corporations are beginning to be underway to create international job pools. Companies also can help spouses find local jobs by enlisting the support of host-country HR departments.

SEARCH FOR BEST PRACTICES: SHELL OIL INTERNATIONALE—Spousal Network

Shell Internationale, the giant oil and petroleum multinational headquartered in both The Hague and London, clearly appreciates that societal trends affect international assignments. A few years ago, Shell believed there were several factors that might block international mobility, and it wanted to quantify those factors that encouraged and deterred mobility. With about 16,000 expatriates, Shell may have more expatriates than any company in the world. Consequently, in 1993 it embarked upon the largest single survey (called the Shell Outlook Survey) ever conducted of expatriates and their partners. The survey was commissioned and sponsored jointly by the Exploration and Production Business and the Corporate Human Resources Group. Sent to 17,000 individuals, the response rate was a whopping 70 percent, indicating how important the issues were to the expatriates.

The Findings

The company discovered several impediments to mobility of employees. The two major ones were: (1) the reluctance by partners to move, primarily because more women have their own careers. Respondents stated that Shell could accommodate the needs of working partners more than it was currently doing and also demonstrate greater understanding of their problems. Spouses also said they felt they weren't being utilized enough and that their expertise was not valued. (2) The next most important concern stated by participants was their children's education. Traditionally, many of

Shell's expatriate children attend boarding school for secondary education because many schools in the typical destinations are inadequate to meet these needs. However, in the mid-1990s, fewer parents than before feel comfortable with the boarding school option.

On the positive side, expatriates believe that these assignments definitely enhance their professional and personal growth. Most view it as an advantage for promotion.

The Actions

Quickly, Shell took action. First, Shell notified the participants about the status of the project. Even before the company had time to complete all of the analysis, it published a booklet with a summary of results and findings. Then, Shell moved ahead onto the next steps. It established six task forces led by line managers with strong representation from staff and spouses, in the following areas: Children's education, spouse or partner careers, recognition and involvement of partners, staff planning and consultation, relocation information and assistance, and health. The policy developed was essentially twofold: a combination of providing direct advice, advice and information through a sort of network, or access to both internal and external networks of information. The second part was financial support. The combination of advice and money put Shell among the leaders.

- *Spouse Employment and Spouse Recognition.* When all the main operating companies supported the findings and conclusions, they decided to put into place several services that demonstrated the company's acknowledgment of the partner's contribution. They added services to address their needs as individuals with careers.

  How did they do it? First, they created the position of Spouse Employment Consultant (SEC), who advises spouses and partners on a broad range of employment issues (paid and nonpaid work). The SEC's aim is to help spouses improve the chance of finding career opportunities and to aid in their career development. For example, a partner may come to the Spouse Employment Consultant because he or she has only a vague idea of what is available in a destination country, or the person may have a very defined career path in mind and speak with the SEC about ways to promote that career. First, spouses receive a thorough assessment that ultimately will lead to career planning. Then the SEC helps spouses to locate employment, aids in acquiring a work permit (when paid employment is possible), and helps them find appropriate educational and volunteer activities that interest the person and helps him or her keep on track when paid employment is impossible. The process can be very difficult because many expatriates who work for Shell International move from one international location to another; thus, one area may be conducive to paid employment whereas the next destination may not. Shell also has a financial assistance policy that covers many of the costs linked to transferring employment skills, such as job search programs, translation and evaluation of diplomas, preparation of curricula vitae or résumés, fees for maintaining professional accreditation if the partner is unable to work in his or her professional capability, other forms of education, intensive language tuition, and specific fees to cover some of the costs of starting a new business.

In addition to employment, Shell recognized the enormous contribution expatriate partners could make to the company. As a result, it created a network of information centers for expatriation around the world, called the Spousal Network, which exists for the entire expatriate family, is staffed by spouses and partners, and offers information on culture, spouse employment, living and traveling in the country, and other issues of concern to expats. The model is in The Hague Center, which has a paid staff of expatriate spouses and volunteers. Each center serves a different community; thus, somewhat different activities are offered around the world. But each Spousal Network is generated and directed by the interest of local expatriate spouses.

- *Children's Education.* After addressing spousal and partner needs, Shell addressed family separation, a serious concern of both employees and their partners. The survey discovered that the greatest facilitator of mobility is the availability of adequate secondary schooling in the host country, which enables a family to live together. To answer this concern, Shell is adding schools in several locations. The company also is strengthening the International Baccalaureate system. All of these options not only help the family remain together, but facilitate solutions to some of the difficulties faced by repatriated children when returning to their home school.

- *Staff Planning.* The task force looked at improving communication between employees, line managers, and HR. One outgrowth will be to talk directly to each expatriate family and attempt to match personal and family needs with those of the business. In other words, Shell is beginning to opt for more unaccompanied assignments, what they call *grass widowers.* Consequently, while the traditional Shell philosophy—keep the family together and, if not, keep the couple together—is still the norm, exceptions will be made if the family and manager believe it is in the best interests of both. This will sometimes occur when secondary education or the partner's career make relocating a hardship. If this alternative is chosen, counseling and additional support need to be arranged, and other types of expenses (e.g., increased travel allowance) are often necessary. The company believes, however, that the mobility and the cost savings of not having to relocate the family are in its ultimate favor. Furthermore, it will place greater emphasis on recruiting and developing an international cadre of staff who will be willing to expatriate. The company is also developing a selection instrument that will help in recruiting.

- *Preparation for Expatriation and Relocation.* Country-specific orientation will be increased in volume and content. The major change in this arena will be from the "Information Centres" and their networks, which will provide help and information after settling into the destination.
- *Health and Medical.* Although these issues do not affect mobility decisions, employees will receive greater communication about medical issues that affect them on assignment. Furthermore, the company will continue to ensure that a high quality of service is maintained worldwide for expats.

SEARCH FOR BEST PRACTICES: HEWLETT-PACKARD COMPANY—Recognizing Dual Careers

Hewlett-Packard counsels and supports spouses before they leave their home country. Hewlett-Packard's (HP) corporate culture is one in which individuals like to take ownership of their own lives and careers. Employees want the company to provide an environment where they can do that. Hewlett-Packard policies attempt to make people as self-reliant as possible and to allow them to channel their energies in some productive way by giving them ideas and access to counseling, education, and other alternatives. HP does this pre-departure through counseling sessions that explore a variety of opportunities for the spouse.

HP's awareness of the dual-career problem, however, doesn't mean the company will do just anything to solve the problem. Solutions must be consistent with HP's fundamental principles about foreign assignments and its corporate culture.

In keeping with that idea, (1) the company doesn't approve of commuter marriages. HP has a very strong philosophy about keeping the family together, so it actively discourages commuter relationships. They could be the basis for not assigning a candidate. (2) The firm will not try to replicate the spouse's income. Although there is great sensitivity and understanding that asking a family to relocate often means that they will give up one income, corporation's policies reflect that concern. The following are HP's policies that affect dual-career spouses:

- One-day session of spouse-specific training which is either career-related or interest related (i.e., it could be academic or it could be a hobby). Usually the counselor researches ahead of time what's available in the host country and provides contact names.
- Financial assistance for the spouse in which HP shares the cost of all types of educational activities up to $2,000 annually (this can include host-location career counseling).
- Assistance with résumé preparation and payment for visas when work is a possibility in the destination.
- Cross-cultural counseling for the whole family.
- Three days of orientation in the host country designed to cover local customs (business and social, history) and ways to become more quickly accustomed to the local environment.
- Language training.
- A spouse who is an HP employee is usually given a leave of absence with a guarantee of work upon return.

FOCUS INFORMATION SERVICES (AND OTHER SELF-HELP GROUPS)

Walk into the London offices of FOCUS Information Services, and you feel the energy, the bustle of activity all around. An enclave of information, this not-for-profit membership organization (supported by corporate donations and individual memberships) was created for expats of all nationalities living in the United Kingdom. Similar organizations are located in Belgium, France, and Switzerland. FOCUS's purpose: to provide expatriates with the information and support they need while living in a new country to enable them to get the most out of the country immediately.

Looking at FOCUS's resources, you can see it is a powerhouse of intelligence. Building on the knowledge of other expatriates (the office has a Danish office manager, French marketing manager, Hungarian program director, and it abounds with Americans, including the executive director, Pamela Drobnyk), newcomers don't have to spend endless days and weeks trying to find services, goods, and even friends. Seasoned expatriates find FOCUS a gathering place for people with similar backgrounds if they simply want to congregate with their compatriots or hear their native language with all its colloquialisms and natural richness. This is exactly what expatriates need. The group has its finger on the pulse of the expatriate community and tries to adapt to changing needs. For example, FOCUS is increasingly appealing to men—both employees and accompanying spouses—who may want career support.

FOCUS offers a phone line staffed by volunteers which provides access to a huge database of information, a bulletin board (for job openings—expatriates can work in the U.K.—volunteer opportunities, and other important information), a newsletter, and a reference library of data about relocation, job hunting, cross-cultural wisdom, immigration, child-rearing, traveling, and the like.

FOCUS is renowned for its seminars and networking meetings whose topics respond to the critical needs of men and women, and are offered in the evenings as well as during the day to accommodate working people. Among the programs are "Relocating to a New Country" (a five-part workshop); "The Movable Spouse" (how moving affects the spouse and employee, how to adjust and build a professional and private life outside of the family); "Networking in Cyberspace"; "Bridging the Cultural Gap in Your Office"; "Long Distance Care Giving"; "Raising Children Abroad"; and "Global Nomads."

For similar organizations, see the Resource List at the end of this chapter.

RECOMMENDATIONS FOR EFFECTIVE SOLUTIONS

1. Spouse Counseling[9]

To address the impact of family relationships on the international assignment, spouse counseling services are a tremendous aid (see Figures 10–1 10–2). These sessions help spouses whether or not they were previously employed. They begin with a needs assessment.

Spouse programs include:

- Managing change.
  Identifying personal strengths.
  Identifying anticipated challenges and rewards.
- Examining cross-cultural values.
  Reviewing cultural impact on life objectives.
  Developing cross-cultural communications skills.
- Creating personal and career goals.
  Determining personal goals.
  Discussing career objectives.
  Recognizing career/life-enhancing educational opportunities.
  Developing a plan and process.
- Maximizing host country activities.
  Arranging for introductions to local resources.
  Identifying local networking opportunities.

F I G U R E   10–1

Spouse Program

- Focuses in three distinct yet interrelated expatriate spouse concerns:
  On working in the new country.
  On effective intercultural management and adjustment.
  On career development during the assignment.
- Includes pre-departure and new country modules.
- Help spouses determine their plans for the duration of expatriate assignment.
- Identify how their lives will be affected by the assignment.
- Develop a career plan if appropriate and possible.
- Provide the spouse with the ability to follow up in the destination country.
- Identify volunteer or professional work opportunities if interested.

FIGURE 10-2

Spouse Program Sequence

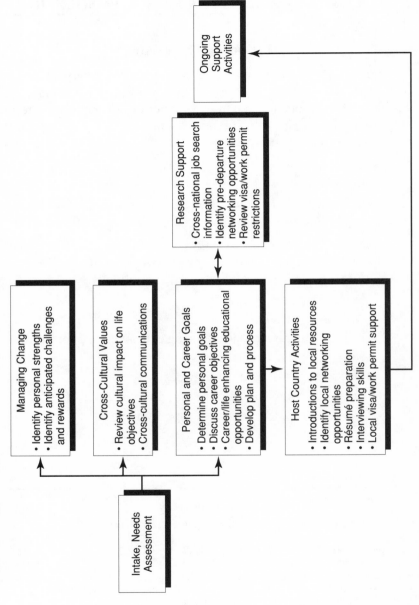

Source: Windham International

2. Dual-Career Spouse Programs Address the Following

- Review current lifestyle and professional situation.
- Identify and prioritize personal and career objectives.
- Conduct a "reality check" to define the impact of the assignment on both personal and career objectives.
- Identify alternatives such as education, volunteerism, and travel and their impact on future professional opportunities.
- Establish a plan to maximize the career and personal benefits of the experience.
- Review techniques for networking, establishing oneself in a new job or activity, and "opening doors" in the new country.
- Research employment requirements and career opportunities to pursue before and after arriving in the new country.
- Develop a personal marketing plan, résumé, and cover letters appropriate to the new culture.

3. Organizational Assistance

- Take a proactive recognition of spousal concerns. By recognizing it, you validate the spouse and relieve some of the guilt from the employee.
- Recognize the economic impact with special allowances for domestic obligations (e.g., housing responsibilities).
- Encourage accompanying spouse in cross-cultural programs.
- Support the effort and reimburse expenses for spouse work permits.
- Make spouse employment concerns the responsibility of host-country HR managers.
- Provide for host country résumé preparation.
- Provide space and systems for spouses to pursue career opportunities out of the host office.
- Allow spouse who has to interrupt career to remain vested in retirement and benefits plans.

These are not big expenses, but they do give you a great many results.

4. Legislative Assistance

- Support lobbying efforts for spouse work permits.
- Lobby uninformed legislators about laws that affect business-re-

lated work permit immigration. Business-related expatriate immigration (which is of a limited duration) is likely to create jobs for local nationals, not take them away. Consider, for example, the jobs created by Japanese automobile manufacturers and the relatively few Japanese expatriates requiring work permits. Consider also the additional jobs lost in the United States if expatriate scientists and technicians are not allowed in, so that the entire chip assemblies are kept here rather than moved to Israel or Singapore. If the United States makes immigration of expatriates so difficult because of dual-career resistance, we make our work environment more hostile. Companies will look elsewhere to locate their plants and expand.

Governments have to recognize two factors: (1) Business expatriates on short-term assignments create hundreds of local jobs and (2) to gain those jobs, we must make our environment friendlier to dual-wage earners. In other words, governments need to separate expatriate immigration issues and recognize the jobs that expatriates bring to local economies. Businesses must lobby to help bring about that change. Although this is an immigration issue (which is not examined in this book), it has a direct and profound bearing on dual-career families. One wonders if London would be the global financial mecca it currently is if the British government hadn't connected spousal work permits to the international assignee.

HELP DUAL-CAREER PARTNERS CREATE A PORTABLE CAREER

Pamela B. Perraud, an international human resource professional and one of the founders of FOCUS Information Service, was the program director for the first Women on the Move conference in 1990. She suggests that portable careers are the outstanding choice. Because traditional career advice may not meet the needs of mobile people who move from country to country where work rules differ from one place to the next, she suggests that individuals recognize the two types of skills they possess: general and specific knowledge. Because skills may not be transferable, they might have limitations in an international setting and require constant reevaluation. Furthermore, licenses, diplomas, and educational certificates are unimportant to global job searches because they are meaningless outside the country of issue. General knowledge, such as verbal or organizational skills, however, will translate nicely from location to location.

Perraud's note of caution is that a portable career should not require special licensing, not be specific to a geographic or cultural area, not depend on seniority for advancement, and not be in a field of little demand. She suggests the following as highly portable career skills: accounting, banking, beauty-related services, catering, computers, conference planning, graphic design, health care, journalism, promotion (PR), research, sales, teaching, and writing.

Figures 10–3 and 10–4 summarize the ways multinational companies can help working partners and what global managers can do in the way of career assistance for expatriate partners.

FIGURE 10–3

Ten Techniques to Help Working Partners

- Strategize about managing change.
- Learn about local values and beliefs.
- Develop a support system in the destination country.
- Identify personal and career goals.
- Analyze the meaning of personal and career success.
- Prepare résumés and develop cross-cultural interview skills.
- Identify skills developed in previous jobs.
- Create a list of general, transferable skills that can be used in many different jobs.
- Plan long-term career objectives.
- Explore job, educational, and volunteer opportunities to complement long-range career goals.

FIGURE 10–4

Expatriate Partner Career Assistance: What Global Managers Can Do

1. Give spouses allowances for spouse counseling.
2. Create loans or grants for entrepreneurial ventures.
3. Provide educational reimbursements.
4. Offer career counseling and pre-departure career planning.
5. Support the partner's job search at expatriation and repatriation.
6. Become actively involved in distributing the spouse's résumé to other companies in the destination country.
7. Create a consortium of business opportunities at the local level.
8. Request local human resources managers to identify departments where they can distribute the partner's résumé.
9. Plan networking opportunities among spouses.
10. Offer free information on getting a job in the destination country.
11. Provide access to on-site career centers or libraries.
12. Distribute information about local career centers at universities or libraries.

RESOURCE LIST

FOCUS
London: FOCUS Information Services
13 Prince of Wales Terrace
London, England W8 5PG
Telephone: 44-171-937-0050
Fax 44-171-937-9482

Brussels: FOCUS Career Services
Rue Lesbroussart 23
1050 Brussels
Belgium
Telephone: 32-2-646-6530

Geneva: FOCUS International Career Services
17 Route de Collex
1293 Bellevue, Switzerland
Telephone: 22-774-1639

Paris: WICE,
20, Boulevard de Montparnasse
15th arrondissement
Paris, France
Telephone: 33-1-45-66-7550

American Women's Club
Brussels
Telephone: 31-70-350-6007

Federation of American Women Clubs Overseas (FAWCO)
Resource Center
Nassaulaan 1
3818 GM Amersfoort, The Netherlands
Telephone: 31-33-4-618-211
             31-33-4-652-937

General Federation of Women's Clubs
1734 N. St., NW
Washington, DC
Telephone: 202-347-3168

Women on the Move
Fax: 212-369-0238
(Contact: Pamela Perraud)

Paradigm Group
Riedhofstrasse 354
8049 Zurich
Switzerland
Telephone: 41-1-342-3606
Women on the Move
Brussels:
Telephone: 32-2-201-6334

NOTES

1. Parts of this chapter were adapted from "One Assignment, Two Lives," *Personnel Journal*, May, 1996 by Charlene Marmer Solomon.

2. Not her real name.

3. *Making Work Flexible: Policy to Practice*, published in February 1996, by Catalyst, the New York-based Workplace Think-Tank. The report is based on a study Catalyst iniated in the Fall of 1994 in which the group identified 31 corporations and professional firms that are nationally recognized as having exemplary flexible workplace policies that are business-driven.

4. Ibid.

5. 1995 Global Relocation Trends Survey Report by Windham International and the National Foreign Trade Council.

6. Reyer (Rick) A. Swaak, senior consultant for ECA Windham and the National Foreign Trade Council.

7. *Competitive Frontiers: Women Managers in a Global Economy*, Edited by Nancy J. Adler and Dafna N. Izraeli, (Blackwell Business, Cambridge, MA, 1994). See chapters 1 and 2: "Competitive Frontiers: Women Managers in a Global Economy" and "Competitive Frontiers: Women Managing Across Borders."

8. 1992 *Expatriate Dual Career Survey*, by Windham International and the National Foreign Trade Council.

9. Parts of this section were adapted from: Schell, Michael S. and Marian Stoltz-Loike, "Importance of Cultural Preparation to International Business Success," *Journal of International Compensation & Benefits*, no. 4 (January/February 1994), Vol. II,No. 4, pp. 47–52.

P A R T

III

⑥　# A LOOK INTO THE FUTURE

11

ⓖ HUMAN RESOURCE MANAGEMENT IN THE NEXT CENTURY

This chapter will cover

- A preview of 21st century organizations and the global managers who will lead them.
- The importance of corporate culture in the global organizations.
- The human resource manager's function into the next century.
- Perceptions of the future from human resource managers.

Elizabeth Adams saunters into the kitchen of her suburban Denver home to prepare breakfast and read her E-mail. She glances at her Internet terminal and softly says, "check E-mail." Instantly, the machine serves up a list of messages to the senior HR VP that have been sent to her from all over the world—New York, Rome, Singapore, Tokyo, and Bombay. All the messages are dated April 25, 2001.

She scans the E-mail, responding to some and forwarding others. Some of the messages offer snippets of video and sound; others offer links so she can access greater detail. By the time she has downed her toast and orange juice, she's ready to head off to work. Since today is Monday, when all important meetings are scheduled, she's required to show up at company headquarters. Although high-speed cable modems have made global

videoconferencing as common as faxes were in the 1990s, most major corporations still prefer to have key people assemble for face-to-face meetings, especially when they require in-depth discussion and detailed analysis. Today's meetings involve a client relations issue with a customer in
Italy who specifically requested Elizabeth as part of the team.

At work, Elizabeth steps through an automated security station where a
fingerprint scan verifies her identity. She logs onto the network from one
of several PCs lining the main employee entrances, which company employees and vendor contractors use and which instantly assigns them a
workstation so they can begin funneling phone calls, E-mail, and faxes to
their PCs. Elizabeth, however, still has an old-fashioned office because she
is the head of the department. She puts the finishing touches on her part
of a multimedia quarterly report about her company, Globex Corporation.
She and other department heads will soon showcase the company, a con-
glomerate with offices in 35 countries, in a teleconference to the client in
Italy.

Globex is considered one of the premier organizations of the 21st century—streamlined, nimble, and boasting an employee population of over
60 nationalities. Global in scope and attitude, departments and entire divi-
sions are no longer encumbered by the location of actual offices. Team
members might just as easily be located in Rome or São Paulo as in Denver. Like Elizabeth, many of them telecommute two or three days a week.
Her department, global human resources, has spearheaded the move toward a virtual company. She marvels that when she joined the company in
1994, there were 100,000 people employed in an organization whose revenue was 40 percent less than today's firm of 60,000, including the 10,000
people who report to Globex on a regular basis but who work for vendor
organizations.

Many of the functions for which Elizabeth was responsible when she
joined the company have been automated or outsourced. Employees update their own records and benefits information via the company's Intranet; recruiting and hiring are accomplished electronically using the
databases available on the Internet; and position postings and internal
openings are filled through the company's Intranet and E-mail. All expatriate compensation and administration, as well as global relocation, are provided by outside service companies whose employees are indistinguishable
from Globex staff.

Her reduced staff is also a reflection of the dramatic change in the corporate culture. It mirrors the training which the organization has provided
over the past several years to change the relationship between company
and employee, and thus eliminate many of the policing requirements her
department used to have.

The meeting begins with Elizabeth and a half dozen department managers reviewing revenue performance data, adjusting strategies to current intelligence, discussing global HR issues, and reviewing succession plans and potential candidates. In the current work culture, what would have been a two-day meeting in 1994 is accomplished in a few hours.

Next is the videoconference with a key customer in Italy, who apparently has some quality concerns about the Globex Series 2000 wireless communicator device and is considering canceling the remainder of the order. The customer has requested Elizabeth's presence in the meeting not only because of her important HR role, but also because she speaks Italian and was an international assignee in his country a few years ago. Apparently the Italians are reporting that parts are being damaged when unpacked from their protective casings. Engineering teams have indicated that the parts exceed specified tolerances and present problems when seated into their casings. Elizabeth has a dual role in this meeting. First, the entire team knows that more than language needs to be translated when dealing across cultures. Furthermore, the suspicion also exists that some of the problems encountered in Italy may relate to hiring, training, and management issues at the Naples facility. Managers at the meeting have each done extensive research in anticipation of this discussion and have carefully prepared a culturally sensitive strategy that will allow enough time for the dialogue necessary to thoroughly understand the root and manifestation of the problem.

The meeting concludes with an extensive debriefing, during which Elizabeth focuses on the challenges presented by the Italian labor unions and the additional training needs that Globex and the Italian employees will require. The other members talk about the engineering problems and an overall plan is put into place. Elizabeth and the head of engineering will visit the Naples plant and discuss the recommended solutions soon.

Elizabeth Adams will tell you she has seen a complete transformation in her company. Only a decade before, she entered a department that was buried in administrative paperwork and was still trying to figure out how to meet the daily demands while making an impact as part of the company's strategic business team. Now, in the year 2001, new ideas—and technologies to support them—have become the driver for an international organization that harnesses the best brainpower it can find worldwide and then builds products of unsurpassed quality. Globex is one of the new breed of companies of the 21st century. Tapping the energy and productivity of talented people through technology and a corporate culture that respects different cultural perspectives, Globex has created an organization capable of responding quickly and effectively to customer needs.

ⓖ ⓖ ⓖ

Globex Corporation, while fictional, embodies the immense change taking place in business organizations, trends that will continue to gain momentum well into the next century. Driven by global competition and accelerated by technological achievements, organizations and their workforces are in an unparalleled transformation process.

In 1987, Hudson Institute's landmark study, *Workforce 2000,* predicted the increasingly diverse composition of the American workforce by the turn of the century.[1] It also examined several of the economic factors shaping these trends. Yet, changing demographics of the workforce is only part of the picture. What about the revolutionary changes in the organizations that these people would staff? Moreover, despite its accuracy, the report forecast demographic trends based on *predictable* events. And while those predictions stunned American business leaders at the time, they pale in significance when compared to the impact of globalization on business in the 21st century.

Hard on the heels of that study, International Business Machines (IBM) and Towers Perrin undertook an extensive survey that examined the role of human resource professionals in helping organizations gain competitive advantage.[2] Building on the findings of *Workforce 2000,* this study, titled, "Priorities for Competitive Advantage," melded the workforce issues with business challenges to explore the implications of both the changing organization and workforce on the human resource management function.

IBM's study predicts that by the year 2000, the four basic components of human resources will be:

1. Responsive to a highly competitive marketplace and global business structures.
2. Closely linked to business strategic plans.
3. Jointly conceived and implemented by line and HR managers.
4. Focused on quality, customer service, productivity, employee involvement, teamwork, and workforce flexibility.

Accurate as those predictions remain in 1996, they did not anticipate the importance of the following:

- The impact of the global workforce and the proactive role that the HR function must assume in order to capitalize on it.

- The need to create a corporate culture with global application.
- The need to build HR competencies into the line manager function—in streamlined, reengineered organizations.
- The urgency to reengineer the HR function to make it consistent with the strategic business mission and structure of the organization.

It is certainly no surprise that many forward-thinking organizations have already embarked on the arduous task of reinventing the human resource function—and that of the organization as a whole—with this paradigm shift in mind. Getting from point A to point B isn't always a straight line. But through thoughtful analysis and ongoing efforts, it is possible to avoid many obstacles and pitfalls while evolving toward a global mind-set.

THE ORGANIZATION IN THE YEAR 2000

The trend toward smaller, independent operating units and smaller companies staffed by employees recruited from a worldwide talent pool will continue as we cross into the next millennium. These firms will focus on—and strive for—an empowered workforce. They will become increasingly flatter, faster, and more facile than their predecessors, and they will move toward a strong corporate culture that binds employees into a unified organization. Managers in these businesses will require global skills and cultural fluency. The human resource function, along with the rest of the traditional staff, will be part of the core business activity.

THE NEED FOR SPEED

Organizations must to be able to adapt quickly to the changing demands of the marketplace. As the influence of technology expands and the business world relies on instant access to information to make quick decisions, global managers must be prepared. Those changes come at an ever-increasing rate accelerated by technology and the simultaneous momentum it picks up. Only a decade ago, a significant time lag often existed between the information and technology available in one country and that available in another. That's no longer the case. Worldwide telecommunications, particularly computer networks, have made the transfer of information—and knowledge—a task achieved in seconds. That makes it possible for companies and even individual workers in Malaysia or India to play a key role in developing new products and making key discoveries on a global team that has other members in the Netherlands and the U.K. To be sure, geography is becoming less of an obstacle than ever before. Moreover, what happens today in the United States needs to be available in Malaysia tomorrow—not six years from tomorrow. In the 21st century, new products and discoveries are just as likely to be generated in Indonesia and will need to be available in the United States simultaneously.

For such a model to function efficiently, however, workers must become more autonomous and business units must shrink. At the same time, just as a video arcade game speeds up and becomes more complex as a player masters each level, so too must a global business manager's proficiency grow as an organization becomes more virtual, fast, and scattered. In other words, what is considered "skill-building" today, is where the game will start tomorrow.

Not only is it suddenly necessary to communicate more quickly, but the entire decision-making process must take place exceedingly fast while maintaining zero tolerance for quality slippage. Leading business executives, such as General Electric's Jack Welch and Intel's Andy Groves already build speed into the organization. They set out to design and engineer business processes and systems that fit into this model. As a result, GE's philosophy of speed is supported by a boundaryless organization that eliminates bureaucracy. It is an organization that steers employees toward actual decision making rather than to approval levels cordoned off by red tape. It allows an organization like Intel to anticipate market needs with such speed that by the time a competitor clones one of its products, Intel has already forced it into obsolescence with its new, faster model.

COHESIVE CORPORATE CULTURE

Because information is the business of the 21st century and the most important resource of an organization is the people who create, synthesize, and use that information, it's important to fully manage this bold new infrastructure. Where will these people come from? How will they fit in?

It is clear that quality education is no longer the exclusive domain of a few fortunate nations. For example, in the coming century, organizations will compete to discover and develop human resources in the same way that oil companies sought new oil fields for development in the 20th century. The difference of course is that no matter where petroleum is found, it can still provide power for an automobile, while people come with a variety of cultural backgrounds and tendencies that cannot be ignored.

Assuming that workers are selected from a worldwide talent pool, then communication across languages and cultures becomes an enormous challenge. If workers fail to understand the cultural messages their colleagues send out, it will be impossible to unify everyone behind a single business mission. Just as an invisible telephone message is sent through a visible wire, corporate culture serves as conduit for messages, both visible and invisible. Without fully understanding the dynamics of the situation, it's impossible to transform all the noise into a corporate symphony.

What fosters communication?

A strong corporate culture.

It is the essential quality of a company that weaves together business strategies and objectives while providing the people skills needed to accomplish goals. Spend only a few hours in a different organization and the power of corporate culture becomes obvious. It sets the tone for dress, pace, mood, and the way offices are configured and decorated. It charges the very air of an organization. Like national cultures, it dictates right and wrong, how tasks are accomplished, and how people deal with opportunities, challenges, conflict, problem solving, leadership, and success. Most of all, it spells out how people deal with each other. And because corporate culture can be so powerful, these actions and behaviors might actually supersede those of a national culture. Therein lies its importance.

Make no mistake, melding a common vision is crucial. If the 21st century organization succeeds in recruiting and hiring the most talented and qualified employees from all over the world, it will emerge victorious because it will have found a way to enable a diverse group of people to join in a common cause. In an information and technology age, where an educated workforce is the most important fundamental resource of an organization, businesses will be staffed by individuals who are reared, trained, and educated all over the world. Coalescing various nationalities and cultures into a streamlined organization capable of speed, teamwork, and flexibility will become essential to ratcheting up profits and productivity.

Corporate culture will be the glue that binds this organization, but the greater the number of elements and the more diverse they are, the tougher it is to hold everything—and everyone—together. Therefore, corporate cultures that transcend national boundaries while violating no core value will be critical for success. How well organizations facilitate the information between their employees and how well the corporate culture complements the business mission is what will distinguish successful organizations.

THE CHANGING RELATIONSHIP BETWEEN EMPLOYEE AND EMPLOYER: CAREER SECURITY VERSUS JOB SECURITY

During the late 1980s and early 1990s, the concept of company loyalty generated great confusion among workers. People who had been raised with the idea of working for a single employer their entire career were stunned by the business realities that forced companies into a "leaner and meaner" corporate model. Suddenly, employees who felt they had made great sacrifices in exchange for lifetime employment were being bowled over by downsizing, a practice they couldn't fully comprehend. It was if someone changed the rules of a game during the competition, but never bothered to notify the players. Confusion reigned as the idea of being a good "corporate soldier" was replaced with the need to possess competence, knowledge, and relevant experience from a variety of organizations. Today, in the new corporate pact, company loyalty is demanded only as long as one is employed by the company and it is good for one's own career.

There is no reason to believe that this trend will subside. In the new corporate order, employees will not seek security with one employer; instead they will capitalize on a new idea: career security versus job security. Individuals will invest in their own development because that will give them greater economic potential. As a result—and to attract the best and brightest—companies must be able to provide workers with skill-enhancing career opportunities that can be carried to the next employer. In the final analysis, the most sought-after employees will be those with entrepreneurial skills and the ability to manage their own careers.

Of course, this has some serious repercussions. Work opportunities will have to present more than financial gain for these highly talented employees. They will have to offer personal and professional growth opportunities. Interestingly, expatriate assignments—almost by their very nature—fall into this category. In most cases, talented employees will look forward to taking on such assignments because of their career-enhancing potential. Ironically, some of these international assignees may not share their new experience and global expertise with the firms that actually sent them on assignment because the repatriation process typically undervalues the expatriate experience. Talented employees will continue to leave if their new growth isn't more highly valued.

HUMAN RESOURCES IN THE 21ST CENTURY CORPORATION

What will become of the human resource function in the next century? How will these changes affect the workplace and people's lives? Will HR even exist as we know it today? These are just some of the questions we can expect to struggle with in the coming global business era. In tomorrow's downsized, restructured, and reengineered corporation, a very different set of demands will be placed on human resource professionals. In truth, the definition of HR is evolving and maturing as we write this book. It is being reengineered every hour of every day.

What are some of these changes?

- Technology is radically altering the way we track employees' careers. Vast databases provide information about applicants, and electronic résumés and online application processes offer advanced ways to receive and store data—and even search for an applicant by education or expertise. Databases also contain records on existing employees, and allow keyword searching to find a manager who, for example, speaks Chinese and understands global compensation. Technology also provides a quick and simple way to deliver information: E-mail, Intranet, or the Internet. That can speed the flow of information and provide powerful communication capabilities to those who use it wisely.
- Administrative functions are rapidly being outsourced to specialized organizations. As companies focus on core competencies, a

wide array of HR tasks—from administering benefits to developing training materials—are being sent to providers who can do it more efficiently. That in turn allows the human resource professional to play a more strategic role and find ways to improve productivity.

- HR staffs are shrinking and being supplemented by contract employees who come to the organization armed with advanced technological skills. These specialists, who can be tapped on an as-needed basis, are driving fundamental change and creating a workplace that is open to new ideas and new ways of tackling work, further altering traditional systems.

Not surprisingly, many practitioners openly wonder whether the human resource profession will actually exist by the end of the century. And even if it does, where will HR talent come from if administrative positions, which have traditionally served as a way to enter the profession and then as a springboard to management, are outsourced? Can an outsourced position retain the corporate culture and the company's spirit of conducting business?

These are significant questions which have an enormous impact on how an organization evolves. Unfortunately, the individuals who are asking the questions are often making inquiries too late because the metamorphosis is already well underway. The fact is that human resource managers of the 21st century may not need a traditional HR background. As business functions become increasingly intertwined, so will the skills and background of those entering the profession and managing within the HR environment. In some cases, that might translate to a broader knowledge base; in other instances, it demands an understanding of specialized suppliers as well as a thorough knowledge of the business.

Not only do today's smaller, more efficient organizations require fewer people and fewer administrative functions than those of decades past, but the fundamental "contract" with employees has changed. Management realizes that in this new era of information, people are the single most important resource for gaining and maintaining competitive advantage. These employees don't need—nor do they expect—the same level of job security and protection that their counterparts of the 1970s and 1980s did. They are perfectly comfortable consulting a computer to retrieve data about their benefits. They take responsibility for developing their own skills and furthering their education, and they no longer expect promotions based entirely on seniority. Not surprisingly, they need portable benefits that they can take with them when they switch companies for what they believe to be better opportunities.

Increasingly, organizations realize that to recruit and retain the talent they so desperately need, they must provide rewarding and challenging career opportunities. They realize that they will retain this talent only as long as employees feel the organization is serving their needs and their career goals. In other words, the organization of the not too distant future will have a far different relationship with its employees than today's company, even with changes that have already become apparent. And that, together with technology and the shifting composition of the workforce, means that the organization of the next century will have different needs to be served by its human resource professionals. Those who succeed will recognize this profound change and offer value and expertise in this smaller, flatter, and faster organization. They will look for ways to further refine—and redefine—what human resources is and what it achieves.

Ultimately, every line manager function will also require the abilities of a skilled people manager. In turn, he or she will need a business partner who possesses the specific HR skills to maximize business opportunities in a competitive global world.

Let's consider the responsibilities of the traditional HR function:

- Recruiting and hiring
- Administration
- Benefits delivery
- Compliance issues
- Training
- Management development
- Performance appraisals
- Labor relations
- Employee communications
- Grievance and disciplinary procedures
- Organization's conscience

Clearly, many of these will still be essential tasks in the organization of the future. However, who accomplishes them, whose responsibility they become, and the way in which he or she manages the work will be vastly different.

Moreover, some of these traditional responsibilities will be replaced by new competencies. These skills will include:

- Cultural fluency
- Global teamwork
- International work experience
- Multiple language capability
- Comfort with ambiguity
- Line function business experience
- Process knowledge
- Self confidence
- People management skills
- Clear sense of corporate values and business ethics

PERCEPTIONS FROM HR PROFESSIONALS

During the winter of 1996, the authors conducted a series of global strategic issues roundtables to explore the direction and define the role of human resource management in the coming century. The participants in these meetings were senior human resource managers from a variety of companies and industries.

The dramatic changes in the human resource function was the most prominent—and pressing—issue to surface. Undoubtedly, the function is already being redesigned. The experts at the roundtables enumerated the primary challenges facing HR in the 21st century.

- For HR to remain a valuable force in the global business environment, it must become more closely aligned to the business, be a partner with line managers, and become a facilitator of the business plan rather than an administrator of employee services.
- The HR function will have to assume a more consultative function, helping the business achieve objectives rather than encumber the process with bureaucratic and legalistic detail.
- The HR function will have to be able to take better advantage of technology to downsize and reengineer itself. It must automate

administrative activities and outsource functions that aren't part of the core competency or that can be handled more efficiently outside the organization.

- Human resources will fulfill the critical role of globalizing the business and creating a global mind-set in a globally competent corporate culture.
- In a business environment where people are the most important asset, human resource development has to become everyone's responsibility. The HR manager must help build skills in the line function.

As an integral partner in the business, the HR function must focus on revenue generation as opposed to bureaucratic administration. That is largely why outsourcing has realized exponential growth over the last few years. In progressive, forward-thinking organizations, HR has already shed itself of the service mentality and either turned these activities over to outside companies or found ways to get the tasks done more efficiently on its own. Once unbound by the chains of endless administrative tasks, HR managers are free to think more efficiently and creatively. They are finally able to fulfill the new role in the new organization.

In organizations where the quality distinction is not in raw materials or manufactured products, where the most recognized valuable resource is people, human resource professionals must continue to view themselves as responsible for line resource functions. Just as a computer company must manufacture PCs or an oil company must pump crude from the earth and then refine it, HR will manage people as efficiently as possible. Instead of having the most efficient drilling or manufacturing equipment possible, it is essential for HR to have the right people who understand the nuances of the global environment and have a language that is understood corporatewide.

The human resource function will assume responsibility for the most important resource of an information age organization: the people. That means equipping line managers with tools to accomplish their task, whether it's developing compensation schemes that enhance the corporate mission, institutionalizing standards of performance and excellence, interpreting corporate strategy into specific HR behaviors, or making their organization the employer of choice for the best and the brightest. Indeed, global HR managers will assume responsibility for profitability— a concept that redefines the very essence of the profession.

WHAT ARE THE ACTION STEPS?

The following ten points are a summary of the recommendations of participants of the roundtables mentioned previously.

1. Take every piece of the HR function and see how technology can affect it beneficially.
2. HR must be a partner with line managers.
3. Educate self and others about business issues.
4. Facilitate change management. Help people prepare and adapt to change and complexity through education.
5. Partnering. Understand customers, products and services. HR must be able to educate others about how the company does business and how HR is helping in that process.
6. HR must be considered on the same level as business development, finance, and marketing. It must be seen as important as these functions. If HR is not reporting to the top, there's something wrong.
7. Be willing to transfer responsibility to employees. By empowering employees, HR can do away with tunnel vision of the function and allow HR to focus on broader issues.
8. Need to identify skills for new HR professional. These will include financial/business skills and sales skills by which HR can sell their partnership to the business manager's world.
9. HR professionals must force themselves to speak the language of business managers. Be aggressive about being included and respected.
10. HR function must constantly prove it is relevant to the project.

As the speed of progress accelerates, managers will become key agents of change. They will have to grow comfortable with ambiguity because navigating through the vast unknown will become commonplace. In the end, talent and skills will override structure and processes. Where someone works, how they work and the chain of command will become far less significant than the basic, but complex, goal of getting the job done with maximum speed and efficiency. As the modern corporation is redesigned and the traditions and practices of the past are discarded, HR can choose to be at the forefront—reexamining, redefining, and facilitating the change.

NOTES

1. Wiliam B. Johnston and Arnold H. Packer, *Workforce 2000: Work and Workers for the 21st Century* (Indianapolis: Hudson Institute, 1987).

2. "Priorities for Competitive Advantage," an IBM study conducted by Towers Perrin, 1991.

An Introduction to the Balance Sheet

The expatriate process is costly, so companies are looking for new ways to minimize those costs. What remains constant is the need to make the best use of expatriate dollars. If companies want international assignments to support the business mission, cost-effective ways to compensate employees that also maximize performance become evermore important.

Developing a total international remuneration package involves many components, each of which requires comprehensive data. Major categories include cost of living, housing, educational expenses, premiums, and taxes—from the United States and host country. When these allowances are grossed up, the accuracy of the data on which the package is built becomes even more critical. This process, although multifaceted, doesn't need to be complicated.

This appendix is an overview of the process and the logic for developing an international compensation package. Section 1 explains the logic behind the balance sheet approach; Section 2 illustrates the elements of a balance sheet and the data you need to construct it; Section 3 provides definitions; and Section 4 is a process map that shows specifically where each part of the balance sheet draws its information. The map assumes your company already has policy and procedures in place and that it has chosen the balance sheet approach. It also shows the buildup process. Section 5 illustrates the total remuneration package.

SECTION 1:
HOW THE BALANCE SHEET APPROACH WORKS

The logic of the balance sheet stems from the idea of protecting the employees' spendable net income. Companies want to be fair to their employees—that is, the employees' standard of living should be similar to their current situation regardless of the destination. Companies obtain information from data service suppliers about standard expenses for items such as food, other goods and services, housing, education, and so forth, and calculate the additional amounts they should give employees to protect individuals against the variable costs of being in another country.

255

SECTION 2: BEFORE YOU CAN DO ANYTHING ELSE

Data Collection

You need to know

- What is a person's base pay in the home country?
- What aspects of the employees' pay or benefits require protection so they aren't financially penalized when they accept an overseas assignment? Some examples are cost of living, housing, children's education, and transportation allowances.
- What are the cost-of-living differentials? Before you can determine the COLA (cost-of-living-allowance), you need to know the difference (called "differential") between the home and host countries in the following areas:

  Market basket of goods and services

  Housing

  Transportation

  Children's education

- What tax concessions or relief are available? For example, it may be advantageous to provide a car rather than give the money for a car because that money will be viewed as income and therefore is taxable at a higher rate.
- What local tax calculation information do you need?
- What statutory information is important? What regulations govern labor, employment, immigration? To determine how to structure benefits, you must know what's mandated in the destination. There are some things that you can take advantage of, such as the country's medical system, when appropriate. When you know what is already provided—and mandated by law—you may not have to duplicate benefits.

SECTION 3: DEFINITIONS

Base Salary

Most companies begin with a base salary that reflects the same level of pay for a comparable position in the home or host country. It may be the current base salary. The base salary also serves as a reference point to establish plan levels of home country employee benefits.

Taxes, Hypothetical Taxes and Gross-Ups

Taxes
U.S. citizens are one of the few nationalities that are taxed on their worldwide income. In addition to paying local host country taxes, U.S. citizens also must file their U.S. federal, state, and local taxes. To offset this double taxation, however, the United States also allows either an income exclusion or an offset of foreign tax against the U.S. tax liability.

Hypothetical Tax
The hypothetical tax is based on a norm of home country tax with exemptions and deductions factored in. It can be the actual tax an employee already pays or a specified projection provided by a consultant. It varies depending upon different salary levels, number of deductions, and so forth. This calculation serves to roughly approximate the home country tax and to reduce the gross before local taxes are applied. About 40 percent of companies use the actual tax rate the employees pay and calculate from that.

Gross-Ups
The term *gross-up* is well known to those in the relocation field. It refers to the amount of money the company provides an employee to offset the additional taxes as well as the taxes incurred on the gross-up itself. The tax gross-up calculation for an international relocation is far more complicated than that of domestic relocation. It requires the help of a professional tax advisor usually provided by the company.

Differential Allowances

The following allowances are usually provided.

Cost of Living Allowance or COLA
Most companies determine their cost-of-living allowances based on information from data collection firms like ECA Windham. These businesses

collect data by determining typical family spending patterns (so they know what goods and services a person in the United States purchases). Next, they price a market basket based on what a typical American would buy. The firms survey these items in the host country to determine the cost differential.

In the United States, and increasingly in other countries, an index is developed by which a portion of the salary susceptible to cost of living differences is multiplied. The result of that arithmetic is the actual cost of living allowance.

The Index Number

Most U.S. based companies use a cost of living "index" number to determine COLA that is developed for them by a compensation data supplier. The index number is the number used by which the spendable income is multiplied to develop a cost of living amount for each expatriate. Obviously, the index is based on income level, and family size. This index is developed based on a series of assumptions that an organization makes as to which items of expenses the company wants to protect and to what levels.

For example, some companies may want to include the cost of eating in a restaurant three times a week while others may limit it to once a week. Some may include the cost of housekeepers while others may not. And some may include the cost of home furnishings, while others may provide a one time allowance and not include these expenses in the COLA.

Obviously, it is important to know what the assumptions are that the data supplier uses in their index in order to make sure that they are consistent with the program's objectives and that they are not redundant with other policy allowances. An example of such a redundancy can be an employee who is provided with a company car as well as a commutation allowance in the COLA differential, or if the company provides a housekeeper and then also includes household help in the COLA. In addition it is important for the HR administrator to know what is included in the COLA so that they can better explain it to the expatriate family.

Of course many busy HR managers either just accept the index or are committed to it by a precedent. In addition, since expatriates from competing companies often compare COLAs some managers are stuck with COLAs that are too high or inconsistent with policy provisions to retain the appearance of competitiveness.

Housing
Most companies provide a substantial portion of expatriate accommodation and utility costs in the form of housing allowances to enable employees to live in a dwelling comparable to the one they had in their home country. Some companies provide free housing; others assume that the employee will contribute part of the rent (often 10 to 15 percent); still others give employees a fixed allowance and tell them if they want something more expensive they will have to pay it out of pocket.

Educational Allowance
Usually a company pays most of the tuition and other educational fees associated with schooling children while on assignment. Room and board are subsidized in few cases, and most education subsidies end after high school or the equivalent.

Home Leave Allowance
It is customary to reimburse a trip home, usually one trip per year for the expatriate and the family. The cost of home leave for the expatriate and the family may not be tax deductible.

Assignment Premium

Organizations often give some kind of inducement to employees to accept an international assignment. Generally the premium is a percentage of the base salary with a ceiling, and it is paid either in a lump sum or at regular intervals throughout the course of the assignment. It is used to recognize the willingness of the employee to leave the home country and isn't associated with any costs the expatriate will incur. Premiums are not generally added to base salary.

Hardship Premium

Expatriates receive this payment when they relocate to countries in which living conditions are considered extremely difficult or dangerous.

SECTION 4: COMPONENTS OF BALANCE SHEET AND PROCESS MAP

Components of the Balance Sheet*

- Base salary
- Less hypothetical tax (U.S. tax)
- Hypothetical net salary
- Plus net allowances
    COLA
    Housing
    Children's education
    Miscellaneous other items
- Net before gross-up
- Gross-up (including tax on tax)
- Total gross
- Net payment to employee

SAMPLE BALANCE SHEET†

Base salary	$100,000
Less hypothetical tax (16%)	16,000
Hypothetical net	84,000
Add allowances (net)	
COLA	10,000
Housing	18,000
Education	20,000
Miscellaneous	10,000
Net before gross-up	$142,000
Gross-up 50% (local tax)	$ 71,000
Tax on gross-up payment	$ 71,000
(local tax on tax)	
Total gross	$284,000
Net payment to employee	$142,000
Incremental cost to company	
or expatriate	$184,000
(Expatriate expenses and gross-ups)	
Total cost to company	$284,000

*Everything paid monthly appears on the balance sheet, but at the end of the year there will have been additional expenses not paid regularly to the international assignee. These might include home leave, education reimbursements (for children and partner), R&R, furniture allowance, medical expenses. While those expenses need to be tracked for total cost calculation (and some are subject to tax and gross-up), we will only identify those here with an estimate number.

† Many of these elements fluctuate because of changes in housing prices, bonuses, exchange rates, expense reimbursements, etc. Common practice is to attempt to keep the balance sheet fairly static and at the end of the tax year, recap all the additional elements that have been paid, including expense items such as home leave, R&R, furniture allowance, medical payments, etc. Typically, this is the time for a tax professional.

COMPENSATION AND BENEFITS PACKAGE DEVELOPMENT: PROCESS MAP

The following illustrates the buildup process:

International Compensation Buildup Process

This chart shows the buildup process required to preserve the international assignee's home country purchasing power. The addition of differential payments (allowances/tax support) to those elements of pay most affected by different living-abroad expenses are approximately equalized between the home and host countries.

Items normally deducted from the gross income to identify spendable and residual pay.

Allowances made in recognition of the cost between home and host countries.

Elements that build up the package to protect purchasing power in the host location.

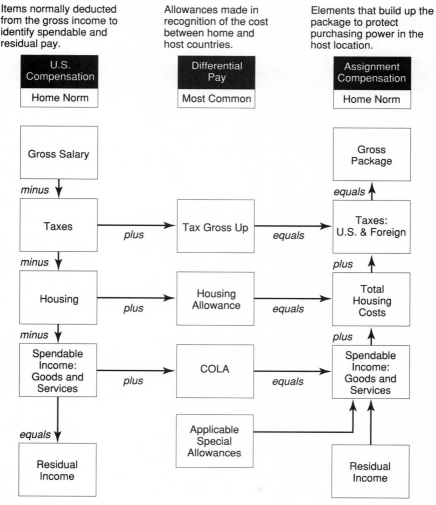

ECA Windham

SECTION 5: TOTAL PACKAGE COST

Compensation Package	Benefits*
Base Salary	Health insurance
Local/U.S. Tax	Life insurance
Differential Allowances	Retirement fund/401 K
Housing +	Business/accident
Reimbursable Expenses	insurance
Premiums	Flexible spending account

PLUS

Relocation Package	Repatriation Package
Move household effects +	Move household effects
Provide housing assistance,	
property management, store furniture	
Homefinding service	Homefinding service
Cross-cultural counseling	Career counseling

*Most companies try to maintain employees in their home country benefits plans when possible. Some host countries provide facilities to opt out of some types of statutory benefits (e.g., pensions or health coverage). Unfortunately, some host countries require participation so that, more often than not, the local benefit ends up as a duplication or is handled as an offset (e.g. leaving indemnities).

REFERENCES

Adler, Nancy J. *International Dimensions of Organizational Behavior,* 2d edition, Cambridge, MA., Wadsworth, 1991.
_____. "Women Managers in a Global Economy," *HR Magazine,* Sept., 1993.
Adler, Nancy J., and Susan Bartholomew, "Managing Globally Competent People," *Academy of Management Executive,* 6, no. 3, (Aug. 1992), pp 52–65.
Adler, Nancy J., and Dafna N. Izraeli, eds. *Competitive Frontiers: Women Managers In A Global Economy.* Cambridge, MA: Blackwell Business Publishers, 1994.
Anfuso, Dawn, "HR Unites the World of Coca-Cola," *Personnel Journal,* Nov., 1994.
Austin, Clyde N., Ed. *Cross-Cultural Reentry: A Book of Readings.* Abilene, TX: Abilene Christian University, 1986.
Bartlett, Christopher A., and Sumantra Ghoshal. *Managing Across Borders: The Transitional Solution.* Boston: Harvard Business School Press, 1991.
Barton, Ronald J. "The Real Issues in International Transfers," *Journal of International Compensation & Benefits,* Nov./Dec. 1993.
Black, J. Stewart , Hal B. Gregerson, and Mark B. Mendenhall. *Global Assignments: Successfully Expatriating and Repatriating International Managers.* San Francisco: Josey Bass, 1992.
Black, J. Stewart, and Hal B. Gregerson. "The Other Half of the Picture: Antecedents of Spouse Cross-Cultural Adjustment." *Journal of International Business Studies,* Third Quarter 1991, pp. 461–77.
_____. "When Yankee Comes Home: Factors Related to Expatriate and Spouse Repatriation Adjustment." *Journal of International Business Studies* 22 (1991), pp. 671–95.
Bloomfield, Katherine. "Stresses on the Internationally Mobile Family," "Strategies for Global Nomads in Relationships" and "Strategies for Parenting Global Nomads." *Transition Dynamics,* Nov. 16, 1992.
Bradley, Stephen P., Jerry A. Hausman and Richard L. Nolan, eds. *Technology and Competition: The Fusion of Computers and Telecommunications in the 1990's.* Boston: Harvard Business School Press, 1993.
Brake, Terence, Danielle Medina Walker, and Thomas (Tim) Walker. *Doing Business Internationally: The Guide to Cross-Cultural Success.* Princeton, NJ: Training Management Corporation; Burr Ridge, IL. Irwin, 1995.
Brenner, Lynn, "The Disappearing HR Department," *CFO Magazine,* Mar. 1996.
Catalyst Report, "Women in Corporate Leadership: Progress and Prospects," 1996.
Caudron, Shari, "Lessons from HR Overseas," *Personnel Journal,* Feb. 1995.
Chesters, Alan. "The Balance Sheet Approach: Problem or Solution." *International HR Journal* 4, no. 3 (Fall 1995), pp. 9–15.
_____. "Constraints on Mobility." *Benefits and Solutions,* in press, 1996.
_____. *Croner's Guide for HRM Professionals,* 1994
_____. "Developing Nomadic Executives." *Mobility,* 1990.
_____. "Social Constraints on Employee Mobility and Company Expenses." *HRM Professionals Briefing,* 1995.
Copeland, Lennie, and Lewis Griggs. "Culture Shock Is Part Of The Overseas Passage," in

OAI: The Overseas Assignment Inventory Assessment and Development Guide. Tucker International, Moran, Stahl & Boyer International, 1993.

Csoka, Louis S. "Rethinking Human Resources." Conference Board Report 1124, 1995.

De Leon, Corinna T. and Diana McPartlin. "Adjustment of Expatriate Children," in *Expatriate Management: New Ideas for International Business,* Jan Selmer, ed., Quorum Books, 1995, pp. 198–214.

Dolins, Ilene L. "International Assignments in the '90s: An Integrated Approach," *International Corporate Relocation News* 4, no. 1, 1993.

_____. "A Look at Trends in International Relocation," *International Compensation and Benefits,* Mar./Apr. 1994.

Eakin, Kay Branaman. *The Foreign Service Teenager At Home in the U.S.: A Few Thoughts for Parents Returning with Teenagers.* Overseas Briefing Center, Foreign Service Institute, U.S. Department of State, May 1988.

Gates, Stephen. "The Changing Global Role of the Human Resource Function," Conference Board Report 1062, 1994.

Geert, Hofstede. *Cultures and Organizations.* New York: McGraw Hill, 1992.

_____. *Culture's Consequences: International Differences in Work-Related Values.* Newbury Park, CA: Sage Publications, 1980.

Global Relocation Trends 1995 Survey Report. Windham International/National Foreign Trade Council (NFTC). Feb. 1996.

Goldenberg, Irene and Herbert Goldenberg. *Family Therapy: An Overview.* Monterey, CA: Brooks/Cole Publishing, 1980.

Graham, John L. "A Hidden Cause of America's Trade Deficit with Japan." *Columbia Journal of World Business,* Fall 1981.

_____. "The Japanese Negotiation Style: Characteristics of a Distinct Approach," *Negotiation Journal,* Apr. 1993.

Hall Edward T., *The Hidden Dimension.* New York: Doubleday, 1966.

_____. *The Silent Language.* New York: Doubleday, 1990.

Hall, Edward T., and Mildred Reed Hall. *Germans, French And Americans.* Yarmouth, ME: Intercultural Press, Inc., 1990.

_____. Understanding Cultural Differences. Yarmouth, ME: Intercultural Press, Inc., 1990.

Hampden-Turner, Charles, and Alfons Trompenaars. *The Seven Cultlures of Capitalism.* New York: Doubleday, 1993.

Harris, Philip R., and Robert T. Moran, *Managing Cultural Differences: Leadership Strategies for a New World of Business* 4th ed., Gulf Publishing, 1996.

Harvard Business Review. *The Evolving Global Economy: Making Sense of the New World Order.* Boston: Harvard Business School Press, 1995.

_____. Global Strategies. Boston: Harvard Business School Press, 1994.

Harvey, Michael G. "Designing a Global Compensation System: The Logic and A Model," *Columbia Journal of World Business,* (Winter, 1993), 28, no. 4, pp. 56–65.

_____. "The Executive Family: An Overlooked Variable in International Assignments." *Columbia Journal of World Business,* Spring 1985, pp. 84–91.

Hofstede, G. *Culture's Consequences: International Differences in Work-Related Values,* Newbury Park, CA: Sage Publications, 1980.

IBM and Towers Perrin, "Priorities for Competitive Advantage: A 21st Century Vision - A Worldwide Human Resource Study," 1991.

Johnston, William B., and Arnold H. Packer. *Workforce 2000: Work and Workers for the Twenty-first Century.* Indianapolis, IN: Hudson Institute, 1987.

Kalb, Rosalind and Penelope Welch. *Moving Your Family Overseas.* Yarmouth, ME: Intercultural Press, 1992.

Kohls, L. Robert, and John M. Knight. *Developing Intercultural Awareness: A Cross-Cultural Training Handbook.* 2d ed. Yarmouth, ME: Intercultural Press, 1994.

Kreicker, Noel. "Global Parenting." *International Orientation Resources,* Northbrook, IL. 1979.

Laabs, Jennifer J. "How Gillette Grooms Global Talent." *Personnel Journal,* Aug. 1993.

Lawler, Edward E., III, "Compensation Strategies for the Global Organization," ACA Journal, Spring, 1994.

Marquardt, Michael J., and Dean W. Engel. *Global Human Resource Development.* Englewood Cliffs, NJ: Prentice Hall, 1993.

McCluskey, Karen Curnow, ed. *Notes from a Traveling Childhood: Readings for Internationally Mobile Parents & Children.* Washington, DC: Foreign Service Youth Foundation, 1994.

McRae, Hamish. *The World in 2020: Power, Culture and Prosperity.* Boston: Harvard Business School Press, 1994.

Mendenhall, Mark, and Gary Oddou. "The Dimensions of Expatriate Acculturation: A Review." *Academy of Management Review* 10, no. 1 (1985), pp. 39–47.

Moran, Robert T. "Culture Shock Can Be a Healthy Experience If You Roll with the Punches." *International Management,* July/Aug. 1988 p. 67.

Moynihan, Michael. *The Economist Intelligence Unit: Global Manager: Recruiting, Developing, and Keeping World Class Executives.* New York: McGraw-Hill, 1993.

Naisbitt, John, and Patricia Aburdene. *Megatrends 2000: Ten New Directions for the 1990's.* New York: Avon Books, 1990.

Nelson, Carl A. *Managing Globally: A Complete Guide to Competing Worldwide.* Burr Ridge, IL: Irwin Professional Publishing, 1994.

NFTC/ Towers Perrin Benchmark Study. "Expatriate Management And Compensation At The Crossroads." June 20, 1995.

Odenwald, Sylvia, and William G. Matheny. *Global Impact: Award Winning Performance Programs from Around the World.* Burr Ridge, IL: Irwin Professional Publishing, 1996.

O'Hara-Devereaux, Mary, and Robert Johanson. *Global Work: Bridging Distance, Culture and Time.* San Francisco: Jossey-Bass, 1994.

Ohmae, Kenichi. *The Borderless World.* New York: HarperCollins, 1990.

———. *The End Of The Nation State: The Rise of Regional Economies.* New York: Free Press, 1995.

Osland, Joyce Sautters. *The Adventure Of Working Abroad: Hero Tales from the Global Frontier.* San Francisco: Jossey-Bass, 1995.

Parker, Gary L. "The Basics of Compensation and Benefits for International Assignments." *Mobility,* May 1995.

Porter, Michael E., ed. *Competition in Global Industries.* Boston: Harvard Business School Press, 1986.

Poulson-Larson, Vicki. "When You Can't Expatriate Your Career." *Mobility*, Nov. 1992, pp.56–57.

Reynolds, Calvin. *Compensation Basics for North American Expatriates: Developing an Effective Program for Employees Working Abroad,* American Compensation Association, 1994.

Reynolds, Calvin and Rita Bennett, "The Career Couple Challenge," *Personnel Journal,* March 1991.

Rhinesmith, Stephen H. *A Manager's Guide To Globalization: Six Keys to Success in a Changing World.* 2d ed., Alexandria, VA: American Society for Training and Development; Burr Ridge, IL: Irwin Professional Publishing, 1996.

Ricks, David A. *Blunders in International Business.* American Graduate School of International Management; Cambridge, MA: Blackwell Business Publishers, 1993.

Rigamer, Elmore, *Raising Children Abroad.* Family Liaison Office, U.S. State Department Video, 1993.

Schell, Michael S. "Basics in Remuneration," *Mobility*, 1996.

_____. "Global Relocation Management, New Challenges for the Relocation Professional." *Mobility,* May 1993, pp. 90–92.

_____. "Integrating International Relocation with Compensation and Benefits Programs." *International HR Journal* 4, no.1 (Spring 1995), pp. 41–46.

_____. "United Kingdom—More Than Words Can Say," *Trade and Culture,* Mar. 1996.

Schell, Michael S., and Ilene L. Dolins. "Dual Career Couples and International Assignments." *Journal of International Compensation & Benefits,* Nov./Dec. 1992.

Schell, Michael S., and Eric Stern. "Outsourcing Your International HR Program: What to consider." *International Journal of Human Resources,* vol. 5, no. 2, Summer, 1996.

Schell, Michael S., and Marian Stoltz-Loike. "Importance of Cultural Preparation to International Business Success." *Journal of International Compensation & Benefits* no. 4 (Jan./Feb. 1994), pp 47–52.

Shaeffer, Ruth G., "Building Global Teamwork for Growth and Survival," Conference Board Research Bulletin 228, 1989.

Shenkar, Oded, ed. *Global Perspectives Of Human Resource Management.* Englewood Cliffs, NJ: Prentice Hall, 1995.

Sheridan, William R., and Paul T. Hansen. "Linking International Business and Expatriate Compensation Strategies." *ACA Journal,* 5, no. 1 (Spring 1996), pp. 66–79.

Solomon, Charlene Marmer. "CEO Mom: The Tie That Binds a Global Family." *Personnel Journal,* Mar. 1996, pp. 80–93.

_____. "The Corporate Response to WorkForce Diversity." *Personnel Journal* , Aug. 1989.

_____. "Expatriate Partners: Dual Career Issues." *Personnel Journal,* May 1996.

_____. "Global Operations Demand That HR Rethink Diversity." *Personnel Journal,* July 1994, pp.40–50.

_____. "Global Teams: The Ultimate Collaboration," *Personnel Journal,* Sept. 1995, pp. 49–58.

_____. "How Does Your Global Talent Measure Up?" *Personnel Journal,* Oct. 1994, pp. 96–108.

_____. "HR Heads into the Global Age." *Personnel Journal,* Oct. 1993, pp. 76–77.

_____. "Managing the HR Career of the '90's." *Personnel Journal,* June 1994, pp. 62–76.

_____. "Managing Today's Immigrants." *Personnel Journal*, Feb. 1993, pp. 57–65.

_____. "Navigating Your Search for Global Talent." *Personnel Journal*, May 1995, pp. 94–101.

_____. "Put Your Ethics to a Global Test." *Personnel Journal*, Jan. 1996, pp. 66–74.

_____. "Repatriation: Up, Down or Out?" *Personnel Journal*, Jan. 1995, pp. 28–37.

_____. "Staff Selection Impacts Global Success." *Personnel Journal*, Jan. 1994, pp. 88–101.

_____. "Work/Family's Failing Grade: Why Today's Initiatives Aren't Enough." *Personnel Journal*, May 1994, pp. 72–87.

_____. "Success Abroad Depends on More Than Job Skills." *Personnel Journal*, Apr. 1994, pp. 51–60.

_____. "Transporting Corporate Cultures Globally." *Personnel Journal*, Oct. 1993, pp. 78–88.

Stern, Eric M. "The Role of Communication in Managing a Group Move Successfully," *Mobility*, May 1995.

Stoltz-Loike, Marian. *Dual Career Couples: New Perspectives in Counseling.* Alexandria, VA: American Association for Counseling and Development, 1992.

Stoltz-Loike, Marian. "Work and Family Considerations in International Relocation." *Journal of International Compensation & Benefits*, July/Aug. 1993, pp. 31–35.

Stoltz-Loike, Marian, and Sondra Sen. "An Eye on India," *Relocation* 9, no. 2 (Summer 1995).

Stuart, Karen Dawn "Teens Play a Role in Moves Overseas," *Personnel Journal*, Mar. 1992.

Swaak, Reyer A. "Expatriate Failures: Too Many, Too Much Cost, Too Little Planning." *Compensation & Benefits Review*, Nov./Dec. 1995, pp. 47–55.

_____. "Expatriate Management: The Search for Best Practices." *Compensation and Benefits* Review. March–April 1995, pp.21–29.

_____. "Issues of Strategy, Structure and Staffing in U.S.: Who Is in the Passing Lane?" 1995.

_____. "Key Manpower Planning For The Global Enterprise," *Journal of International Compensation & Benefits*, Jan./Feb. 1994, pp. 38–42.

_____. "The Role of Human Resources in China," *Compensation & Benefits Review*, Sept./Oct. 1995.

_____. "Today's Expatriate Family: Dual Career And Other Obstacles." *Compensation and Benefits Review.* January - February, 1995, pp.21–26

Swaak, Reyer A., and William Sheridan. "Turmoil in the House of Expatriate Compensation," *Journal of International Compensation & Benefits*, May/June 1993, pp.7–13.

Tilghman, Thomas S. "Beyond the Balance Sheet: Developing Alternative Approaches to International Compensation," *ACA Journal*, Summer 1994.

Toffler, Alvin. *Future Shock.* New York: Bantam Books, 1970.

_____. *Power Shift.* New York: Bantom Books, 1990.

_____. *The Third Wave.* New York: Bantam Books, 1980.

Trompenaars, Fons. *Riding The Waves of Culture: Understanding Diversity in Global Business.* Burr Ridge, IL: Irwin Professional Publishing, 1994.

Tucker, Michael F., "Human Resources Management in a Global Environment, " *Mobility*, Oct. 1989.

_____. *Overseas Assessment Inventory*, Tucker International, Boulder, CO.

Tung, Rosalie L. "Career Issues in International Assignments." *Academy of Management Executive,* 2, No. 3, (1988), pp. 241–44.

_____. "Expatriate Assignments: Enhancing Success and Minimizing Failure." *The Academy of Management Executive,* 1, no. 2, (1987), pp. 117–126.

Werkman, Sandy. *Bringing Up Children Overseas.* New York: Basic Books, 1977.

Windham International and the National Foreign Trade Council, *Expatriate Dual Career Survey Report,* Sept. 1992.

Windham International and the National Foreign Trade Council, *Global Relocation Trends 1995 Survey Report,* 1996.

Windham International, National Foreign Trade Council, and the Society for Human Resource Management (SHRM), *1996 Survey Report on Expatriate Human Resource Program Outsourcing,* September 1996.

"Working with China" ITRI Video, 1750 Buchanan St., San Francisco, CA 94115.

"Working with Japan" ITRI Video, 1750 Buchanan St., San Francisco, CA 94115.

INDEX

Index number, 258
Indirect cost analysis, 92–93
In-house professionals, 107
Initiative. *See* Overseas assignment inventory
Intercultural adjustment, 155, 157
Intercultural coaching, 206
Intercultural success, 31
Intercultural training. *See* Ongoing intercultural training
Interdependence cluster. *See* Societal interdependence cluster
Internal operating procedures (IOP), 93–98
     information, 95–98
International assignments, 69, 106, 182, 184, 188, 223, 229. *See also* Line managers
International business, 150
International compensation, 118
     packages, 106
International management, 117, 131
International marketplace, 9
     operation challenges, 6–8
International markets, 14
International policies, 84
International relocation management/coordination, 108
International relocation policies, 84, 92
International work experience, 250
International workforce, 129, 136
Interpersonal interest. *See* Overseas assignment inventory
Invisible culture, 11
IOP. *See* Internal operating procedure

J
Jin Dian Nau (JDN), 14, 16, 17, 22, 47
Job security, 246
     comparison. *See* Career security/job security

K
Kellogg School of Business, 19
Knowledge. *See* Balance sheet; Culture
     base, 248

L
Language, 170
Legislative assistance, 231–232
Letter of agreement (LOA), 84

About the Authors

Michael S. Schell is the president and founder of the Windham Group, which includes Windham International, ECA Windham, and Windham TRAC, headquartered in New York City. He is also the coordinating partner of the Global Relocation Partnership (GRP), a group of companies that provide expatriate and family support services in more than 60 countries.

The Windham Group was created to mirror the responsibilities of the international human resource management function as it is emerging in the contemporary organization. It addresses the spectrum of global human resource deployment issues, ranging from selection, compensation and preparation of expatriates through comprehensive relocation support, both domestically and internationally. The firm provides cross-cultural preparation, home finding, and settling-in assistance for expatriates as well as global awareness training, intercultural team building, and expatriate administration services for global corporations. In addition, it provides its member companies with information on expatriate compensation and benefits, cost-of-living and housing data, and provides consulting services on the development and implementation of international HR programs.

Before creating the Windham Group, Mr. Schell was the founder and president of Moran, Stahl & Boyer (MS&B), a preeminent consulting firm in business and human resource deployment. The firm was responsible for many of the innovations that are standard in the relocation industry today. He was with MS&B for 25 years.

Mr. Schell is a frequent speaker at international human resource conferences, is a member of the Editorial Board of Advisors for the *International HR Journal,* and has written extensively on global business and international relocation for professional publications. The Global Relocation Trends Survey, which is cited often in the media as an important industry benchmarking instrument, is conducted each year by Windham International and the National Foreign Trade Council (NFTC).

In order to stay abreast of the constant and rapid changes in the international business arena, Mr. Schell travels extensively and conducts focus groups with expatrites and international business leaders around the world. His experiences are reflected in the anecdotes in this book.

Charlene Marmer Solomon is an award winning author who has written six books and hundreds of magazine and journal articles. She is a contributing editor to *Workforce* magazine (formerly *Personnel Journal*). Her magazine credits include: *Life* magazine, the *Los Angeles Times*, *Los Angeles* magazine, *Omni*, *American Way*, *America West*, *Publisher's Weekly*, *Black Enterprise*, *Parents*, *U.S. Air*, and *The San Francisco Examiner*, as well as many trade and business publications. She is a recipient of several *Maggies*, a *Lowell Thomas* award, and awards from the *American Society of Business Press Editors* and the *Community Action Network*.

She has been a commentator for "Marketplace" on American Public Radio, has been featured on radio shows (including the top-rated Michael Jackson talk show on KABC Los Angeles), and has appeared on numerous television news and feature programs. Specializing in global business, human resources, work-and-family, and human behavior issues, Ms. Solomon has also been a lecturer at many conferences. She also worked for several years as the editorial director and managing editor of three trade and consumer magazines, and is the former president of the Southern California chapter of the American Society of Journalists and Authors.

She lived and worked in Nagoya, Japan during which time she studied Japanese language and culture, and also developed curriculum to facilitate language acquisition for Japanese adults. A student of British literature, she also taught cross-cultural studies in Japan. She resides in Los Angeles with her husband and two children.

Contributing Authors

Contributing author to the Chapters: 2, "The Influence of Culture on Global Business"; 3, "The Time/Relationship Cluster: Time, Relationships, and Communication"; 4, "The Power Cluster: Hierachy, Status Attainment, and Space"; and 5, "The Societal Interdependence Cluster: Group Dependence, Diversity Receptivity, and Change Tolerance" Marian Stoltz-Loike, Ph.D., is vice president of Windham International and author of *Dual Career Couples: New Perspectives in Counseling* and has written numerous articles on culture, international relocation and work-and-family concerns. She is cocreator of the Windham International Cultural Model ©.

Contributing author to Chapter 7, "Globalizing Compensation," Alan Chesters, is operations director of ECA International and Member of the Board of ECA Windham. He has worked in international compensation and benefits for 20 years and prior to his current role, was responsible for the global compensation function in the British Petroleum Company. He has written regularly on the strategic use of compensation to support the business process.

THE GLOBAL LEADER

Terence Brake
ISBN:0-7863-0821-4

Global competitiveness requires continuous attention to core capabilities of an organization. *The Global Leader* addresses one of the most critical capabilities needed for winning in this business environment: a company's ability to develop global leadership resources throughout its organization. Through interviews with pracitioners of leading organizations, the author demonstrates how leading companies are seeking to maximize the collective intelligence of their people around the globe and build leadership communities.

GLOBAL IMPACT

Sylvia Odenwald
ISBN:0-7863-0958-X

Americans managers and trainers, long accustomed to searching within U.S. borders for solutions to complex performance challenges, are quite often finding the best answers across the globe. *Global Impact* serves as an invaluable resource and as an "idea bank" for any professional looking for fresh perspectives and approaches to both new and age-old problems.

A MANAGER'S GUIDE TO GLOBALIZATION
Revised Edition

Dr. Stephen Rhinesmith
ISBN:0-7863-0545-2

Have you joined the perceptive managers, preparing now for the 21st century? Begin adapting yourself and your company for 2001 and beyond by reading the second edition of Stephen H. Rhinesmith's best seller, *A Manager's Guide to Globalization*. After training over 5,000 managers in 35 countries, Rhinesmith passes along new knowledge of companies changing successfully from national to global orientation.